We Are All Targets

Other books by Matt Potter

Outlaws Inc: Flying with the World's Most Dangerous Smugglers

The Last Goodbye: A History of the World in Resignations

We Are All Targets

How Renegade Hackers Invented Cyber War and Unleashed an Age of Global Chaos

Matt Potter

NEW YORK

Hachette Books
Hachette Book Group
1290 Avenue of the Americas
New York, NY 10104
HachetteBooks.com
Twitter.com/HachetteBooks
Instagram.com/HachetteBooks

First Edition: January 2023

Published by Hachette Books, an imprint of Perseus Books, LLC, a subsidiary of Hachette Book Group, Inc. The Hachette Books name and logo is a trademark of the Hachette Book Group.

The Hachette Speakers Bureau provides a wide range of authors for speaking events.

To find out more, go to www.hachettespeakersbureau.com or call (866) 376-6591.

The publisher is not responsible for websites (or their content) that are not owned by the publisher.

Print book interior design by Six Red Marbles

Library of Congress Control Number: 2022946342

ISBNs: 9780306925733 (hardcover); 9780306925726 (ebook)

Printed in Canada

MRQ-T

10 9 8 7 6 5 4 3 2 1

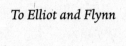

To Elliot and Flynn

Contents

PART III

Metastasis

(How Total War spread from the East and took over the world)

And now I will tell of one of my feats with this antique implement of war which will strain to the utmost the credulity of the reader.

—*Nikola Tesla*

We Are
All Targets

PART I

Empire of the Invisible

*(How the Eastern internet
was born)*

Pandora's Box

London, 2000

I know it's them straight away, even from up here on the second floor, looking down through the window onto the hubbub of the crowded Soho street. The two men whose job it is to take me in for questioning stop, look around, and go through what look like previsit rituals—checking their pockets for paperwork, looking at watches, making a last call on the mobile. If their dark-gray suits, mackintoshes, and black brogues didn't scream intelligence services loud enough, their movements do. These are no office workers on lunch break.

They look up toward my corner window.

Now they are threading toward me between tourists and taxis, now standing at the curb outside Planet Hollywood, now crossing Coventry Street, clogged with lunchtime crowds. I twist my neck, look down at an angle. They are directly below my window on Oxendon Street. Now they are entering the dark shadow of my building.

I didn't get much of a warning, only a tip-off from a journalist contact that word had gotten around about the documents on my computer. "Oh," he said, almost as an afterthought, "and, by the way, MI5 are on their way over to chat to you about that."

In the few seconds left before my world changes, I turn my face from the window and survey the office. It's a normal, busy work-place. My workmates are working, typing, making calls, making tea, having meetings. Nobody else here on the editorial floor of my magazine office knows anything, not yet.

I work for a magazine. It's a branded travel thing for an air-line, and I'm pretty junior on staff, but it's experience, and the free trips are okay, and they help me keep change coming with jour-nalistic side hustles, like some reporting trips I've taken to Eastern Europe. My employers know what's going on, but so long as I keep it out of their lives and don't start making a spectacle of myself, everyone's happy. What I shouldn't do is anything that would embarrass them. Such as, for example, having two men from MI5 come to interrogate me on suspicion of espionage on a Wednesday morning.

As I survey the calm beige-and-gray editorial office, its pods and cubicles, designers in headphones, and slowly dying succu-lents, one trip I made a couple of years ago is bothering me. Red flags I never saw at the time, unfurling and flapping at the edges of my vision.

I have a minute left, maybe two if the receptionist is on the phone or talking to a motorbike courier when the MI5 men come in.

Some discoveries turn on coincidences, tiny shafts of light, the smallest of accidental details. Something like opening the wrong email. It had begun like any other day in the office. I was on a dead-line and at my desk early, and the strip lighting only made the gray outside the windows feel murkier. March was bone-dry, cold, and dark, as if London still hadn't fully recovered from its millennium-night hangover after almost four months. There was the familiar five-note "incoming email" sound. I'd been expecting a load of copy to arrive, so while the name wasn't familiar, that wasn't unusual. Click. Open.

"Hello."

"I am Anti-Smyser-1."

Weird name. I still wasn't concentrating. Outside, a sweeper truck whirred past the building. Scroll down.

```
' Thus_001
' Anti-Smyser
' This virus is an alteration of a virus which was
    designed to delete all files from one's C: drive on
    Dec 13th.
' Application.Options.VirusProtection = False
```

Shit. Garbled text, reams and reams of the stuff. Then something that stopped me dead:

ANNEX E TO OPLAN 31402 DATED 23 DEC
    99: RULES OF ENGAGEMENT FOR LAND
    OPERATIONS
INTRODUCTION. The Rules of Engagement (ROE)
    contained in this compendium are for the use of
    the Kosovo Force (KFOR) land forces, when autho-
    rised in accordance with the procedure described
    in paragraph 3.a. (2). of Annex E.
KFOR: NATO's army in Kosovo.

Scanning down now, faster, words jumping out. Deadly force. Electronic jamming of enemy signals. Military Restricted Areas. War criminals.

I was concentrating now all right. These were military plans, commands issued to NATO troops currently on the ground in Kosovo and elsewhere in the former Yugoslavia. The seventy-eight-day bombardment aimed at making Serb forces withdraw might have been over, but the ground occupation, the firefights, the round-ups, the armed peacekeeping, the hunt for war criminals, the shoot-to-kills, the time of sabotage and terror had barely begun.

These documents seemed to cover all that. They contained endless sets of commands, going way beyond the public briefings NATO or the Pentagon had been issuing to the press detailing the terms and goals of the mission, beyond what President Bill Clinton, Secretary of State Madeleine Albright, or Prime Minister Tony Blair had been saying in front of the TV cameras. Even as President Clinton and his aides talked of "zero-casualty" operations, these plans detailed under what circumstances US and allied soldiers should shoot to kill. In some cases, they seemed to directly undermine the president's public statements.

The commands came and came and came. Here were the circumstances in which "deadly force" could be used against unidentified attackers; here were instructions to NATO troops on apprehending suspected war criminals for handover to the International Criminal Tribunal for the former Yugoslavia; here were specific commands setting out the procedure for riot control to media transmissions; authorizations for attack helicopters, tanks, order on the laying of mines.

My mind raced, back through my time in Russia, my exposure to spies in Serbia, the country with whom we were at war. Whatever I'd done, whatever I'd said, had mixed me up in very bad trouble indeed.

Maybe I had just been in the wrong place at the wrong time. But I couldn't help worrying I was not entirely blameless. I'd always been fascinated by Eastern Europe, wondering through my childhood under the all-pervading, paralytic shadow of nuclear annihilation just how it could be that life was so black-and-white. I taught myself Russian after school, managed to get to Russia as a student, just in time to see it implode. I taught briefly, hitched around the Wild East, and watched in horror as Communism's borderlands— first the Caucasus, then the Balkans—toppled into horrifying wars. Communism's promise of an allegiance greater than nationality or religion had stitched together postwar wounds that now erupted once more, each livid and bleeding organ of the former USSR now rejecting its force-grafted neighbors, old wounds erupting. Chechnya, Armenia, Azerbaijan, Georgia, Moldova, Transnistria, North and South Ossetia, Tajikistan, Uzbekistan, Abkhazia, Russia itself.

In Yugoslavia too, the promise had fallen away with the completeness of an illusion discovered. Like the USSR, it had contained multitudes: a Communist Party–ruled union running from Alpine Slovenia down through Catholic Adriatic Croatia; mountainous, Muslim Bosnia; Orthodox Serbia, teeming and urbanizing, the capital, Belgrade, rising from its wartime devastation in concrete and steel; its tiny coastal neighbor Montenegro; the contested Greek-Bulgar-Yugoslav lands of Macedonia; the majority-Albanian Kosovo. Now, the way those lands had blurred and bled into each other during the Cold War fostered in each a sense of septic betrayal.

Communism had not addressed the betrayals, real or imagined, of one ethnic or religious group against another, whether Croat nationalists had seized on the advance of Hitler's armies in the name of "liberating" themselves from the Serb-dominated Kingdom of Yugoslavia and collaborated in the brutal extermination of ethnic Serbs, or whether Bosnian Muslims were now potential leverage for a surge upward from Turkish power. It had covered them. Now, where Communism's stitch-up-and-hope had failed, the nationalists brought cauterizing fire. The term "ethnic cleansing" became a surgical euphemism for the hysteria of incineration that laid waste to cities and villages, woods, fields, families, and generations in Bosnia-Herzegovina as Croatian and Serbian soldiers and militia put them to the flame. What remained was the aftermath of slaughter and atrocity in Bosnia; an independent Slovenia, Croatia, Macedonia, and smoldering Bosnia-Herzegovina; and a rump Yugoslavia—Serbia, with Montenegro as its junior partner, and Kosovo as something it now refused to cede to its Albanian majority, claiming it as part of Serbia.

By 1997, I'd taken some leave for a side hustle and flown to Serbia as a journalist as the next round of violence gathered. Serbian militias and military units had now begun ethnically cleansing Kosovo, slaughtering Albanians just as they'd massacred Bosnian Muslims just a couple of years earlier. Belgrade itself—liberal and youthful, yet the seat of a mad-dog regime—flickered between the daily banalities of rampant inflation and protest and the twilight world of a city under siege. Out went everyone who could still leave. In came soldiers, spies, diplomats, TV news crews, US-led negotiating missions.

Around me, the city was melting into a vortex of drugs, guns, nationalism, crime, and patronage. I met a lot of people—media moguls working for Milošević's mouthpiece channels, antiregime activists. I'd undoubtedly been on the radar of dozens more. And then I'd done what journalists do: I'd flown home, filed my work. NATO had launched its bombardment on Serbia and its forces in Kosovo, destroying targets in Eastern Europe during the spring and summer of 1999 for the first time since World War II, US bombers soaring over the former Communist world in a way that had been unthinkable.

The bombardment had lasted only seventy-eight days. As a Westerner, I was lucky. I'd been able to move on. A new millennium. A new job. New stories, new things to think about.

Only now, in the first spring of the new millennium, here was something from my past, floating up again.

I'd read the reports in the press in the aftermath of the bombardment, like everyone: throughout the conflict, NATO had been plagued by the suspicion that a spy was in their midst, transmitting NATO plans to enemy positions in advance. US Tomahawk missiles had rained down on empty fields, or the wrong buildings. A missile attack had hit the Chinese embassy in Belgrade the previous summer, killing Chinese journalists and diplomats and bringing the world, briefly, to the brink of a larger war of the superpowers. NATO had consistently supplied the media with anonymously sourced briefings to the effect that any data breach that had taken place—and it was increasingly obvious that it had—was the result of a human spy. The briefings hadn't stopped with the bombings. Word on the hunt was everywhere from the *Guardian* to *Jane's Defence Weekly*. General Wesley Clark's office began briefing on the hunt for a spy. Anyone caught with information like this was going to have their lives taken apart.

I looked about me at the still-empty office, then recalled the advice of a friend who'd handled leaked material for one of the newspapers: *You can't hide from this.* So you infect the public space with it. Make it visible to as many people as possible, as quickly as possible. Right now, if this got out, it could have come only from me. I had to change that.

I printed out five copies and went on a quick walk around the office, "absentmindedly" leaving printouts in different public locations—two on filing cabinets, one in the bathroom, one on top of the printer itself. Just enough to leave room for plausible deniability. If this blew up, and my bosses panicked, I could just about deny I'd been the one who sparked the visit. If only for a few hours, it might buy me time while I figured out what was going on.

I called one of the few names in my Rolodex who I figured might be able to help me test what I had on my hands—and potentially protect me from any blowback if it was as serious a security breach as it looked. I didn't know Graham, but he was a friend of a friend, an editor at the *Sunday Telegraph*. I told him what I had on the screen in front of me, and he went quiet. He let out an oath under his breath, then said he'd look after it, make some calls, just to establish it was genuine. I should sit tight and not talk to anyone.

Less than five minutes later, he called me back. He sounded agitated. It sure as hell sounded as if it was genuine, he said, because NATO had called the Ministry of Defence and now all hell had broken loose. Oh and by the way, I'd need to answer some questions.

The army was on its way with some military intelligence officers—the ones who were now on their way up to my office.

I asked him how to handle what was coming, but the phone clicked and the line went dead before the words were out. I was on my own.

Seconds left now. I skip across from the window to check my desk—strange, but I want to look natural and busy when they come in. I told one close colleague, the guy I sit next to, what I'd found, and what I'd done. He seemed pretty freaked out, and now he's nowhere to be seen. The phone on my desk rings. "Your guests have arrived."

Fumbling uselessly now: keys, pen, wallet. And there, right by my desk when I look up—as everybody in the office around me looks up—are the spooks from across the street.

"Good morning. Mr. Potter, is it?"

Their handshakes are firm, wooden, awkward. The officers are both white men, heavily built, middle-aged, and suited. They're wearing ties.

While they introduce themselves—"I'm MI5, I received the notification, and my colleague here works closely with the Ministry of Defence, so I've brought him along"—I notice details. Their shoes are policemen's shoes. Heavy, dull black, sensible. The men are both chief-inspector tall. One is a Yorkshireman with a mustache and receding hair and looks like a TV cop from my childhood. The other is a Londoner and has thick-cropped hair and a lower forehead. Their voices are that strange mix of chummy, indulgent, commanding, and coldly professional you get when a policeman asks you to turn the noise down, or explains why he's stopped you today. The Londoner frowns when he speaks. He speaks less often. I will find out only later that he is not who he seems to be.

The Yorkshireman takes the lead. "Now, I understand you've got something that you'd like to show us, and perhaps after that we can have a chat about it all. It's sensitive obviously, so we've got somewhere we can use. It's not far and we're parked just around—"

"Yeah, I know, I…," I blurt, pointing toward the corner window, and immediately wish I hadn't.

There is a moment of silence. From the corner of my eye, I see colleagues' heads pop over their monitors. Two or three get up and scoot out of the office.

"The email, then," says the Londoner, nodding. As I call it up on the screen, he's comparing it with some paper he's unfolding. He's already got a printout.

"This a work computer, is it?" says the Yorkshireman. "Doesn't leave the building?"

I nod and they seem satisfied. "Okay, that's all we need to see here. Our car is waiting. If you have everything, then perhaps you'll come with us, if there's anybody you need to tell." It isn't phrased like a question.

I can't catch anyone's eye on the way out, so I ask the receptionist to let my boss know that if I'm late back from lunch, I'm on an errand and I'll make the time up.

"Sure," she grins, cocking one eyebrow at me, then following our strange party with her gaze until the door swings shut, and the cold air and shadows of Soho swallow us up.

Twenty minutes later in a temporary questioning room borrowed from an office hire company—tea in plastic cups, cheese plant, ergonomic chair, copies of property magazines—we sit. Now they are ready for me. The interrogation—their word—can begin.

Whoever's been breaking into NATO and leaking battlefield plans to the enemy, it wasn't me. But since I'm the one holding the classified documents, it seems I've got some explaining to do.

Click.

"Let's just begin at the beginning," says the taller officer.

I take a sip of water, then a deep breath. And I tell them everything.

"And then, a few minutes later, the receptionist called me about two guests. And there you were."

They're exchanging looks, and clearly there's something they're expecting to hear that they haven't.

"I see, thank you." The Yorkshireman walks to a window, then turns and looks at the ceiling, as if in thought. "All that techie stuff doesn't really answer some of the questions that arise, does it? For example, why would someone inside NATO be sending these sensitive documents to *you*, in particular? You've been to Serbia. Around the time of the bombing, wasn't it? Friends there?"

My mind flashes back to Belgrade. All those people, on all those sides. Had I said anything I shouldn't have?

The Londoner senses something's up and interjects. "This is *war* we're talking about. This is a sensitive document. These things aren't public for a very good reason. People get hurt. *Think*, please."

I want to tell the men from MI5 what I've really seen. I want to tell them what they should really be looking for, and it isn't me, or anyone I know, or any one person at all. Because I suspect already that the classified information I've received doesn't mean what they think it means at all. That the Serb spying network they are now certain has penetrated NATO's forces both in Brussels HQ and on the ground in Kosovo, and is sending classified information out from under the noses of the United States, United Kingdom, and their Western European allies, is the least of their worries. I want to tell them about the real threat out there. How this tidal wave is going to change everything— for me, for the West, for the way we fight wars, for the post–World War II order, and for these two officers in front of me too.

My thoughts are racing ahead. If this high-level security breach—in the spooks' words, not mine—is what I think it is, then there's more to it than they can begin to imagine, and they will soon wish the threat was as simple as an enemy spy in their midst. But that's not what comes out of my mouth.

"I don't know why it came to me, but it looks like it got sent to a lot of people." I've thought this through, but my mind's spinning. "Maybe . . . maybe I was just in someone's email address book."

"Whose do you think you're in?"

"I don't know. Like you say, I was in Serbia on a job a few months ago, just before we began bombing it. Russia before that. I met...a lot of people."

"I see. Well, we'll be needing to talk to you about those people. You see, documents have been going missing for some time, information stolen—the Americans were suggesting throughout the Kosovo conflict there might be someone passing information like this on to the enemy. We need to know who the spy is. Who's giving away secrets to the enemy."

The Londoner leans in. "Perhaps you know something about that?"

I know one thing. Either they're not being straight with me, or—and as the realization dawns that the unthinkable is even a possibility, an absurd euphoria rises—these two middle-aged spooks *really don't know* what they've got on their hands.

Because to me, this looks like they've been infiltrated, NATO's battle plans stolen and leaked, not by a flesh-and-blood spy at NATO headquarters or the Pentagon, or anywhere else, but by someone sitting far away, in front of a screen. Someone whose name they've never even heard. Someone who doesn't show up on any CIA database, or any nightly news bulletin.

There was one detail I had left out of the account I gave the spooks.

Before calling the editor, I'd acted on a hunch and called a programmer friend. We had a quick chat. A brainteaser for him, a little clarity for me. So as I talk to the two spooks, I already know that everything about Anti-Smyser-1 screams "Trojan."

Trojans are a cheap, low-maintenance, and almost risk-free way for hackers to get a backdoor into their victims' computers—and, once they are in, to take over. Run undetectable programs in the background. Search for documents of certain types, for example, or containing certain terms—say, "Kosovo," or "KFOR," or "coordinates." Spread them to selected recipients—such as me.

Easy to distribute, self-replicating, and self-installing, a good one can take the hard work out of hacking. Once the recipient clicked on whatever it was that would execute them, they would start running inside the infected computer.

Between their first appearance in 1975—when artificial intelligence (AI) pioneer John Walker tested the concept with a nonmalicious subroutine he called PERVADE to hijack the popular computer game ANIMAL on the computers of Dartmouth College, in New Hampshire—and the 1990s, Trojan viruses had become a key tool in the arsenal of the hacker. They haven't evolved much since 1975 because they haven't needed to. Like sharks and scorpions, they hit their perfect predatory niche early and just sailed on even as everything else—operating systems, networks—changed around them.

A Trojan comes as an attachment—in an email or a web download, or on a drive. It might be an .exe file, or a PDF, or in this case, a Windows 97 Word file. Trojans want to be opened. Trusted. But there is an army hidden inside an innocuous-looking "horse" file. The Trojan will trick you into clicking, thereby unwittingly executing a hidden program. Once the program is running—and you might never know it's running—it can perform any number of tasks, whatever its creator tells it to do, looking for documents on the now-breached computer that match certain criteria. Then it might send out whatever matches the thing it's looking for, potentially to anyone whose email address is stored in their system, or anyone who uses a file created by, or altered within, that system.

This Trojan appeared to be hunting for something specific. Documents containing certain terms, perhaps; users of machines running Windows—meaning not just most home PC users, but every significant department of global government, military, business, and finance. Having found what it was looking for, it leaked it, and spread at the same time, by sending itself along with its payload as an attachment to a list of recipients. And for reasons I need to find out—me.

Trojans are the archetypal subversive attack: asymmetrical in their low-risk, low-maintenance ability to cause damage behind fiercely secured barriers, just like the mythical horse they're named after. Their scattering of documents and data works just fine against individuals. But against corporations, countries, military institutions with masses and masses of sensitive data and thousands of staff, each one of whom represents a potential way into the system if they can be tempted to click just once, they are loose cannons whose effects can be anything from embarrassing and costly to devastating. And for soldiers on the ground or spies in the field whose plans or locations are compromised, they can be lethal.

And instead, the government is looking for a spy, and these two men are looking at me. But this is MI5, for goodness' sake. Surely they're on top of this. They *must* know more than they seem to.

I try explaining it to the spooks. This Trojan *is* the spy—or at least it will lead you to them. The malware has tricked someone at NATO. And now there's a program running, in secret, inside NATO's computers, and who knows where else, and it's sending out the secrets of KFOR—the NATO army made up of combined forces from the United States, United Kingdom, Netherlands, Germany, Sweden, Norway, Denmark, Italy, and countless other allies—to who knows where. But they stop me before I have a chance, steer me back to people. It's not flesh and blood, and they can't see it.

Either they know more than I do, or they know nothing.

I've said that the Trojans found their optimum form early, while the world evolved and changed around them. This isn't quite true. What hasn't evolved is the authorities' defenses, or its knowledge of them.

While networks—from military and academic networks to the global internet—have gotten bigger, faster, and more popular, they haven't gotten any more sophisticated. Ultimately, they are just conduits between machines controlled by people. And while the code running on those machines is vetted and securitized, and every vulnerability and back door audited, exploited, patched, fixed, they are almost irrelevant. Humans are as easily tricked, their defenses as easily turned to weakness, as they were thirty-two hundred years ago by the original Trojan horse.

Then again, sometimes it's easy to believe you can leave your door open.

Anti-Smyser-1 was just another speck of foam on a wave of millennium madness. By the late 1990s, the internet was indisputably American territory, dot-com its stars-and-stripes. Between 1995 and 2000, the NASDAQ stock market rose 400 percent, with a price-earnings ratio of 200—dwarfing the previously unthinkable high of 80 for the Japanese asset bubble of 1991. Internet start-ups sprouted at a rate of more than sixteen thousand every single day. Companies with .com in their names could go public and rake in investment via initial public offering (IPO), making every shareholder a paper millionaire, without ever specifying how, or when, they expected to make a profit, or having ever realized any material revenue at all. Y2K bug preppers dug and stocked shelters in the Nevada deserts. NASDAQ soared, then crashed. Microsoft broke up on the rocks of US antitrust laws. The same week the NATO plans hit the press, NASDAQ fell 25 percent. Stock markets everywhere panicked and crashed.

The 1990s had turned the world into an Anglo-Saxon capitalist casino. As far as the Western military alliance was concerned, history had come to an end. Now the internet had grown too fast, too far for even its investors, even its developers, to know what worked and what didn't. And for Western intelligence agencies and economies alike, that meant a fatal blind spot.

As my interrogators pushed, I noticed with fascination and something like dread that they appeared to come from the pre-internet age. We had all read reports—seen NATO spokesperson Jamie Shea admitting in his wartime briefings—that the Kosovo conflict had seen cyberattacks on NATO. We knew that its servers had been flooded with spam, until its systems had seized up, unable to cope with the traffic. NATO had upped its capacity to get online. They surely can't have believed the attacks had ended with that? Spamming the email addresses of an attacking force was one thing; infiltrating NATO's servers so thoroughly that you are still inside, wandering around the innermost workings of the world's mightiest military alliance and its constituent militaries, copying and distributing classified material from its computers during the fragile hot peace and occupation of combat zones that followed, is another. They seemed entranced with the idea that only a human spy could have leaked the documents.

So did others higher up. In March 2000, just a month before my questioning, unnamed "senior US defense officials" had briefed the BBC's *Moral Combat: NATO at War* investigation that their plans had been leaked by a pro-Serbia spy belonging to one of the national delegations to NATO. Supreme commander of NATO's allied forces US general Wesley Clark himself was reported to have been "convinced" that America had an urgent flesh-and-blood spy hunt on their hands.

They asked again: What were my personal links with "states we might call hostile," perhaps members of the current forces in Serbia? I'd been there as the Kosovo conflict ramped up, and immediately before our latest bombardment as troops massed. Then it was on to links with Russia: I had contacts there, had spent time there in the lawless 1990s. Then China: I'd worked in Hong Kong around the time in 1997 that it reverted to Chinese rule. One of them even remarked sardonically, "You seem to follow trouble, don't you?" He laughed, then stopped. "Or the other way 'round." Any theories I might have? The men from MI5 kept looping back to whether I knew anyone, whether I'd been into the NATO office, to any of its military facilities, whether I'd had clearance, been passed documents, been blackmailed.

They took my life story, my numbers, my recent travel history, my interests, my travel plans. Then they let me go. The whole thing had taken just over an hour.

I ambled back to my office, sat back at my desk. Lunchtime was over, with its sandwich boxes and empty soda cans. My colleagues looked at me strangely for the rest of the afternoon.

Graham asked me to write a report together with a young *Sunday Telegraph* staff reporter, Adam Lusher. He checked up, hustled for reactions, called NATO, then the army, about the Trojan. A British army officer called him back and agreed that seemed to make more sense than the spy theory: "If it looks like a duck, and it quacks like a duck, it's probably a duck, right?" He promised an investigation. The next to call was NATO's chief spokesman, Jamie Shea—the man who'd been issuing the press briefings throughout our bombing of Serb positions the year before. Shea expressed alarm, and tried to dissuade us from publishing the documents or revealing the breach. "If this proves true that a NATO document has got into the public domain, it will be a matter of great concern to us," he said. "These are sensitive NATO documents. We would like to keep them classified and prevent them being compromised."

I met Adam that night outside a pub next to London's Charing Cross station. It was a warm spring evening, and the crowds of sunshine-happy young Londoners milled past us as we stood with our beers and notebooks. We made a couple of quick decisions. How to protect me as the origin of the story, and that we'd quote Shea's warning verbatim in the piece.

Things moved quickly after that. Adam received another call—one that he would later describe to me as "astonishing—pretty unheard of." The voice on the other end introduced himself as a colonel in the British army. Throughout the short conversation, he seemed to be trying to distance the British military from any security failure. "It is a security breach," he said. "But not one of ours." When Adam pressed him, he reiterated: "It has been determined to come from outside the UK." No, not the United States either. The colonel hinted that it may have come from a NATO partner nation, but in any case, its origin was somewhere in Eastern Europe. And the guys from MI5? Their hunt for a spy? His team is behind the curve, playing catch-up: "We are only looking into it because we are the local security agency," he says, implying that they are involved only because I reported it in London.

The pressure intensified. I received two unusual phone calls in the hours that followed. The first came from a woman who just wanted to check the number was the one for my work address, but wouldn't say why and rang off. A few minutes later, I received a second call at work in which the male caller failed to introduce himself but told me to "be very careful, lest you find yourself caught up in any investigation."

Despite—or perhaps because of—the pressure, the story ran on the front page of that weekend's *Sunday Telegraph* newspaper, dated April 2, 2000, complete with a quote comparing my officers to Mulder and Scully from the hit TV series *The X-Files*. Then it hit the BBC. Then the newswires. Then, as the United States came online, Yahoo! and MSN, then CNN and the other news media, then everywhere else.

That changed things. The interrogators were about to be interrogated.

The phone went crazy. Suddenly, Anti-Smyser-1 was cropping up everywhere. It had infected not just NATO HQ computers and KFOR computers across Kosovo, but US government and military computers as well. Then the British military. Then the Czech Ministry of Defence. Then systems belonging to other NATO members, partners, and staff. Word went around about more breaches, some confirmed, some rumored, some first confirmed and then denied. But every time, something connected the breach to the same places. I began writing, putting crosses onto a map, working on it at lunchtimes and in the evenings. Serbia. Russia. China. Serbia. Russia. China. I knew a pattern when I saw one.

NATO launched its investigation in a hurry. It emerged that American sources had been quietly raising concerns with NATO during the conflict that a spy at NATO headquarters was leaking details of US Air Force (USAF) bombing plans to the Serbs. From Shea and his colleagues' reaction to my find, the discovery of the Trojan had clearly stung. If the Pentagon's concerns had seemed over the top at the time, NATO's focus on a physical human spy now looked humiliatingly out of touch. With this much-trumpeted investigation, at last the focus could shift from flesh-and-blood spies to viruses. At last, we'd learn how far the work—even the lives— of American and allied aircrews, military, and civilians had been compromised. Apart from anything else, I wanted to know whose handiwork had inadvertently put me in the frame as an anti-NATO spy for the Serbs. I waited for the flood of follow-up stories.

But the flood never came. Because at that point, NATO chiefs suddenly did something very strange.

Barely had the investigation started when the investigating team was abruptly ordered off the case by NATO secretary-general Lord Robertson—a personal confidant of President Bill Clinton, Prime Minister Tony Blair's close political ally, as well as Britain's secretary of state for defense throughout the Kosovo bombardment and deployment. Robertson then ordered the half-finished report itself be classified. The report, its findings, and its conclusions remain buried to this day, more than twenty years later.

In a curious stroke of timing, on the exact same day in June 2000, NATO's press office abruptly changed its story too.

In a bare and brightly lit meeting room deep inside the blue-glass wave of NATO's HQ off the busy Boulevard Leopold III in Brussels, the big guns emerged to brief the press. This time—unusually— Robertson stood before the cameras alongside Shea. Together, they announced that the summarily abandoned and classified investigation had been closed not because there was anything to hide, but simply because there never had been any attack or breach after all. Rather, they said, it had all been a silly misunderstanding.

"Following an investigation into the leaks, I can now tell you that this was started at KFOR by our own people and subsequently spread to NATO headquarters and to other NATO members," Shea told the ranks of reporters in their plastic chairs. There were easy smiles. Sheepish faces.

It was a virtuoso briefing: It gave a great stereotype-enforcing, dopey-scientist narrative, irresistible to short-staffed newsrooms who really just wanted a story people would enjoy. An irresistible pitch that would be sure to make more noise than the initial story. Over refreshments, low-key laughter was shared by NATO staffers and press pack alike.

It was also a lie.

They judged it perfectly. The following day's reports, across newspapers, TV, and radio, took their cues—even their words—straight from Shea and Robertson's briefing. They were eerily similar, down to the language. The phrase "bungling NATO boffins" cropped up like a fingerprint. Those always irresistible figures of tabloid fun, the backroom eggheads, had created a powerful piece of spyware for NATO to use on its enemies, but it had "got loose" and created havoc on their own servers. Cue trombones, cue canned laughter, and fade.

To this day, the NATO website's educative global "History of Cyberattacks" leaves a strange, complete blank between 1988 and 2006, between Massachusetts Institute of Technology (MIT) scientist Robert Tapan Morris's "Morris Worm"—an innocent experiment to establish the size of the internet—and December 2006, when NASA was forced to block email attachments before shuttle launches for fear they would be hacked. It was as if those years in between never happened. Like real-life Men in Black, Shea and my visitors had done their work, and killed the story off.

Yet their account didn't add up. For one thing, this virus had first been spotted in the wild by a young cyber-forensics researcher named Katrin Tocheva almost a year before NATO claimed its own team had created it.

Fiercely intelligent with a penchant for fluorescent nails, rock jewelry, and sleek jet-black chic, Tocheva could have slinked from the pages of a Stieg Larsson novel. She'd headed up the Bulgarian government's Laboratory of Computer Virology through the 1990s, partied with hackers and cyber cops from Hong Kong to Moscow, and had the numbers for CEOs, hackers, and cops across the globe in her phone. She also spoke several languages. Transferring to the prestigious F-Secure cyber-investigation agency in Helsinki to work directly with its founder, Mikko Hyppönen, she became their eyes and ears in the East. She'd first spotted and identified the new strain of malware in a Windows email attachment a year previously. She named it "Anti-Smyser" after its first line, just as you'd name a poem—with the F-Secure lab giving it the official name W97M/Thus.K, for the host software and part of the code's payload. She tracked the Trojan for months, like a virologist or epidemiologist tracking the progress, spread, and new mutations of COVID-19.

Like new variants of any biological virus, these new strains were given letters as they were identified. W97M/Thus.G emerged first, then I, then K, then AD, then more and more. But amid all the strains attacking computers through 1999, the K variant—the one I received in 2000—was the only one with the classified NATO documents as its stolen payload. Not only did the virus not originate when NATO said it did, but it had originated outside and gotten in, not the other way around, as they claimed.

NATO's cover-up was either desperate stuff or contemptuously poor. Fearing I was going crazy, I began sense-checking my misgivings with cybersecurity researchers. "That's horseshit," laughed one when I called him the night of NATO's claim. "That's not a bungle. If that is what occurred, then it would have been an act of deliberate and repeated sabotage, not an accident." The reaction from another when I read her the text of NATO's denial was even more damning. "NATO said that, did they?" She spoke slowly, as if trying to make sense of the words. "And... you *believed* them?"

Having briefed what appeared to be a dummy story to kill the speculation as to the motives, identities, and extent of the security breach caused by the real attackers, Shea's office—the whole NATO apparatus, from Washington, DC, to Brussels—closed down on the subject. The press was looking for easier stories. My *Telegraph* team declared the investigation closed. The bungling-boffins angle had done its job.

I called the spooks' office just to ask for an update. I never got through to anyone, and never got a call back. I began calling daily, with the growing suspicion that I had been played. Eventually, the phone number just stopped working. It felt for all the world like my erstwhile interrogators were now hiding from me.

It was clear that something bad had happened to NATO, that it had to do with the documents on my computer, and that it was something they didn't want to talk about.

This was just odd. The world knew—NATO had briefed on it steadily during the conflict—that crude cyberattacks aimed at the United States and its allies had downed systems at the US Department of Defense, air-traffic control, shipping, the Pentagon, the US Air Force, the US Navy, even the White House itself; it had at one point made the Federal Bureau of Investigation's own archives inaccessible to the FBI itself. But if they had been open about being impeded by cyberattacks then, why were they so anxious to treat this differently?

Against the odds, I had liked my MI5 interrogators. They had come across as solid guys, doing a difficult job under pressure. Even

Jamie Shea had seemed sincere. But even though I suspected that they were holding back on me, I also felt bad for them. Because while they may have known more than they were letting on about what had happened, so did I.

Someone out there was playing havoc with the systems of the most powerful military alliance the world had ever seen. If my hunch was correct, then NATO's discreet canning of the investigation was very much not the end, but a beginning. It was also a terrible mistake.

My questioning had shown me that NATO was chasing something that didn't exist. In the first year of the new millennium, something had happened to them that heralded an entirely new form of conflict. This was anonymous, distributed, and seemingly undefendable. Yet here they were, trying to establish human hierarchies of command and responsibility, as if it was an army they were fighting.

If an unknown hostile power could play for months inside US military computers without being detected—and do it in a way that even when it was, its targets couldn't be certain of its origin or extent—then I wanted to know what it was. Maybe I could help them to understand it. Even to defend against it.

The term "Total War" had circulated in military command offices worldwide since Goebbels first coined it in 1943: a war unlimited in scope, prosecuted on any front, to any extent, by all means necessary. What if the new and borderless world of cyberspace was opening up a front, a new set of weapons, whole new generations of combatants, global and faceless, that nobody had even noticed yet? Total War in cyberspace—carried invisibly on currents of zeroes and ones, through the walls of missile silos and governments, homes, and airbases—was dizzying to contemplate. A new kind of conflict had arrived, and the Western alliance's face-saving obfuscations were wasting valuable time.

This is a story about that conflict, and where and how it started, and why it spread to become the dominant mode of war in today's world. It's also a story about that decision by NATO to cover up the damage, to kick the can down the road at the critical time. And what that decision cost us.

Chapter 1

Rebel Code

The one thing the incursion should not have been for NATO was a surprise.

But to understand how the new era of cyber war dawned, and how it led to the world we think we know, we need to step across the tracks. And I'll need to show you something that I never told the men from MI5.

That January morning, rain swept Belgrade's slums in a hard drizzle. The capital of the former Yugoslavia was smeared by lowering cloud. Even in 1998, it was hard to avoid the feeling of an expectant lull, the moment of inhalation. Not just the eve of war, but the eve of a new millennium.

I stepped across the disused railway tracks now overgrown with grass, past the rusted shells of wagons. The drizzle came in drifts, making the broken concrete and rusting corrugated iron shimmer like ghosts under a gray descending sky. The old docks of Dorćol, Belgrade's drug-addled district of wharves, warehouses, and creeping reclamation by the young, lay in dereliction, abandoned after almost a decade of war, scavenging, plunder, and hyperinflation. The doorways of railway sheds and concrete bunkers along the waste ground spewed soaking bodies, ragged clothes, sleeping bags, beer bottles. The sign on the dripping, rubbish-littered concreted doorway I sheltered under was illegible. There was nothing to indicate to the archaeologists of future civilizations that this had ever been one of the buildings in which the internet age was birthed.

The former Yugoslavia is a patchwork of lands, peoples, and home religions—from Catholic Croats and Slovenes to Christian Orthodox Serbs and Montenegrins, as well as Muslim Bosnians—its postwar existence a supreme effort of will. During World War II, the occupying Wehrmacht had found the governing authorities of Croatia and Alpine Slovenia more amenable and had exercised particular savagery against the Serbs. The postwar government was populated and led by resistance fighters. Its charismatic, wily, and pugnacious president, Jozip Broz Tito, had led perhaps the most successful resistance movement of World War II against Wehrmacht occupation and wore his military uniform even as he helped found the postwar country.

But the founding myth of this Communist state was very different from that of the USSR. All workers were brothers and sisters, of course; nationalism and religion were dangerous follies that had plunged the country into slaughter and division. But there it deviated from Soviet Communist teachings. Yugoslavia, held Tito's Communist-guerrilla leadership through the 1950s and 1960s, could never be occupied again. It would be an untamable, punching-above-its-weight land of *hajduks* (bandits) and *partizans* (freedom fighters) that shot first and asked questions later. From school, children would lead two lives: one, as a citizen; two, as a potential guerrilla fighter, always ready to be pressed into service if the country needed them. The two national archetypes are so deeply ingrained on the collective psyche that two of the former Yugoslavia's biggest football teams, Hajduk Split and Partizan Belgrade, bear the names—something akin to Manchester United and Chelsea being called "Manchester Bandit Clan" and "London Resistance Guerrillas."

The Soviets were none too pleased to have an independent-minded neighbor, Communist or no. Tito's relationship with Stalin disintegrated spectacularly, and after a decisive falling-out in 1948, the country frantically sought to position itself as home to an alternate seat of Communist power, wholly outside of Soviet influence, exerting its own power on neighboring Albania and Greece, taking Western aid. This put Tito on top of Stalin's hit list. Five assassination attempts later, Tito penned his famous note to the Soviet leader: "Stop sending people to kill me! We've already captured five of them, one of them with a bomb and another with a rifle....If you don't stop sending killers, I'll send a very fast-working one to Moscow and I certainly won't have to send another."

Yugoslavia had something that seemed to the Kremlin like a giant liability for any fellow Communist neighbor. Its constituent lands had been overrun, ruled, invaded by everyone from the Hapsburgs to the Ottomans, the Nazis, and the Romans. That had left it with an age-old problem with authority. By 1961, Tito had rejected the whole premise of a Cold War face-off entirely and founded the Non-Aligned Movement of states with India, Egypt, Libya, and Indonesia. It was a ballsy move because it meant Yugoslavia was unaligned and able to dance across the lines of acceptable policy and behavior.

In the way of borderlands everywhere, it also looked both ways in cultural terms. Throughout the Cold War, Yugoslav teens grew up learning about Communist doctrine in school and went into jobs allocated by the state. But they also wore Levi's; listened to Western rock, pop, and rap; and could travel to other countries more or less freely in a way that their fellow Communist youths behind the Iron Curtain could never even hope to. Trieste in Italy, close to the border with Slovenia, became a retail park for Yugoslavs keen on buying up the latest Western branded goods to sneak back home beneath the seats of their cars. Border guards were supposed to limit the amount of Western stuff brought back in, but they were in on the hustle as much as anyone—as was the Yugoslav Communist Party itself.

The party liked to keep an entrepreneurial eye on Western trends too. After all, catering to those trends would mean more microchips could be imported.

This tendency for monitoring American and Western European trends showed in other ways. Yugoslavia had always been proud to offer its citizens American and British imported pop music and Hollywood movies. President Tito himself was a western and science-fiction fan—even hiring the rockier, sunnier parts of constituent republics Croatia and Montenegro out to Soviet and East German film crews who wanted to make "Red westerns" approximating Arizona and Dodge City, and occasionally alien planetary surfaces too.

But while westerns were entertaining, it was science fiction that swept Yugoslavia like a fever. The reasons for the public's embrace of it are many and range from the historical to the economic. For one thing, a technologically enabled future free of petty national grievances was central to the promise of Communism, so it found ready backers in the government, who marked it an approved genre. For another, Yugoslavia had already pioneered the same aesthetic in its own response to history. Especially mindful of the danger of looking backward or ethnic signifiers in a country that united so many states, religions, languages, and historical feuds, Yugoslav architects and artists had pioneered science fiction as an aesthetic for the famous World War II memorials, the *spomeniki*. These alien totems sprouted up across the landscape, each looking more like the Starship *Enterprise* or H. R. Giger art than anything religious or folkloric.

By the late 1960s and the Apollo missions, the final frontier occupied Yugoslav TV schedules and cinema listings morning to night. *Doctor Who* (1963), *Star Trek* (1967), and *2001: A Space Odyssey* (1968) were all popular sensations, defining the national conversation for months on end, as would *Space: 1999* (1975) and *Star Wars* (1977). Government-funded magazines produced editions based around themes in last week's episodes, while schools would build discussion of them into lessons.

In early 1972, in an astonishing PR coup, Communist Yugoslavia became the first nation to host a tour of Europe by NASA's Apollo 15 crew, fresh from their successful August 1971 moon mission. The American astronauts stopped in three capitals—Belgrade (Serbia), Zagreb (Croatia), and Ljubljana (Slovenia)—giving talks, meeting classes of schoolchildren, and attending dinners and cultural events, before being sent on their way to their next stop in the West with Yugoslav weaving and handicrafts. The US government was delighted. Wooing an alternative center of Communism to the Soviets could help weaken the Eastern bloc's unity. Yugoslavia too was thrilled. It was the country both East and West wanted to win over. It was a position with powerful leverage.

But nonalignment was also a lonely furrow. Without backers, without becoming a fully funded, armed, and backed puppet state for either the United States or the Soviets, there was nobody to fill the holes that began to appear more and more frequently in the budgets: a bad crop here, a faulty piece of machinery there. As the September 9, 1971, edition of *New Scientist and Science Journal* remarked: "This brought the realisation that Yugoslavia's main hope lay in becoming a substantial trading nation and that it was necessary to change from product to market oriented industry. With continual fear of becoming dependent on any country, and the Soviet Union in particular, the Yugoslavs set about eradicating a by then huge trading deficit." As recession bit, the declared foreign policy of Yugoslavia was subordinate to one aim, and one aim only. Get hard currency, and quick.

Around this time, the League of Communists of Yugoslavia held a series of meetings. The individuals changed, but the elements were consistent. On one side of the table would be party leadership, the Ministry of Finance, and the police. On the other were their old contacts from the Balkan criminal underworld.

The result of these get-togethers was a loose alliance of the ruling Communist Party, organized crime, free enterprise, and the
intelligence services. Between them, they decided to outsource the
matter of state wealth acquisition to enterprising private citizens—
in this case, criminals—and on a plausibly deniable basis. It was to
become a blueprint for its later approach to cyber war.

The month that *New Scientist* editorial was published, September
1971, the Yugoslav government emptied its prisons of anyone convicted of organized-crime activity, issued them travel documents and
business contacts from the diaspora, and sent them West to work.
They would be encouraged to make money in any way they could—
bank raids, blackmail, private security services, business, whatever—
and have their paths eased with diplomatic letters, papers, passports,
anything that cost nothing to give. There were three conditions. The
first was that they stayed away—by exporting crime, there would
be less of it to police at home. The second was that they send plenty
of hard currency back to the Communist state's coffers, a kind of
agent's commission to keep the status quo sweet. The third was that
if needed, they could be called on. There was no limit to the number
of mouthy dissidents overseas who needed liquidating.

The immediate effect—a sudden and frenzied crime wave from
Western Europe to South America, and from the United States
through Australia and South Africa—seemed to take the authorities
in each of the countries it swept into by surprise. The police reports
from West Germany, Italy, France, Belgium, the Netherlands, and
Scandinavia make particularly grim reading, as they struggled to
cope with the sudden wave of cigarette smuggling, drug trafficking, arms dealing, bank heists, hijackings, kidnappings, armed robberies, and illegal gambling pulled off by recently freed Yugoslav
inmates sent across the border by the Yugoslav Communist Party
on moneymaking sprees—to liberate as much cash in hard currency as possible. Their orders were to keep some and send the
rest to the Ministry of Finance back in Belgrade. That way, not

only would the money arrive as hard currency, but the Communist Party itself would become its laundromat. In it flowed in duffel bags, diplomatic consignments, and car trunks, from heists, protection rackets, heroin shipments, and prostitution; out it went again, spent by the Communist Party on food, farming equipment, arms, and, increasingly, technology parts.

The scheme was extraordinarily successful. But fairly quickly, the security services ran low on actual prisoners to free and criminals to send abroad. At that point someone had a brilliant idea: they realized that Communism's big product post the 1960s—bored and disaffected youth—could be leveraged in the same way. They began to work with the police at the municipal level to identify what they termed "talented delinquents" and to groom them for trouble on a global scale.

The archetype for the kind of all-around troublemaker the Yugoslav state preferred to keep on a loose leash and pointed at the West was a young delinquent by the name of Željko Ražnatović. Born in 1952, Željko was a bad lot at school, and by fourteen was a career mugger in Belgrade's parks. In 1969 he was sentenced to three years in a young-offenders institution. On his release, his despairing Yugoslav air force colonel called up some old contacts in the Yugoslav Federal Secretariat for Internal Affairs and set up a meeting. Shortly afterward, Željko was hopping across Europe on a series of fake Western European passports issued by the Yugoslav Communist Party. Soon after that he was cutting a trail of high-stakes armed robberies through Germany, the Netherlands, Belgium, and into Scandinavia. He was first caught and jailed for armed robbery in Belgium in 1974, but he escaped from a high-security prison. A couple of years later, caught and jailed again for armed robbery, this time in Holland, he escaped again. He made yet another successful jailbreak in Germany, serving yet another term for yet another armed robbery. Barely had these headlines subsided when he freed a fellow armed robber from trial in Sweden by walking into the courtroom and pointing a gun at the judge.

His entire team—the entire generation-wide identification of talented criminals and their gentle direction toward jobs the Communist Party wanted doing—was handled by the Yugoslav secret police, the Uprava državne bezbjednosti, or UdBA. Today Ražnatović is best known as Arkan, leader of the Serb Volunteer Guard, a paramilitary force during the Balkan wars notorious for its trail of war crimes across Bosnia. (Several decades later, capturing him alive would be a key focus of the NATO rules of engagement that popped up on my computer.)

But despite the relative success of their "workers," the Communist Party was stuck. The yields from violence were far too low for the mess it was creating. After one botched assassination in Scotland when state assassins disguised as football fans shot a dissident to death while his dog raised the alarm, UdBA's chief was frostily reprimanded by none other than Margaret Thatcher (albeit reportedly with a sotto voce "You do what you have to do" after the public dressing-down). The Yugoslav security services realized they were attracting too much attention. More efficient, more thoughtful, and farsighted moneymaking schemes were needed. Maybe, they thought, the public's enthusiasm for science fiction could help.

It was proposed at a party committee meeting in Belgrade that summer that they seriously consider not just making computers but becoming a self-reliant Eastern European version of Silicon Valley. That was where the real money was going to be made in the 1980s and beyond, not Little League bank raids. And if the predictions were true, it would also form the defense of the future. A cyber front, to protect them on all sides. Until they became expert, they could import parts from the Americans—which the Russians or Chinese could not do—and learn how to copy them. The same with code. They'd sell to all the nonaligned states like India and the Arabs, who'd rather not be seen buying American. And while they were at it, they could set up their own computerized defenses.

It was a stroke of genius.

There was just the small matter of how to import parts from America without arousing suspicion among the Communist neighbors. That's when they hit upon the idea of baskets. One young Yugoslav company made computers, which depended on microprocessors that in turn needed to be imported from the United Kingdom. They consulted the regulators. Because they were creating an imbalance in import/export, that same company had to export something. So the biggest computer company in the Communist world at the time merged with a company that made rustic woven baskets. The high-tech/raffia-work industrial complex was born. A joint venture between high-tech engineers and developers and elderly countryfolk weaving handmade baskets could now import the microprocessors on a strictly monitored basis. One processor in, one basket out.

In one of the more curious episodes of the Cold War, directives were issued by the Yugoslav Communist Party to pivot to Western consumer fashion, which with the advent of mass package tourism was suddenly in love with all things that smacked of Mediterranean, rustic, and ranch style. If they looked at the records, it would be easy for future historians to conclude that, at some point in the mid-1970s, the world underwent a craze for raffia baskets, with one in every home, defining in their quietly totemic way the Latin-style ranch decor that swept the United States and the rattan and weave textures of interiors and lifestyle magazines across the world. And in fact, those historians would not be far wrong. Only, the *estancios* many of these ranch-style raffia-work pieces came from weren't in Andalusia, or Mexico, or the Argentinian pampas, but concrete silos in Communist Eastern Europe. The West might have fallen for rustic crafts, but they had no idea how many of the straw donkeys and sombreros, woven wastebaskets, and rattan chairs that suddenly flooded home stores and living rooms, markets and TV sets, were part of a Communist plot.

It was the perfect smoke screen for a secret move into high-tech.

Yugoslavia's Soviet neighbors would object once they realized it was importing microprocessor technology from the USSR's capitalist enemies in the West. When they did, the Yugoslav government would simply point to the rules. We sold a lot of baskets, it would shrug. It wasn't that we went *looking* for computer parts. We just had no choice but to accept them to balance the exports according to Communist Party policy.

The USSR was flirting with computers too, but in a way that was as paranoid as Yugoslavia's was utopian. Kremlin-backed movies, books, and other propaganda explored a brave new world of electronic human machines, artificial intelligence, and science fiction–style communication that electrification would provide. AI and a worker's paradise proved uneasy bedfellows, and if the country had been an early pioneer, the central control the Soviets had placed at its core had turned it into a different beast entirely.

The very word "robot" is Slavic in origin—it is the root of the word for "work" across most of Eastern Europe—and originated in the 1920 science-fiction play by Czech writer Karel Čapek, *RUR—Rossum's Universal Robots*. In the play, scientist Rossum creates a drone cadre of synthetic humans, programmed to follow orders. Initially, they seem happy to work for him, though the play ends on an ominous note, when a robot uprising dooms humanity to extinction. The work was an international success, and, like *WarGames* in the 1980s, sparked both concern and excitement of a level so high that the word "robot" had entered usage globally—from Russia to American English—by 1922 and spawned a whole branch of culture, taking in science fiction and industry. The USSR particularly was entranced, the robots becoming an instantly recognizable cultural meme. The 1935 Soviet propaganda movie hit *Loss of Sensation; or, Robot of Jim Ripple*, adapted from Ukrainian playwright Volodimir Vladko's *Iron Riot; or Robots Are Coming*, featured robots with the instantly recognizable logo "RUR" emblazoned on their tin sides, and became a hit across the Soviet Union with its story about a man who hatches a plot to bring down capitalism. Robots would, went the story, make human labor unexploitable.

Yet the Soviet authorities could not countenance machines that transmitted information between peers or acted in any way autonomously; they had enough trouble with flesh-and-blood humans doing that. To the Kremlin, information technology felt opaque, suspect, and decidedly *un-Soviet*. Cybernetics was regularly held up to ridicule, in newspapers and speeches. Stalin himself had dismissed the field as "one of the worst bourgeois deviancies."

As for Communist China, it too was decades behind. In the wake of the Tiananmen Square protests and massacre—not to mention the global attention they had garnered—Chinese premier Deng Xiaoping would clamp down hard on the sharing of information. As late as 1995, there were just three thousand internet users in a country of almost a billion people.

This unbridgeable void in the worldview of America's most powerful strategic opponents would see it almost entirely bypassed by the first years of the information revolution. In the period in which the West produced ARPANet, Sinclair, the internet, Tim Berners-Lee, Commodore, Microsoft, and more, the Soviet Union and its neighbors behind the Berlin Wall would achieve little more than a reputation for the confiscation and destruction of photocopiers, China a series of official clampdowns on fledgling information networks.

Yugoslavia was different. In the creation and equipping of a culture of potential cyber warriors, the West saw an opportunity to undermine Russia and China. In this wayward, freewheeling Eastern European state, it would create a generation of modern Prometheuses. Tech specialists who would help bring the Communist world to its knees.

The whirlwind love affair between Yugoslavia and everything science fiction extended to party headquarters, where the perils, technologies, and dystopias of *Doctor Who* and *Star Trek* were considered not as remote fantasy, but as dry runs for potential near-future scenarios. The appearance in *Doctor Who* of figures from MI5 and the British army, not to mention the fact that the BBC is funded by the state, seemed to amplify the idea that, somehow, these were not just dramas, but theoretical maneuvers. And so, in one of the more curious moments of Cold War history, the Yugoslav government countered it with their own real-life version. Inspired by the army of man-machine hybrid invaders who first appeared in a 1966 episode of *Doctor Who*, Zagreb University renamed the research arm of its technology faculty the "Group of Cybermen."

These Communist-funded Cybermen were to be led by a robotics visionary named Branimir Makanec. Makanec was obsessed with the fighting capability of cyborgs. As early as 1962, he had built an early remote-controlled humanoid robot called TIOSS that had roamed the city centers performing manual tasks in front of excited onlookers. With its eight-foot humanoid frame, shining metal body, articulating arms, and unblinking stare, TIOSS looked eerily similar to one of the Doctor's cybernetic nemeses. But it was the programming that most excited the Communist Party, and the country's military. Its actions were directed by rudimentary AI and it could be directed to perform simple tasks, such as operating machinery, walking about, communicating from an expanding menu of programmed phrases in response or as directed—for warning purposes, for instance—or, as it was often commanded to do in colleges and at expos, handing out leaflets to children and passersby.

But TIOSS was not a toy. For the Communist Party, it was viewed very much as an inspirational blueprint for a new way of fighting wars. For army chiefs, the Cybermen were its shorthand for automated digital-defense capability. A legion of directed machines that could keep the country safe from aggressors.

At least part of the party's excitement about TIOSS (and Yugoslavia's fascination with space-age tech as a whole) was in the promise of machines to fight future battles for them. Wasn't it a Serb—Tesla himself—who had pioneered remote control for an astonished world in Madison Square Garden in 1898?

This vision of the future was given weight by real-world developments, which seemed almost to keep pace with the most fantastic imaginings of sci-fi writers. The very year HAL appeared onboard Kubrick's spaceship at the cinema, MIT unveiled the Apollo Guidance Computer, which not only would interact with the Apollo astronauts' punched-in commands in real time, helping them steer and command their craft, but also reduced the size of the Apollo spacecraft's onboard computer from an impractical seven large refrigerators to a compact unit of less than one cubic foot. Just three months after Apollo 11 touched down in July 1969, the US military's cyber-tech research-and-development lab, the Defense Advanced Research Projects Agency (DARPA), connected ARPAnet—the first large-scale, general-purpose computer network able to connect different kinds of computers. The military internet had arrived.

The Yugoslav Communist Party's plan was simple. Yugoslavia would stop relying on crops and harvests. Instead, it would become a global player in the brave, shiny new world of cyber capability. While the superpowers were stockpiling nuclear warheads and racing for space, Yugoslavia could birth a nation-size force of machine-enabled warriors.

Report after report from Tito's spies suggested that the great, looming bulk of the USSR, obsessed with superiority in battalions and megatonnage, appeared to be missing the computer's potential. The Soviets, with their rigid approach to censorship and the sharing of information outside official channels, struggled with the idea of giving anyone at all access to information technology. In the words of a 1972 report in the *New Scientist and Science Journal*, "[Yugoslavia] has now become fully aware of the benefits that can be derived from computerization, with a particular emphasis on communications. . . . Yugoslavia has now turned to the West—and any question posed on the possible use of Russian computers is met with the shrug, 'What computers?'"

The United States was only too pleased to court the prodigal tech-obsessed nation with an anti-Soviet streak. If this country was serious about developing computer technology as a national defense, then better the Cybermen were mentored by DARPA. Within a week of asking, Makanec was dispatched by his government to the United States on a series of "cooperative fact-finding" missions. He was entertained at DARPA, the US military's Defense Advanced Research Projects Agency in Arlington, Virginia. On one of his school outreach trips to the United States, he met the teenage Bill Gates, who was already making a name for himself as something of a computer whiz.

Makanec would return inspired by ideas of networked computing power, and with a mission unheard of, even in America: Yugoslavia, he proclaimed, needed to teach its children to code. The masses would become cyber citizens and, if necessary, cyber warriors. With the party's backing, he set up a government-funded experimental lab in Zagreb, and set about emulating DARPA's own outreach networks in schools.

High-tech traffic, parts, and know-how began to flow between the United States and Yugoslavia. Military weapons developers such as the Lola Ribar Institute began designing and manufacturing a generation of small Yugoslav computers fit for both civilian and military use, with toughened bodies and battle-proof keyboard designs. Discreetly supplied by American microchips and processing units received in payment for their burgeoning raffia-work trade with the West, Communist computer companies soon stretched from the Alpine Yugoslav republic of Slovenia down through Serbia and Croatia.

Without realizing it, the United States was creating a digital mujahideen—a resistance network—and arming it with the skills it would one day use to turn on its mentors.

But the Yugoslav tech sector ran its own risks too. The Soviets were alarmed by Yugoslavia's sudden buildup of US-backed capability. And with the Cold War entering its most tense and deadly standoff in the early 1980s, they came calling.

A long-haired young network geek named Janez Škrubej had caught their attention. Slovenian-born Škrubej was part of a new generation of coders and tech heads in Silicon Valley East who admired Microsoft's vision of putting computing power at the fingertips of every citizen—a vision that took on added resonance as it crossed eastward into a land whose government saw computers as the new frontier in national defense.

Škrubej's supply routes from the United States had helped him found and grow Iskra Delta—now Yugoslavia's biggest computer developer and manufacturer. The Communist PC company was so popular, its machines, with their IBM parts and proprietary operating system, still have their own committed fans today, with conventions, blogs, books, and a feature film dedicated to them.

While Škrubej's mission had backing from parts of the government, as well as the military and intelligence services, the party leadership remained skeptical. That official skepticism changed with one telephone call. An astonished voice calling him from the party HQ in Belgrade told Škrubej that an order from the Chinese government had come through—"a very big one." The order was to make the first citywide networked computer systems in Beijing and Shanghai. It was a surprise not only because of its sheer size—it would bring enough money to keep whole cities in the Balkans in fuel and electricity for months—but because the networking capability it specified was still supposed to be a secret. If that order made the remaining skeptics in the ruling Communist Party sit up and listen, it also served notice that Yugoslavia had, inadvertently, become the go-to providers of high tech to the world's have-nots—anyone with whom the United States would not deal.

The Communist Party treasury was rolling in cash. The

military wanted more. But the intelligence services were worried. The Soviet Union had noticed too. So it was that in 1984, Škrubej found himself in the crosshairs of the Cold War's most peculiar high-tech standoff.

In private, Soviet government and military officials were becoming worried about cyber war. The 1983 Hollywood movie *WarGames* imagined the potential for global catastrophe if a kid could hack into the Pentagon Nuclear Command Center's computers. It was a fantasy movie—with its origin in writer Lawrence Lasker's fascination with Stephen Hawking's use of computerized voice technology—but it quickly began to have real-world repercussions. President Ronald Reagan, a family friend of Lasker, not only watched the film but treated it as a credible piece of speculative scenario generation. Horrified by the possibilities, he swiftly convened a series of meetings with members of Congress, his advisers, and the Joint Chiefs of Staff to discuss the film. Indeed, his interest in the film is thought to be directly responsible for the enactment eighteen months later of NSDD-145, a flagship Reagan initiative and the first presidential directive on computer security.

But it rattled the Soviet leadership too. They were convinced that the movie contained more genuine research, and betrayed more real US cyber-war capability, than the Americans were aware of.

They realized with a cold flush of panic that whatever their respective nuclear warhead counts, a terrifying gap had opened up in computing power. Through the 1970s and 1980s, the Soviet authorities had focused all of their high-tech energies into the idea of information technologies that were defiantly top down instead of network based. The very idea of a PC in the home—something that made work, thinking, playing, and communicating so unobserved, private, *personal*—went against everything they could countenance. (Putin's backdoor monitoring of the Russian internet today can be seen as the direct successor to this mind-set.)

The Soviets had computers—but they were huge centralized-mainframe workplace affairs. Of course, espionage had procured the odd individual PC—the deputy director of the Kurchatov Institute of Atomic Energy was known to have an early Apple machine in his office—but such was the suspicion and contempt with which these "toys" were seen by the Politburo that they existed as curios only, never networked, never connected. Their owners were suspect. It was a bad career move to show too much curiosity. The Soviet Union's own ability to adapt with the times—to detect emerging threats—was choked by its centrally directed structure. But the writing was on the wall. Now, belatedly, they were ruing the "reverse Missile Gap" that was opening up with the West in computing. And it wasn't only the USSR's ability to fight wars that depended on it; it was economic survival.

Now, there was this chatter around Yugoslavia. China, India, even Libya were buying into network tech. But with relations as they were, how could they hope Yugoslavia would sell their know-how to the USSR?

They decided to send in what might just be history's worst mystery shoppers.

KGB agents began turning up at Škrubej's company receptions. He and his colleagues found it funny at first, these people arriving on planes from Russia, sending faxes, always calling, wanting to buy their computers and know-how.

Buying computer systems and hardware from Belgrade or Ljubljana meant they would be able to get hold of Yugoslav machines, software, and consultancy fit for dual military and civilian use. The technologies and know-how were the equal of (and in some cases almost identical to) the very latest and best American products from Silicon Valley. For the Soviets, buying off-the-rack from Yugoslavia seemed to be the only way they could close the computing gap without international embarrassment. This was a fellow Communist country, after all. The computers weren't US made, or US labeled, in any way, even if they did have US parts. So there was no embargo. And even better, there was no way the Americans could use their purchase as a PR coup. Still, the Russians wanted to minimize their exposure to ridicule. So they first adopted a series of disguises and cover stories for their shopping expeditions.

The KGB officers' cover that they were cool-dude tech entrepreneurs from Moscow was hamstrung from the start by the fact that they hadn't a clue how a cool-tech entrepreneur might look or speak, not having any at home. "They would pretend to be from Russian computer companies," recalls Škrubej. "I knew that it wasn't true, mainly because the Soviets didn't have any damn computer companies."

The Soviets became desperate. At one point, the KGB went so far as to set up a computer shop in California itself—it was real in every detail, except it didn't have any computers—purely so that they had an address there and could pretend more convincingly to be Western purchasers. Being trained KGB, they began adding depth to their cover to allay any suspicions. Instead of sending Škrubej's office and that of the trade ministry in Belgrade simple business communiqués, they began attaching selfie photos of themselves sunbathing in Speedos on different beaches in California. "That's how they thought a real American purchaser would communicate with any overseas business they were working with," laughs Škrubej. "They just . . . *weren't very good* at it. They behaved like KGB people when they were supposed to be acting like computer people. So, eventually, they just gave up pretending. They came and said, 'OK, here we are. We are the KGB. And now: we want to buy your computers.'"

In doing so, the Soviets were walking straight into perhaps the last, and most audacious, trap of the Cold War. It was a coup de grâce that showed just how well free-market advantages could pay back national strategic goals for America—and one that would play its own little-known but central part in the Soviet Union's downfall.

The KGB's proposal put Škrubej—and Yugoslavia—in a tricky position. The Soviet spies were prepared to pay a lot of money—money that nonaligned Yugoslavia sorely needed. Government contacts began putting soft pressure on Škrubej and his colleagues. Couldn't he sell to the KGB just this once, and be discreet about it? Just treat them like any other customer? Škrubej resisted. Everything he had built—not just his company, Iskra Delta, but Silicon Valley East itself—depended on the supply of microchips from IBM and the indulgence of the Americans. He couldn't risk putting that in jeopardy by just passing tech on to the KGB like that.

Škrubej's phone call to his contacts at IBM headquarters in Armonk, New York, was exactly what IBM's own handlers at the CIA in Langley, Virginia, had been waiting for.

IBM had worked with the US government for decades as the suppliers of computing power for sensitive federal programs, from the military to policing—and, by 1985, powering not just the CIA's information processing but NASA's too. In reality, its involvement in US government work went deeper than most Americans suspected. Central Intelligence Agency records show that as early as 1971, the CIA's liaison team was given the extraordinary authority to carefully vet and approve any and all testimonies and depositions IBM was required to make to American courts in any and all business disputes, lest the computer giant accidentally let slip any information that would blow the cover on their CIA work. So when the IBM team in New York took Škrubej's call, Armonk's CIA liaison team was all ears.

While the Americans conferred, the KGB became restless. Their increasing agitation made Škrubej nervous. He insisted on being chaperoned by UdBA officers for meetings with his would-be clients. The officers would come along disguised as computer-nerd colleagues of Škrubej's at Iskra Delta. The meetings became excruciating. "At any moment there was at least one KGB present whose role was supposed to be to coerce or threaten me, so our own agents never left me alone with them."

Finally, he got a call direct from IBM headquarters in Armonk. The CIA had a plan. They would work with Iskra Delta to supply and quality-assure the parts for any Yugoslav-made machines that were to be sold to Russia. But there would be a twist. Every one of the microchips destined for Russian end-user machines would be specially doctored before shipping. Parts installed in the machines for Russia were specially made to rebel in any one of a variety of ways weeks after activation—from self-destructing to becoming illicit bugging or keystroke-transmission devices on US spying frequencies. Škrubej could hardly refuse.

Over the next few years, untold Soviet messages were intercepted and government offices put out of action by listening devices, transmitters, and gremlins installed in Škrubej's shipment. Russian government and military computers would catch fire for no apparent reason, or blow up seemingly spontaneously. The CIA was delighted, while in Russian leadership circles, computers developed an undeserved reputation for being unstable death traps, further dimming Soviet views of their prospects.

By the 1980s, Yugoslavia was in the grip of computer fever. Yet a genuine Commodore 64 or ZX Spectrum imported through the raffia-work basket-exchange system would still cost the ordinary Belgrader a month's salary. Faced with a supply bottleneck, the party stepped in. To supplement the machines and software that companies such as Iskra Delta could produce, the government's fearsome network of arms manufacturers would begin producing cheaper domestic versions of all the military computing immediately.

These were technologies the government and military had already invested in refining, so the cost of pumping out more was minimal. The most popular model, the Lola-8, was built by the Ivo Lola Ribar weapons institute in Belgrade. When it arrived in homes, even its keyboard still bore the standard military layout, with rectangular key caps laid out orthogonally to minimize dust intrusion under combat conditions. Many of the state weapons makers' computers verged on being pirated copies themselves: cloned designs and ripped-off coding from Apple, IBM, and other American tech businesses. The ubiquitous Ivasim Ivel Z3 computer was an Apple IIe copy and a core part of the Yugoslav army's field-support technical kit. The consequence was that weapons-grade state production of these machines, once it had started, was the most efficient way of trickling out computers to the public. What was good enough for the army was good enough for kids, and army surplus machines began to flow into classrooms, workplaces, bedrooms. The result was a mind-set—a badass cachet—light-years from the way Western PC users experienced the products of Silicon Valley. The East's first generation of computer geeks grew up training on military computers, with sand-proof keyboards and field-grade interfaces that they would know by heart by the time they entered compulsory national military service.

The national project didn't stop at use, though. Kids would learn how to make, strip, and adapt domestic machines in minutes.

In the long, hot summer of 1983, Voja Antonić, a journalist for *Galaksija* computer magazine, was holidaying in Risan, Montenegro. Antonić had been letting his mind spin off on tangents under the electric blue skies for days when he had an idea. Just as thirties Germany had introduced the Volkswagen as the national People's Car, or America had the Winchester rifle—a simple, reliable model that everyone could not only afford but repair and service themselves if needed—Yugoslavs needed a People's Computer. Only this one would be infinitely scalable. It could be made from scratch, out of household hardware. It would turn even the humblest villager into a DIY programmer. He set about designing his DIY machine on a piece of Hotel Teuta notepaper. Within a couple of hours, his product was ready to patent. But that wasn't what Antonić had in mind. He would release the design into the public domain, free for anyone to use. He called his contacts at *Galaksija* and planned a special issue of the magazine called "Računari u vašoj kući"

(Computers in Your Home) featuring the designs, plans, and parts directions to hit the newsstands for Christmas. While the rest of the world used computers, Yugoslav kids would be at work inside them.

These glossy magazines were a curious refraction of global male-fantasy imagery through the lens of a country all too aware of its status as Cold War outlaw and modern borderland. Dominatrices stood astride computers, while their shattered male worshippers collapsed in heaps onto their desks, having narrowly escaped the internet's global cops—usually America—by crawling back out through the PC in the nick of time. Glamorous female spies held electronic devices as if they were Zastava pistols, or reclined like leggy, miniskirted Communist Steve McQueens astride the iconic Soviet army motorbike, the Minsk M1A. But something happened to them as Yugoslavia tipped closer and closer into ethnic cleansing and war. As darkness gathered, computer magazines started to look less and less like the aspirational fantasies of the rising online generation and more like instruction manuals for cyber warriors. Just as grunge had swept the high 1980s hair-spray rock aside, the armed-and-bedraggled cyberpunk couple on the cover of *Igara 10* magazine in May 1992 look less like lifestyle fantasies from a high-living technofuture, and more like Lola Ribar tech-packing vigilantes roaming the Bosnian countryside. *Računari*, from March, simply has a woman bound and blindfolded in an empty room but for a single disconnected screen on the floor beside her—a noir scene straight from the pages of *True Detective* and the grimy underworld thrill rags of 1950s Los Angeles. These magazines promised the keys to a very real-world demimonde that could, depending on your choices, bring the excitement of artistry and a career, cybercrime and vice, espionage, dissident status, or military defense. By providing hacker tips, stories, and networks, they were the keys to a Choose Your Own Adventure game that took place in real life.

Like early hip-hop fanzines, they also became the talking shops for hackers across borders of the former Yugoslavia, a place where Croatian, Slovenian, Bosnian, Macedonian, Montenegrin, Serbian, and other hackers and computer aficionados and cyber enthusiasts could face off, inspire, or carry out games of prestige one-upmanship with each other. As new lines appeared on maps, and those lines determined whether you or your neighbors were the ones who would be hounded from your home or worse, the sense of liberation for the young in joining a borderless thing called cyberspace cannot be overstated.

And as the 1990s wore on, teenagers, students, and high school kids were increasingly swept up in a world of hackers sticking it to the Man, geeks liberating money from banks, tech-enabled citizen militias and mafiosi, smuggled computers, and illicit livelihoods.

As early as 1993, those families whose parents worked for weapons institutes, for computer firms themselves, or in other government or military roles were able to get—and share—access to their own internet connections. Going online to carry out secret jobs, to hack, to cause chaos among your enemies became the next best thing to a UdBA badge or wiseguy status.

The kids who watched *WarGames* took the hint. They were powerful. They were elite. America needed them, and this movie—Ronald Reagan's favorite, no less—laid out why. They were the strategically vital center of the world, a fully funded Silicon Valley East with the resources, money, computer tech, and connections on all sides to be whatever they wanted.

The dream could go on forever.

And then, suddenly, everything went wrong.

Chapter 2

Enter the Web

Nobody in the West spotted the slow formation of this strange, leaderless national cyber force as it knitted and coalesced.

The late 1980s were frenzied years, the years of the strange, hybrid military-technological-criminal complex that would become Yugoslavia's defining contribution to twenty-first-century warfare. An odd, millenarian frenzy gripped the country's youth as they felt the Cold War stasis coming apart. The action in the most popular Yugoslav computer game of the eighties, *Kontrabant*, revolved around the player being a smuggler trying to get illicit computers across the border from Italy, past Yugoslav army border guards and inspections, so they could assemble it at home, get coding, and begin fucking with the Man.

Communist Party leadership was not just okay with that. It was *behind* it. These DIY coders' de facto HQ was a concrete Communist Party complex in New Belgrade's gleaming, postwar-brutalist suburb, and it still stands today, gray and defiant. The House of Youth—Dom Omladine—was built on Tito's orders in 1964 as a statement: this was a Communist Party like no other. Yugoslavia wasn't afraid of the flat-networked, youth-powered silicon future like the USSR was. It was *betting* on it.

While the USSR suffocated beneath a blanket of Tchaikovsky and trad Communist doctrine, Tito's House of Youth became a petri dish for a strange, new Eastern European breed of cyberpunks. The party celebrated their look—even commissioning photographers to chronicle the movement in clubs and bars. This was cyberpunk not as the anarchic, joy-in-dystopia statement it was in the West, but as psyops. The guarantors of Yugoslav peace and prosperity would be Communism plus the asymmetric power of futuristic, pulsing computer networks. Out of Cybermen, there came a new fashion and pop culture tribe, rave-inspired cyborgs.

But since a connected network like the internet did not exist, it proved necessary to invent one. Instead of fiber-optic cables, microchips, and private equity, the most intriguing homemade proto-internet bodged together by these technopunks used radio waves and funding they wrangled from the oblivious oldies in the Yugoslav Communist Party. The popular Belgrade new-wave rock radio show *Ventilator 202* ran from 1979 to 1987, hosted by ebullient Belgrade personality, DJ, and aviator Zoran Modli. Razor-cut and flamboyantly dressed in punky PVC jeans and leather jacket, by 1983 Modli was trying to figure out ways to connect all those DIY coders. He began turning to computer code as much as music for his radio show's playlist. The DJ would excitedly hype and play the audio of program code over the airwaves, as if they were tunes, for the kids to tape at home. He interspersed the latest songs by unsigned indie bands with the bleeps and fizzes of code. *Ventilator 202* quickly became the most popular youth broadcast in the country, taking the free downloading of software into homes. Listeners would send in their own computer code for Modli to queue up and broadcast to home tapers, or they would make requests—for lines of code people wanted and that others would supply to be played and downloaded. By 1988, *Ventilator 202* had become the world's first large-scale peer-to-peer file-sharing network, stretching from the Alps to the Black Sea.

But it was the Communist Party–funded youth radio channel called B92 that finally plugged this generation of hackers into the worldwide internet. Founded on May 15, 1989, just as the Cold

War stasis was disintegrating, the channel was run from the Dom Omladine by youths themselves. Its founding manifesto was the UN Declaration of Human Rights: the rights to personal liberty, justice, freedom from discrimination, freedom of movement, free elections, and a free press. It was a dangerous time to say any such thing. Ironically, it would set them at odds with a new set of political leaders in a way that would create the big bang, turning the cyber generation loose online.

The late 1980s were tense in Yugoslavia. A rabble-rousing Communist Party apparatchik turned populist named Slobodan Milošević had swept to power amid rising nationalist sentiment in each of the country's republics, combining the Communist Party's embrace of organized crime with rabble-rousing rhetoric, stoking grievance among a population stripped of the unifying blanket of Communism. In March 1991, the country finally tipped into a brutal decade-long series of wars that pitted neighbor against neighbor and former comrade against comrade. First Croatia, then Slovenia broke away, then Bosnia. Belgrade fought to keep whatever it could—the vision wavering between preserving a rump Yugoslavia and scrambling to create a Greater Serbia.

It's almost impossible to untie the many and complex knots of cause and effect around the impact on ordinary people of the sudden economic squeeze, plunge in living standards, brain drain, desperation of the ruling Socialist Party—the rebranded Communists of the totalitarian state—to hold on to power at all costs and the plunge into nationalistic war. But the numbers hint at the sheer scale of it. By the start of February 1993, inflation was at 200 percent. By August it had soared past 1,880 percent per month. Your morning's work was almost worthless by evening. Yet the bottom had still not been reached; it was nowhere close. The central bank began issuing 50-million-dinar notes. By January 1994, monthly inflation was running at 313 million percent, a figure never seen before in recorded history, anywhere in the world. The currency was not merely worthless at that point; its very existence was absurd. An audit in 2001 consolidated 1993–1994's annualized inflation at *286 billion* percent.

Milošević and his government cronies combed through the newspapers' and TV channels' personnel files, weeding out those who were members of trade unions, critical of their rule, troublemakers, or just suspect. Belgrade clamped down on the media—accusing them of lies and fake news, stirring up populist anger at their "elite," "globalist," "cosmopolitan" stances.

Now a vestige of another era, B92's youth- and resistance-oriented operation kept being shut down. So far it always came back. They knew it was only a matter of time before it went off the air for good. Enter young university lecturer Drazen Pantic. Wiry and gregarious, he had traveled with Belgrade University and seen how academics in the United States were using email and bulletin boards. One night in 1995 he was drinking with students who ran Radio B92's antigovernment shows. He turned to them and asked why, if they were so scared of being shut down for good, they didn't just turn themselves into an online group that would be harder to trace. He talked about private networks and distributed servers called mirrors. Nobody was doing that. Not Russia, not China. Not even many Americans. The Serbian weapons facilities labs might know about it, but sure as hell not the goons in government. The kids rolled their eyes. Great idea. But the only internet connections were given out by the regime, just like broadcasting licenses.

Pantic shrugged. He'd met some people from Amsterdam on his travels who claimed to lead a professional hacker organization. If they wanted to become real resistance fighters, maybe a call to them was a start.

The Dutch group was XS4ALL. Part business, part counterculture operation, the group was ahead of its time. It was founded by Rop Gonggrijp, a hacker himself. Shaven headed, wiry, and imposing, Gonggrijp had been editor and founder of one of the original hacker magazines (along with *2600 Hacker Quarterly* in the United States), *Hack-Tic*. Later, he would become part of the Wikileaks team that leaked the infamous *Collateral Murder* video bearing witness to the US military's atrocities in Iraq. Launched at the same time as B92 in 1989, *Hack-Tic* was as a semisecretive underground publication—fifty copies only of each issue, all made with a photocopier. Its articles are shocking to read today and amount to something like instruction manuals for technologically enabled crimes.

But word of mouth grew, and the underground went overground. By the early 1990s, it had grown to a print run of several thousand. When *Hack-Tic* morphed, providing a similarly anarchic internet service provider (ISP), Gonggrijp and the team realized they needed someone with a business-strategy background. His cofounder was a handsome, sandy-haired former restaurant worker from Amsterdam in his midtwenties named Felipe Rodriguez who had stumbled into the internet just as Pantic was now doing, and was full of missionary zeal for the equalizing power of hacking. Rodriguez saw Belgrade's youthful cyber legions as a secret weapon in the fight for an open internet that wasn't controlled by American corporations.

On the day Pantic visited Rodriguez at his flat in Amsterdam, he got a taste of the kind of attention he could expect. As he made his way up the block staircase and onto the landing where the plan told him he'd find Rodriguez's apartment door, he found the stairwells, flights, and hallways clogged with around fifteen men, all clad in near-identical black suits and sunglasses, "like members of the Blues Brothers." As he rounded the landing, he was surprised to note that they were filing out of Rodriguez's apartment—and the boxy figure of Rodriguez was shooing them out. The legions of suits spilling out of the flat, he explained, were all Church of Scientology lawyers. XS4ALL were in a legal fight with them, Rodriguez laughed.

It wasn't just the Scientologists beating a path to Rodriguez's door. Dutch telecom monopoly PTT was trying to get *Hack-Tic* shut down for instructing young people, issue after issue, on exactly how to hack PTT's networks. Pantic expected to be grilled, but they stopped him before he could begin his presentation. "No problem," they laughed. "We're gonna get your young people the internet for free. Just get a telephone line. We'll take care of the rest."

The very first investor in the post-Communist internet was not a government, or a business, but a Dutch hacker organization and piracy collective. The Eastern internet born in those fraught weeks would not be a safe, corporate environment as it had become in the West, floated in on stock-market optimism, military testing, and the promise of e-commerce, global community, walled gardens, and high-res erotica for all. Instead, its first introduction would be as a tool of dissidence, one that could be leveraged to decenter official power.

Through everything that followed—even as governments took it over and the Russian authorities under Vladimir Putin embarked on their campaigns of sabotage and disinformation in Georgia, Estonia, Ukraine, and ultimately America itself—the Eastern internet remained a very different beast from the American strain precisely because of the way it was introduced to Belgrade.

Because it was introduced by hacktivists, it was, perhaps more honestly, always defined as a fundamentally partisan tool rather than as an essentially neutral set of protocols. Here, it was not a mainstream industry, but a tool for destabilizing the mainstream.

For Pantic, there remained the even more basic problem of getting a phone line. Under the increasingly dictatorial Milošević regime, as under Communism, this meant going to the regime-controlled telecoms monopoly and asking for approval. But where the formal structures represented hurdles, informal connections could help. One of Pantic's university colleagues heard him talking about his plans for a dissident internet. The colleague was a keen chess player and mentioned that at his weekly chess club, he sometimes played against a paunchy regime apparatchik whose job in the government would almost certainly mean that he could approve an internet connection line on the quiet. The problem was that he was, warned the friend, "an old-school, an ex-Communist, and one of those guys who drinks neat slivovitz for breakfast. The worst kind of tin-pot functionary."

Come the day, Pantic sat in the apparatchik's smoky office and asked for his help bringing public internet to the kids. The man smoked and drank steadily through the presentation, his face stern and impassive. At the end, he pointed his finger at Pantic, leaned forward, and thundered, "You are an enemy of the state!" Pantic froze. "But," murmured the official, holding up his hand, "I have a son. And my son talks about this 'internet' thing all the time." He poured another vodka. "Your request is therefore approved."

This first group of rebel connections in the dingy upper-floor office of a threatened radio station was the spark from which the twenty-first century's conflicts would grow. But for now, nobody was watching. Even in Belgrade, it was a closely guarded secret, a clandestine ops room where, day and night, young Belgraders would slip up to the landing and queue and then catch one of the six terminals. It became known as the place where those without military connections learned hacking skills from each other.

It couldn't stay a secret for long. As February 1996 rolled around, the hacker collective got a call to say that the country's two most feared regime-backed oligarchs—Belgrade tycoon brothers Bogoljub and Dragomir Karić—were intending to pay a visit to the supposedly secret office, with their own security.

The brothers had been in business together since the 1960s, in everything from construction to banking, and were now Balkan éminences grises who not only could make or break Milošević, but had the power to make things happen in Russia, China, Ukraine, Belarus, and the Middle East. Their banks held the Milošević clan's money. Dragomir was one of Slobodan's negotiators in Bosnia.

They were widely believed to be bankrolling the development work of the army itself. Now they were concerned about reports of a young hacker collective in the heart of the city.

To everyone's surprise, their interest was not in shutting down the secret room, but in supercharging it and taking it nationwide. They were in on what could be achieved through communications sabotage; they had seen it in the weapons institutes. But they were canny enough to know that nothing could be achieved against Russia or the West with the odd incursion. A citizenry of young cyber warriors? That might just give Serbia some muscle.

One of the first things the brothers learned as they scrambled to set up their own high-powered ISP for the whole population was that infrastructure was just the first step. Next, you had to find people who could administer your network. But how to find all those admins in a country where there was simply no ready pool of users?

The answer was schoolkids.

While China and Russia were carefully selecting occasional bright engineers from universities to become part of their own government cyber-war capabilities, Yugoslavia's tech-savvy school teens were only too ready to get stuck into technological issues with the cool efficiency of a garage mechanic changing your oil, thanks to people like Voja Antonić and the coder and game designer Žiga Turk, creator of *Kontrabant*. On top of that, kids would work for pennies. They could be recruited through parents in government jobs, through schools, through universities.

One of the first crop of admins to be recruited through parents was Zoran Rosic. Rosic was a burgeoning hacker by the age of twelve. Both of his parents were computer scientists, his dad working at the government's high-tech weapons, aerospace, and computer lab, the Institute Mihailo Pupin in Belgrade, and through them he'd grown up on one of the few early military/government-employee home internet connections from 1993. That year he'd heard a new English term going around: "exploit." The idea of a

piece of code that worked on a vulnerability in a program to sub-
vert the system was full of dark excitement in the former Communist republic. When the first exploits had started to emerge that
year, he'd watched and then found other curious kids online and
began a hacker group. They would spend hours over the phone on
chat, figuring out how to hack early sites and servers, in Serbia, the
United States, and Western Europe.

It provided an escape from an increasingly alienating daily
reality. But it also provided him with his first taste of power. The
smart, bright-eyed little kid with his mop of black hair began to
enjoy social cachet—and be accepted by a core of cool, rebellious
hacker kids from elsewhere in Belgrade who were all some five
years his senior.

Rosic had already cut his teeth on disk drives and closed systems and played with some of his father's access. Recruited through
the institute's workers like most of the children who fronted the
Eastern internet, he jumped at the chance to work with an ISP. His
parents encouraged him, provided he could manage schooling during the day and working for the new internet service at night.

Like the rest of his school-age colleagues, he found there was
little real administrating to do and set about engaging in hacking
activities through the nights. He got half the money he'd been told,
but far more freedom. The oversight was almost zero.

The first time he pulled off something risky was 1996, when the
first Unix servers came to the university. Like the older members
of his hacker group, he had asked for an account. But the system
admin refused, sneering that Rosic was "just a kid" and writing
that he should get lost. Rosic was incensed. He was not just good;
maybe he was the best hacker of the lot of them. So later that evening, he returned, hacked into the admin's server, and deleted the
whole thing.

The following day at lunchtime, Rosic was walking to McDonald's in the city center when one of the older hackers who led the

group recognized him and called out, "Hey, little guy! Did you hear about that hack yesterday? Do you have any idea who did that? Hear any rumors?" Rosic said he hadn't heard anything. The older kid laughed. "Well, I didn't do it, and I cannot think of anyone else who *could* do it except me." Rosic nodded. "Right, I guess it had to be someone smarter than you," he said, and walked into McDonald's for his fries.

The university, meanwhile, launched its own investigation.

■ ■ ■ ■ ■

Flame haired, leather jacketed, and blessed with the kind of voice that usually accompanies glamorous Eastern European spies in Hollywood film noir and twenty Marlboros a day, Professor Mirjana Drakulic was a lecturer at the university's law faculty. With a reputation for straight talking and for getting the stiffs and regime apparatchiks higher up to do what she wanted, she was fascinated by the idea that cyberspace was a new dimension of human reality, that it was growing fast, that it looked certain to become a major field of everything from war to business, yet in Serbia at least, not a single law applied to it.

It was this that had led her to the information technology faculty, where she'd met a similarly spooked informatics lecturer with a mustache and an infectious laugh called Ratimir. They married and quickly became a duo—two researchers, tracing the intersection of cyberspace and trouble. Crime fighters in a place where nothing was a crime. They were enlisted to help the university's IT head, the cropped-blonde computer pioneer and anti-Milošević dissident leader Srbijanka Turajlić, to establish just what had happened to the university's server and to identify the hackers.

Turajlić isolated the network, and the investigating team got a fix on the intruders' access points. The investigation led to two specific computers at two different locations. The team was surprised to discover that the hacks had come from the home computers of two of their colleagues at the Belgrade University. Confronted with the file of evidence, the owners of the computers seemed baffled, not to mention horrified at the thought that they had carried out the country's first major cyberattack on a state institution. Drakulic and Turajlić took them through the times and durations of the intrusions, matching real-world data with network evidence in a way that would become standard. And that's when the penny dropped. The intrusions had occurred when their children had access to the room housing their computers for extended periods.

Mirjana Drakulic had half expected the perpetrators to be university students, but the list of possible candidates for the hack revealed even the oldest of them to be just sixteen years old. The youngest had just turned thirteen. The investigators and the parents paused in silence for a moment. Drakulic explained that there was nothing in the criminal code of the country about it. There wasn't even a university policy. It simply did not exist as any kind of offense. The father of the youngest child just laughed. "Well, great. So what do we do?"

The thirteen-year-old Zoran was relaxing at home when the downstairs phone rang. It was his father, calling from work. His family was friends with Turajlić. He paused, then said in his sternest tone, "Zoran, I have been speaking to Srbijanka from the university." Then he paused. "It seems some shit went down in the computer center. Some hacker broke in, cleaned out the server, and deleted everything else. They have made the list of potential suspects." The thirteen-year-old replied, "I see. Who is on the list?" "Well, *you* are on the list, Zoran. In third place." "Well," replied the child. "They should put me in first place."

Mr. Rosic gave his son a telling-off, though he admitted that the skill was unexpected and commendable. Rosic could tell his son was proud, but "he tried to hide that reaction from me. Although there were no laws or rules, I was supposed to believe it was wrong."

The arrival of the internet and the sudden blossoming of a

cadre of trained and savvy schoolchildren to run it was the fuel that the established networks of code junkies, file sharers, hackers, and software crackers had been waiting for. The hack was just the first faint spray of what became a tsunami of hacks, against government sites, university servers, sites abroad and at home. Time and again, intruders brought networks down, in the former Yugoslavia and elsewhere. Time and again, the perpetrators were juveniles—young Belgraders, driven by kudos and curiosity. Drakulic and her colleagues watched. "We didn't believe it at first. We thought it was just a freak. But this was a movement, and it was building in secret."

Like Rosic opining that he deserved to be "put in first place" on the list of hacker suspects, they began to publicly claim responsibility for exploits. It even became fashionable to announce in advance that at a premeditated time, in a certain way, and for a certain purpose, you would hack a certain target—and then proceed to do just that. The child hacker behind the job would leave their name in the code for good luck, or excitedly phone one of the country's glossy computer magazines and tell the editors to go look at the hack, being absolutely sure they got your name spelled right for the write-up before you rang off.

Within weeks, what began as groups of peers and school or college friends morphed into citywide networks. They gave themselves nicknames, codes of conduct, brands, more akin to those used by street gangs, secret societies, and pirate ships than citizen militias. In hacker code, some defined themselves as "black hats," hackers whose intent was malicious or criminal. Others emerged as "white hats," whose motivations were either to improve security and point out or close up exploitable holes or to battle against black-hat intrusions, oppressive security, and other online bad guys. Most were gray hats: adventurers driven by curiosity over principle to explore the strange, new world that was opening up to them.

In Serbia, one teenage crew that arrived in 1996 grew fast, through a particularly close relationship with the intelligence services, and was named Crna Ruka (Black Hand). It had quickly established itself at the center of black-hat action and often nationalist, proregime information warfare and hacking ops. It was named after the nationalist group of which Gavrilo Princip was a member when he shot Archduke Ferdinand in Sarajevo and ushered in the Great War. They swiftly became known for nationalistic defacements and criminal actions. Black Hand even claimed to be the same organization that Princip had become part of, hinting at a *Da Vinci Code*–style existence in the shadows through the years since World War II, until they were needed to ride out like King Arthur and save the nation once again. C1337ORG emerged alongside them: shadier, less overtly nationalistic, and infinitely less keen on being identified.

"There is no doubt that the brand name was the Black Hand's protection," says Drakulic. "It was a sign to Milošević and the thugs that they were on the same side." Others are more pointed. "The Black Hand was an operation from the start," said one former hacker claiming Black Hand affiliation. "We were groomed by the military. We were never paid, but were we mentored? Did they connect us with others? Make sure we got what we needed? Provoke us? Yes they did."

But not everyone was quite so happy to let this gang of Serb nationalist hackers have their own way. The wave spread to the surrounding former Yugoslav republics, where homegrown crews would attempt to sabotage and disrupt the Black Hand's pro-Serbia work. Kosovo Albanian crews organized to fight back against Serbian hackers' pro-Serb defacements of Albanian websites, with some of the Albanian diaspora's funding drive—not just among Albanians but the global Muslim *ummah* from Turkey, Saudi Arabia, Libya, and Syria—going toward the swift upskilling and equipping of hacker crews. Other Balkan neighbors followed suit. Mindful of the rising online nationalist actions and scarred by a half decade of conflict with Serbia, the former Yugoslav republic of Croatia's government was sponsoring its own hothouse of hacks and information ops in the form of the Croatian Mind Hackers, led by two teenagers going by the code names Positive 0 and Negative 0.

One who seemed to have a charmed life was a kid called Goran Katlevic, who styled himself the King of Croatian Hackers.

After Croatia's secession from Yugoslavia in 1990 alongside Slovenia, the country broke down in a series of horrific internecine and sectarian wars to carve up the spoils, notably Bosnia-Herzegovina. What had been an ethnic patchwork state tipped into ethnic cleansing as the two sought to claim "majority Catholic" or "majority Serb" areas as theirs, butchering any others—especially Muslim Bosniaks—whom they saw as undermining their claims. By 1996, only Serbia and Montenegro still called themselves Yugoslavia. The very fact that Katlevic hacked in the name of Croatia was enough to raise Black Hand suspicions that he was a Croatian government operative. Then, on the second day after the remainder of Yugoslavia put up an official country website as a way to push information and diplomacy, Katlevic hacked into it and took it down. He rubbed salt into the government's wounds, announcing in the hacker pages of the Serbian computer magazines that it had been "ridiculously easy."

Amid protests from Milošević, the authorities in Zagreb announced that Katlevic would be taken in and investigated for causing a serious diplomatic incident. Yet within days, he was hacking Croatian National Television and flooding the screens with trash talk about Serbia. Then he interrupted online news schedules across the Balkans, replacing reports on Serbia with rapid-fire sequences of full frontals from *Playboy*.

It is impossible to imagine the excitement this move generated. Before the great *Playboy* takeover, it was possible for the hacks to have passed regular people by. Now everyone knew their names.

What followed was nothing short of a frenzy. Schoolchildren, students, seemingly everyone began daring each other, initiating public beefs via the hacks, and undertaking more and more public, and security-sensitive, challenges. A reliable pattern emerged, similar to gang warfare conducted over servers instead of zip codes or blocks. A public spat or a challenge would erupt. At this point, a website would be attacked, passwords stolen, and documents liberated for the bragging rights.

But for the more conscientious in that pre-Google age, it was a chance to gain and exchange experience on what quickly became a sort of informal degree in hacking. The forerunners of today's internet, the Bulletin Board Service (BBS) model involved each physical server running software that would allow users from anywhere in the world to connect to it. To do so, all you needed was a terminal program. Through the early 1990s, they were the internet, at least as far as the public was concerned, accessible with nothing more than a phone line and a low-cost modem that could deliver good performance given the graphics-light nature of BBS content. Many Bulletin Board Services were also prime, global exchanges for the code set pieces beloved of hackers known as scripts, with Eastern Europe's burgeoning nationalist collectives plundering them. "We used to obtain user names and passwords for some hack of a BBS in the United States," recalls one Belgrade hacker, "and then we would use a dialogue connector so that we could connect to it, find scripts, and so on." All of this was below the radar.

Emailing lists were the major source of scripts. Tips became explanations, explanations became demonstrations, demonstrations became impromptu flash mobs carrying out cyberattacks. The emails became popular currency offline too, in playgrounds and streets. A secondary layer of hackers amassed—so-called script kiddies, or inexperienced hackers who only take pieces of code other people have made and deploy them. They are often dismissed by the skilled hackers and coders, but they are the infantry of cyber war, often critically swelling the numbers in actions like DDoS attacks. DDoS stands for Distributed Denial of Service. It

involves inundating servers with traffic from all quarters until they
are overwhelmed and crash. Such attacks are able to cause as much
chaos and confusion as any defacement. Soon, kids from all over
Serbia were organizing in secret during the day, then logging on in
the evenings to carry out joint attacks on chosen targets by night.

Incredibly, little or none of this activity was picked up by Western intelligence services. What did come to their notice was chalked
up as mischief, or at worst vandalism or cybercrime. Simply, in the
view of America and its allies, they had bigger fish to fry dealing
with military and diplomatic matters.

Yet to ask whether these attacks were acts of cyber war or simply criminal hacks is to attempt to place modern definitions on an
environment that simply had no need to differentiate. While the
first wave of hackers in the United States and the West typically
chose targets for a reason—whether grievance, protest, political
motives, criminal intent, or simply mischief—this distinction was
largely absent in the hacker scenes of the East. To a nation of impoverished kids raised on a cocktail of bandit smarts and technological
utopian dreams, only to have their nations torn apart by nationalist
politicians on the take and mafia and businessmen close to power,
liberating hard currency from the Man through cybercrime was at
least as political an act as taking down a government target, there
or abroad.

Yet back in Belgrade, this was a lightbulb moment—for the military, for hackers, for the regime. The intelligence services began
watching the young admins, reaching out for help—and even
attempting to join their ranks in the chats, to see if they could infil-
trate protest marches or online antigovernment sentiment.

The first intelligence service in the world to adopt a policy of
infiltrating online groups in the name of national security was
the Serbian Yugoslav UdBA. It pioneered the mentoring and trolling toward action of cyber warriors online from these first incursions in 1996 as part of its shift away from running purely physical

criminal networks for neutralizing dissidents, setting provocations, and netting revenue in hard currency—and in direct response to the arrival en masse of the hacker children.

Their approach would become, in time, the conscious and studied template for the Chinese government's cultivation of its own cadre of independent hackers for the nation and for the Russian security services' running of dual-purpose criminal-defense cyber networks. Even what the FBI does now, running its own undercover presences on extremist-friendly networks like Gab and 4chan, it started scrambling to achieve only after 9/11. The internet was, after all, not something they knew they should catch up on. Yet even on the ground, domestic intelligence agencies remained strangely uninformed as to what was going down.

In fact, they were stumbling against an unusual gap in their ability to trace and monitor the networks. Most of their admin hackers were schoolchildren. This meant they were known to each other "irl"—from school classes or regular hangouts like the McDonald's in Belgrade's city center. Any new voice claiming to be one of them online was almost immediately verified, falsified, assessed, and struck off in schoolyard gossip or physical after-school meetings. The birth of this new generation of cyber warriors, and its resistance to infiltration, was aided by the ultimate secure, two-factor identification protocol: paper notes passed along the rows of desks in class.

But while the intelligence services scrambled to bring their latest recruits into the fold and stop them from straying, many in the government still did not connect these online kids with the long-held national dream of an army of cyber warriors to defend the country.

The few vestiges of Soviet-style central-planning thought in the system quailed at the idea that they couldn't control what was done over private internet connections quite as easily as they controlled what made the TV news or got printed in regime mouthpiece papers. Was this new internet going to become the long-hoped-for citizen cyber militia who would leap to their computers to defend the homeland? Or was it a boon for traitors and fifth columnists?

This was the conundrum on which the Soviet Union's aspirations for a Communist internet had floundered and on which Russia's and China's authorities remained resolutely stuck. The two giants were now aware of the technology, and its potential. They were witnessing the dot-com boom. But they were simply unable to countenance a world without gatekeepers.

Even in Serbia, the former Communists in government zoned in on the fact that organizations like OpenNet received international assistance from journalistic and democratic organizations overseas—from the Voice of America to the BBC and George Soros's prodemocracy Open Society foundation. While they were lionized in magazines and opposition media, regime TV, radio, and newspapers denounced even independent bloggers as "mercenaries" and "traitors." The atmosphere for the hacker kids was febrile.

For the intelligence services, though, the reward of stewarding the Black Hand and of tolerating the others was greater than the risk.

One directorate particularly took an interest in their information-war potential. It was a department with no official name, because it was supposed not to exist, but informally it was known as the Department of Chaos, or sometimes the Ministry of Comedy. During the Communist era, its specialism had been in sowing chaos among dissident groups by measures such as printing fake dissident newspapers that purportedly "confessed" to resistance leaders' corruption, collaboration with the government, or other evils. They became known for pranking dissident meetings with stink bombs, for arranging mock funerals for regime critics, and for adding playful twists to their many assassinations. Itself staffed by a mix of career spooks and ex-journalists, the Department of Chaos saw before anyone—China, Russia, the West, and even the hackers themselves—the form of the wars that were to come in the new century.

The form of these future wars was a question nagging at the minds of a few niche workers in the US military too. At the National Security Agency headquarters in Maryland, there was a new director. A gray-haired Texan USAF career man, Lieutenant General Kenneth Minihan had arrived in February 1996, straight from his previous posting as commander of the Air Force Information Warfare Center in San Antonio, Texas. He'd seen close-up the probing of US military networks by hackers and was anxious to put the issue of cybersecurity at the top of the National Security Agency's agenda.

In San Antonio, the tech crews had reported frequent attempts at incursions. On the hoof, they'd repelled the attacks. But it did not strike Minihan as the way things should be done. Admins on the ground were working hard to keep the networks secure and integral, but they were doing so in the almost complete absence of strategic leadership. It was, for too many senior USAF officers, an unglamorous problem. It was too gnarly, too technical, too hard to get a hold of. They seemed to zone out as soon as the tech teams started talking about servers and code. It felt like that dread thing in the military, more housekeeping. But for Minihan, now at the NSA, that added up to a dangerous blind spot. He resolved to use the annual Pentagon Joint Staff exercise called Eligible Receiver as a test case. The next opportunity would be for the one to be held in June 1997.

Eligible Receiver was an exercise that involved some form of live simulation that would highlight an emerging threat, weakness, or opportunity for the US military. Minihan pitched for the June 1997 exercise to probe US cyber infrastructure's preparedness for a state-sponsored cyberattack. But Minihan's pitch went further in scope and realism than any previous exercise. "He'd heard about small-scale exercises of this sort, against battalions or air wings of the Army or Air Force," wrote Fred Kaplan in his account in *Dark Territory*. "In these war games, he'd been told, the hackers *always* succeeded." This had made Minihan less than confident in the value of a simulation. The attacks Minihan proposed for Eligible Receiver '97 (ER97) would be real.

To his satisfaction, the Pentagon agreed. Moreover, the exercise was to last ninety days, an astonishing amount of time for such a maneuver, in which the attacks could come from any vector, against any target in the US military or civilian infrastructure.

The participants were a roll call of all the great and the good in the US cyber community. The CIA, FBI, US State Department, Defense Intelligence Agency, National Reconnaissance Office, Defense Information Systems Agency, and Department of Justice all joined the NSA's own "attackers" in the exercise. So did a number of civilian infrastructure companies, from power-generation and utilities providers to telecoms networks.

The NSA itself formed a number of two-person "Red Teams," each consisting of one hacker and one observer, who were to role-play North Korea, Iran, and Cuba as the key state actors the agency judged likely to launch such an attack. These teams were set the objective of targeting and compromising specific pieces of US infrastructure, defended by interagency "Blue Teams." There was an additional twist that pointed to the NSA's suspicions as to the prime vector of attack, even then: while the Blue Teams were unconstrained, the "hostile" hackers were permitted to use only hacking tools easily found and obtained on public areas of the 1990s internet.

First came attacks on the civilian infrastructures of eight major US cities, ranging from disabling 911 calls to bringing down power grids. Phase two was military command and infrastructure. It was, wrote Kaplan, "a massive attack on the military's telephone, fax, and computer networks—first in US Pacific Command, then in the Pentagon and other Defense Department facilities. The stated purpose was to disrupt America's command-control systems, to make it much harder for the generals to see what was going on and for the President to respond to threats with force."

For twenty years, as far as reports went, that was as far as the exercise went. In fact, there had been a third phase, the existence of which was successfully kept secret until a Freedom of Information request from the nongovernmental NSA Archives project at George Washington University forced the release of records in 2018. Part three involved simulating conventional terrorist attacks, in the physical space, mounted with the benefit of information gained online by the Red Teams.

The exercise unfolded in a way that should have changed everything. The NSA hacking teams, with minimal head count and using only publicly available freeware, managed to gain privileged access to more than thirty-six target computer systems—including that of US Pacific Command based in Hawaii, which at the time oversaw command of some one hundred thousand troops stationed throughout Asia. The hackers had control of the power and utility grids of every single one of the US cities. They had taken over the USS *National Pride*, making a cyber hijacking at sea. They had changed and added user accounts and been able to reformat hard drives across every one of the compromised targets. "By the third day," recalled one Red hacker, "we had the Blue Team on the run."

Worse still, as the dust settled, it became clear that the scope for America to be plunged into disorder was tantalizingly broad. Downing emergency lines, power, and telecoms across military and civilian targets, and interrupting command chains, meant complete paralysis of troop deployment on the ground. There would be chaos in the streets. The potential for damage and loss of life was incalculable. Even reporting and assessing damage—even flying to it—would be impossible. Confusion and bloodshed would reign.

ER97 did cause consternation among observers. Startled by the level of penetration, the US military hurried to redefine its Cold

War–era Defense Condition footings (known as DEFCON) with a new variant: Information Condition, or INFOCON. Like DEFCON, this could be raised or lowered—INFOCON 1, INFOCON 2, and so on—as threat and readiness levels changed. It also pushed the Department of Defense to create the first joint cyber command, the Joint Task Force–Computer Network Defense (JTF-CND), reporting directly to the deputy secretary of defense, in December 1998. The plan was for JTF-CND to encompass STRATCOM, CYBERCOM, and a number of other functions so that, in the words of one military insider, "the left hand would know what the right hand was doing—and hopefully, the brain would tell both of them what to do."

They did not have to wait long.

One morning in late February, the alarm sounded at Wright-Patterson Air Force Base, Ohio. Someone unauthorized was inside the military's computer networks. The mystery hackers were installing back doors, then coming and going almost at will. The files being opened were sensitive, but not earth-shatteringly revelatory, often technical specs on aircraft design and so on.

But the more the newly trained US team looked, the stranger the hacks seemed. This hacker wasn't just popping in and messing about like a teenage badass—or intelligence agency—simply showing off their chops. They weren't just messing with files; they were taking them. This hacker was swift, but they were thorough, navigating purposely, and sticking around inside for long periods. And when they left, they were always careful to rewrite the logs so that their incursion, their very presence, would be covered up.

The cyber sleuths set a trap: they inserted a tiny piece of code called a digital beacon, not unlike the modern Facebook pixel, into some suitably tempting files. It was a technology that would go on to become ubiquitous: from the digital beacon the US team inserted back in 1998 come all the trackers that today give you everything from location-specific ads in your Twitter timeline to home-ware store locators. But back in 1998, this tiny slice of "beacon" code was hot from development and still cutting-edge enough to stand a very good chance of going undetected by the hacker. The team hoped it would give a trace to the geographical location of the hacker, and, sure enough, hours later, it stabilized on the Russian Academy of Sciences in Moscow—part of Russia's own governmental attempt to replicate the work of Silicon Valley. Teams at the academy work on everything from AI, image recognition, robotics, software, and defense to space dynamics, a close match for the topic areas covered in the stolen files. Then digital forensics managed to decrypt some of the code the hacker was using and found Cyrillic characters.

The idea that the Russian government itself, in these post–Cold War years of collaboration, was prioritizing its few internet lines for the theft of US military science beggared belief inside the Pentagon, and opinion was split as to how to handle it: Was it a diplomatic, military, or criminal case? The answer would depend on whether this was a rogue incursion or something officially sanctioned. Eventually, the FBI took over and sent a delegation to Moscow under the auspices of seeking Russian help to solve a crime. The FBI investigators met a Russian delegation, who seemed as crestfallen as they did; one general brought out academy computer logs for examination. When they were found to match the US records of the hacks, he hurled insults at what he called "those motherfuckers in intelligence." While the investigators soon had their probe shut down by the Kremlin, the incursions—the US team dubbed the series of hacks "Moonlight Maze"—stopped.

Yet even in these steps, the United States was still prepping for a theoretical foe who cyberattacked much as traditional armies would attack—all at once, and from a particular angle, with some form of strategic goal in mind. While the make-do-and-freeware approach of Eligible Receiver '97 had been spot-on, the next global attack, when it came, would come without warning.

It would be a strangely distributed network—a hydra of vectors, methods, tools, interests, targets, and objectives, unlike any that the United States had prepared for.

The Belgrade hackers now enjoyed unofficial protection from UdBA and the assurances that they would remain free from consequences for hacking anything—especially targets overseas—so long as they shared how it was done. They were, after all, equipping the national defense that Tito had dreamed of.

One former UdBA officer summed up the argument for letting the nation's tech-literate kids have free rein on the internet. "We said, why not let them use it? They will show us what it can do, and we can use what works ourselves. Nikola Tesla who was a Serb, he talked about inventing the Death Ray, but the plans were never found. So maybe this is its time. Maybe this is where we will find our own electronic weapon."

But if this approach was visionary, it was also timely.

What nobody could have foreseen back as 1997 rolled over into 1998 and the kids ran riot through the jungle of the rapidly spreading internet, with not a single international body or intel agency in the West watching them, was that the coming war in which they would use it was one against the combined might of America and its NATO allies.

Chapter 3

Hacker Nation

Through the hot summer of 1998, electricity hung in the air. It felt as if the power of the electrical zeroes and ones pulsing through schools, homes, intelligence, militaries, and universities was generating the dry storm clouds that swept in over the mountains for evening.

America was in flower. Its map was bursting with new wires and exchanges, the internet bringing the country to itself like the railroads and the auto routes had for the past hundred years and more. This was Al Gore's information superhighway all right. If it existed, there were websites for it, partly because there had never been anything like this and partly because interest rates were falling and low interest rates were going to make money free, and borrowing to invest would never be so gloriously untethered from risk. Through the summer, Go.com, Boo.com, Pets .com, and Flooz.com blew the bricks-and-mortar companies from TV ad slots, took over the Super Bowl, stormed the news, torched the stock market. It was the new mall. The new space. The new battlefield. The new dating. The new leading business sector. Every day, a new something else. That summer, the Naval Institute's Proceedings published a paper called "Network-Centric Warfare: Its Origin and Future" that sounded a chilling warning. "Here at the end of the millennium we are driven to a new era in warfare. Society has changed. The underlying economics and technologies have changed. American business has changed. We should be surprised and shocked if America's military did not."

In fact, the internet's biggest single investor was the US government. For the past three years, it had funded an initiative called Google. The initiative was the first really big test of a project that the US intelligence community had founded in 1995, as part of a US government–Silicon Valley partnership that they hoped would secure American interests online into the new century. It was borne of the realization that the internet, if it grew at the rate they predicted, would itself become a form of voluntary mass surveillance.

Funded jointly by the CIA and NSA, computer scientists at CalTech, MIT, Carnegie Mellon, Harvard, and Stanford formed the Massive Digital Data Systems (MDDS) project. It predicted that like flocks of birds or colonies of ants, like-minded groups of humans would coalesce on the internet around certain nodes. Among the communities that would coalesce around certain click patterns, you could spot anything. People who were interested in a certain idea, or product, or political position. People who weren't, but matched those people's other online behaviors so might be worth targeting. Demographics. Communities of interest. Political and religious persuasions. Potential sex criminals. Terrorists. Potential terrorists.

The first two DARPA/National Science Foundation grants under the initiative funded research by Larry Page and Sergey Brin, a pair of Stanford graduate students who were making rapid advances in the science of interpreting that data at scale. Google launched to the public in September 1998. But to become the world's eyes and ears—to be of help in a crowdsourced cyber war—it would have to achieve the massive coverage in the East that would make its patterns mean something. That would take time.

Time was in short supply.

Kosovo, the wild borderland between Serbia to the north and Albania to the south, was a simmering cauldron. A rural, hilly land populated mostly by ethnic Albanians, it has long been considered by Serbia to be Serb territory. Typically for the area—and in common with the Bosnian wars—the issue is clouded by enclaves of populations within populations, and by history as much as diplomacy, myth as much as fact. Through the mid-1990s, the Albanian-sponsored Kosovo Liberation Army (KLA) had been carrying out acts of sabotage and attacks against Serbian authorities and installations in Kosovo. By February 1998, the Serbian response had escalated beyond mere enforcement. A series of summary executions and civilian massacres in early 1998 tipped the scales toward full-blown conflict, with Secretary of State Madeleine Albright warning Serb president Slobodan Milošević that on the current trajectory, the crisis was no longer "an internal affair." Where ultranationalist paramilitaries from Serbia and Croatia had shelled, burned, tortured, raped, and massacred their way through Sarajevo, Srebrenica, and the rest of Bosnia through the 1990s, now Kosovo was in Serbian nationalists' sights. Slowly, but with terrible, slipping inevitability, it began tipping toward war.

As the world turned its attention toward the possibility of another full-blown Balkan conflict in which Milošević was the antagonist, waves of hackers began breaching Albanian-language websites in what seemed increasingly like focused, if not organized, fashion. During "visits," the Serbian coat of arms would be placed on the home page together with suitable messages. They wrote in both Serbian and English languages. One read: "Welcome to the website of the world's biggest liars and murderers." Another one: "Albanian brothers, this coat of arms will stay on your flag as long as it exists." Their next target was the Kosovo Information Centre site, on the basis that it was "enemy propaganda" angled against Serbian interests.

Far larger storms were brewing offline. A series of massacres apparently committed by Serbs, skirmishes with the Kosovo Liberation Army, and warlike rhetoric from Milošević were turning the mood ugly. They were whipped up by increasingly crazed regime news reports of American plans to install a New World Order with a putsch in Belgrade, or mystics reporting visions of New York on fire, or proregime historians warning that the Muslim hordes were massing again for a final assault on Christendom in Kosovo, "as foretold in Revelation," with far-right agitation orchestrated daily, and the public mood turned ugly and fearful. As diplomatic pressure mounted for Serbia to pull back from the brink of another full-blown war and stop ethnic cleansing in Kosovo, the regime also tried to direct opposition frustration against the West that had it under sanctions.

The sanctions seemed to magnify the madness that gripped the country. Though it was now under the world's tightest lockdown—sanctions so strict and so universal that in theory nothing came in or went out—Serbia's rulers in government and crime, its airstrips and four-by-fours, streets, and speakeasies spun in a blizzard of illicit guns, cash, ecstasy, cocaine, bootleg goods, *warez*, and hacker code. On one memorable evening, a gigantic chopped-cocaine swastika the size of a dinner plate became the pièce de résistance at a party held by Marko Milošević, the Kendall Roy look-alike hoodlum-playboy son of President Slobodan Milošević, now an aspiring internet entrepreneur and hacker groupie himself. It was meant as a fuck-you to America, likening it to the last outside oppressors from the Wehrmacht. It was cheered as it was unveiled, like a chef's special creation, and again as it was hoovered up by the gangland power brokers in attendance, like everything else in the land.

More than the cocaine itself, the very atmosphere in which such things were possible was a drug. For a legion of the kids, it was not PCs from parents with clear rules of creative engagement, but playground stories like the young Milošević's party, full of dangerous glamour and the trappings of power and fear, that became the cues as to what could make you successful in this world of escalating savagery. Everybody knew even if you had no home internet or your parents were watchful, college and university tech faculties had the fastest connections and were almost completely unsupervised. Then schools began opening internet connections in class, and the wave of kids grew unstoppable.

The army began cyber-war outreach to children as young as nine. One former pupil recalls his middle school class in Belgrade being visited by a man from the Lola Ribar Institute, who told them about robots and a new kind of technological frontier that would make the horror of human-fought wars obsolete. "Robots, drones, and lines of code are going to fight the next wars for us," the man had said. "They will not be fought on battlefields. The front line will be inside our enemy's computer systems. Without those systems functioning, they cannot communicate. They cannot fire rockets or give orders. They cannot attack or defend." Then, in a soft voice, the speaker asked the class who would be interested in fighting such a war, as cyber defenders. The classroom transformed into a forest of raised hands.

The hackers took on pen names and online aliases and were so confident that they now wrote and talked about their raids, hacks, breaches, and incursions increasingly openly, in print and online. They would talk to the journalists on message boards. There was no way they could be touched. Those computer mags—*Računari* (Computers) and others—had evolved and were now like nothing else on earth, then or now. Some became bulletin boards, publishing challenges, trash talk between hackers, announcements by the hackers themselves of impending hacks, and subsequent reports on how they had done it. Others became de facto sports pages for a sport that was illegal in the West, hardly known at all in Russia and China, but had the status of national sport here—for participants and spectators alike. It would be the late 2000s before Twitter gave the world anything like a comparable public forum, with its real-time announcements of hacks versus admins by the likes of Anonymous and Lulzsec, dumps of raided info from Wikileaks, and even terror groups like al-Shabab and ISIL.

Once they got access to the internet, the first thing the children learned was to copy source code and amend it. In the United States and the West, the internet experience was often mediated by big businesses—AOL's CD-ROM walled gardens, or the context of office work or e-commerce. But in the East, like computers themselves, it was something to interrogate, break into, remake, and weaponize. For some, learning that you could simply collect source code and mess about with it was a eureka moment. Organizations' home pages would become hilarious, the image replaced with something else, or a rude word inserted into the main text. It was pure joy. In retrospect, they realized they were being taught how to deface websites.

Between their time on the terminals, the kids would write down ideas, just jotting them in exercise books, and take some things off the blackboard. You could learn lines of code and operations, by heart, like card tricks or jokes. Sometimes, you swapped ideas with other people, like sticker cards for football or superheroes. None of the kids concerned had any idea that they were training for cyber war; it was just fun. Yet somehow, some felt that they were doing something good and officially approved.

As an Eastern European land with a thriving personal computing industry, Yugoslavia had been a strange test tube for mass computer technology under Communism. So while Western countries with comparable uptake had introduced laws to protect private and intellectual property (IP)—the United States had introduced its first federal computer-crime statute back in 1984 with the Computer Fraud and Abuse Act as a result of Ronald Reagan's *WarGames* viewing—Yugoslav leaders had been doggedly resistant to introducing any specific laws whatsoever relating to computers. After Communism had come war and penury; now, as NATO threatened action over Kosovo in 1998, the very idea of introducing laws stopping its citizens from using the internet to get ahead was so unpopular as to be absurd. Hacking into protected systems simply wasn't recognized as a criminal act. It simply did not register with parents as something to query. It became a burgeoning cyber resistance, often unsuspected even in the homes of the hackers themselves. And the locus for its high weirdness and skulduggery was the university computer rooms.

Dr. Mirjana Drakulic's dapper, mustachioed husband, Ratimir, was one of the information tech lecturers at the university. The computer rooms' notoriety had grown fast, maybe too fast. They became a free-for-all. Nonstudents were haunting the rooms by the dozens. When they were barred, the doors to the terminals suddenly mysteriously became jammed open. These rooms, beyond monitoring and now patrolled by cops, kids, and hackers, became open house for anyone wanting to flex their newly acquired hacking skills. Outsiders, even people who reeked of intelligence or military, drifted in and out freely like scouts and spectators at a Little League tournament.

The university, like the media, had been hollowed out and staffed with nationalists and regime loyalists whose time was largely taken up not teaching but compiling dossiers on other members of staff and students.

Now, as NATO deadlines came and went and 1999 arrived, new organizations calling themselves things like Serbian Angels and Guardians of Serbia positioned themselves as white hat, propeace, and believers in the idea that publishing authoritative information— obtained either by hacks or by citizen reporters—would expose the gap between what governments said and what they did.

Kosovo was a tinderbox. As the last year of the millennium dawned, the January nights lit up with gunfire from the borders of Serbia itself down to those of Muslim Albania, and through spring the talks went from constructive to last-ditch. In June, Madeleine Albright's deputy Richard Holbrooke visited Kosovo. He'd already warned Milošević that if he didn't step back, "what's left of your country will implode"; now he was photographed with KLA fighters. Russia, meanwhile, called for a "mutual cease-fire." The United States countered that Serb forces were the ones who had to desist, regardless of what they claimed the KLA was doing.

This ushered in a stage of phony war known colloquially by diplomats as "the expo," when all sides begin to court global opinion in the hope of ramping up not only diplomatic or military support but the donations of diasporas and sympathetic communities across the world. For the Serbs, this meant turning their attentions toward the affluent English-speaking diasporas in America, Canada, and Australia. And the hackers got in on the action. On Halloween 1998, the Black Hand hacked the Croatian news agency Vjesnik and defaced its site with the words, "The Black Hand wants to change the false image which orbits the planet that the Serbs are villains." The intelligence services, now installed across a hollowed-out media and academia, pushed them to amplify the successes of their "cyber auxiliaries." The Serbian regime hailed them as public folk heroes, as in this government report: "A hacker war started that was proclaimed a good one in Serbia, and was publicly celebrated."

The teens' fame was spreading overground. Chat rooms and email lists exploded with their work. Magazines never looked at by the straight world led with hackers as cover stars and lead stories—using their screen names and blurred and hooded portraits. Incredibly, issues would regularly hype preannounced hacks as upcoming events. They'd review actions as if they were sports matches and carry screenshots of compromised sites. University terminals and servers, government offices, home computers buzzed with it. City radio stations thrummed with it. Walking through Belgrade in 1998, from the university to Novi Beograd's towers, flyers on lampposts and walls, graffiti tags, songs playing on the radio cried out what was happening, who was doing what, and where to find it.

Even for kids raised on the ubiquitous, violent, and sexualized shores of urban culture in the West, it is almost impossible to imagine the outlaw status these teenagers enjoyed. They were not only saboteurs and rebels in a place fallen to lawlessness and despotism; they were the *equalizers*, working with the tacit approval—even the protection—of their guardian angels in Eastern Europe's most feared intelligence service. They felt invincible. "Like superheroes."

In the race to unmask the Black Hand's superheroes, two reporters from *Svet Komputera* (World of Computers), a Belgrade-based magazine that had become the hackers' offline gossip sheet, showcase, and networking bible, finally managed to get a messaging session with two Black Hand members pseudonymously in a chat room. In an atmosphere that now felt higher stakes than it had before the intelligence services got involved with the hackers, sides in the proposed chat had to go through a series of ornate proof-of-identity tests involving simultaneous offline and online actions with verified individuals before the talk could take place. The reporters wanted their story. The Black Hand was wary in case US intelligence was manipulating them under the guise of an online interview.

At one point the journalists asked the Black Hand hackers to prove they were authentic by hacking and sabotaging a website live, while they watched. In almost any less lawless environment than Serbian cyberspace, such a challenge would have landed both hackers and journalists in jail. The hackers were only too delighted to oblige. When the reporters finally asked why they had done it, especially if they were going to remain incognito and so miss out on the personal prestige, the attackers' answer was a taste of things to come, and a phrase that would become the government's cyber-war motto against America. They replied simply that they wanted to "stand up and mount an electronic defense of Serbia's interests."

Nobody could have guessed that they would do it so successfully. Or that in doing so, they would write pages of history that we are still reading now.

Part II

The Children's Crusade

(How cyber war was won and lost—and not in the way we'd imagined)

Chapter 4

Electronic Child Soldiers

At the sound of the first explosion, Zoran Rosic starts in his sleep so violently that he falls out of his bed. He stares into the darkness of the apartment bedroom for a moment and the orange beyond the curtains, then jumps out of bed and run across to the window. The March night air is chill against the glass.

The sounds of American planes and US-made Tomahawk missiles can be heard overhead—the crackle that fizzes above jet-engine noise and the distinctive "crump" of more explosions—and Zoran pays close attention to the booming and roaring in the darkness around the high-rises.

Sometimes, a flash and a trail light up the black, followed by the dull, sickening sound of impact. It could be on the bridge, the Embassy Quarter, the next street, the next block. Even the next building. The crump of explosions is close now. One shakes the floors and windows, sends light shades wobbling, and makes the heart jump and the rib cage contract in fear.

More noises now. Sirens, yelling. They can hear more because someone's loud TV has been turned off. Footsteps, voices on the staircases and the streets below. From his window, Zoran sees people in doorways, in T-shirts and nightgowns. Everything shakes. That livid Halloween glow over the buildings by the river looks especially bad.

But tonight, it is not yet the turn of the building where he lives.

Up and down the street, he can hear babies crying; parents are up, comforting younger siblings, talking in low voices, calling from windows at passersby. But as the roaring echoing around the sky dies away for the last time, their voices do too. There are still sirens and alarms outside, but farther off.

His heart is pumping hard. School starts in six hours, but he isn't sleepy now. Besides, the five explosions mean there's something important he has to do.

The orange is still flickering through the slats in the shutter as he switches on the computer.

Across the city, others like him are logging on now. Young kids, older teens, students, grown-ups, everyone who can. The routine they follow differs in a lot of ways. Some kids hold a pillow over the modem to stifle its pings, crashes, and bleeps as it connects. Others run a game in the background so that they can pretend they're up doing something their parents wouldn't mind instead of something you can be targeted for. Others are left alone. They're on, connecting. The chat box blinks. The first message appears. "Who are we going to hit?"

"Was I *frightened* when NATO started bombing us? Are you *kidding* me? I was *excited*," recalled one. "It felt like we had been prepared all those years. And finally, this was going to be *our moment*."

That moment would be a pivotal one. Not just in the evolution of cyber war, but in the very idea of the always-on internet.

The flood of kids online to fight took everyone by surprise, not least the internet companies, who watched the usage patterns switch from evenings and weekends to all night long during the bombardment, as kids stayed up until morning at their PCs.

Word spread to families, teachers, intelligence services. While the government clearly had no plan, the spooks knew an opportunity when they saw it. The way they saw it, Total War and the citizen militia were never about relying on established hackers alone. They would mean leveraging every one of the motivators for being online and inspiring and equipping a citizenry to become vectors in the unceasing, entrepreneurial, networked, and spontaneous push for advantage and the degradation of the enemy's physical, emotional, financial, and intelligence capital.

There was only one way to achieve that, and it was the Serbian regime's control of the phone network, and its military and government ties to the internet companies, that made it happen. Within days of NATO's planes taking to the skies, PTT, the Serbian government telecoms provider, also under the command of Milošević's cadre of ministers, opened up their network to everyone—pay or don't pay, you suddenly had internet access. Within days, more internet service providers and telecom companies were turning themselves over to the hackers, 24/7, gratis. Under the heading "Kosovo," provider Infosky's leadership also declared that it would henceforth be providing completely free, unlimited internet for everyone in the country, "until the end of the aggression, for better information, and for spreading the truth."

It's easy to forget, in this age of ubiquitous Wi-Fi, how genuinely unheard of and weirdly exciting free, unlimited internet access was in the dial-up days of 1999. Consumers and households across most of the world still paid for their internet by the minute, like they paid for long-distance phone calls. They accessed it on a dial-up basis—going to their PC, switching it on, and connecting, so that the modem made its familiar twanging, crashing noises as a pair of arrows thought about whether they could connect you. Once you were connected, the bill was running, so time online was limited. Emails arrived in "flash sessions"—a user would go online just for a moment or two of paid time, during which their "waiting" emails would download into their inbox. The second they had downloaded, the user would hang up, and read them offline. The 1998 Hollywood rom-com *You've Got Mail*, starring Tom Hanks and Meg Ryan, was an up-to-the-minute view of two fairly committed, heavy internet users in the United States at the time. In the movie, they check their email like they would go out and check a physical mailbox.

While many businesses had access deals—and an office job in the late 1990s often came with internet access as a perk—for most of the world, using the internet meant hijacking your phone line. The commercial setup of dial-up was a brake on hacking as leisure activity, as it was on any other form of connected creativity. While connections were dial-up, only a tiny percentage of users would ever cause mischief on anything like the industrial scale that needed serious defensive consideration from the US military. In this sense, Eligible Receiver had it right. If there was going to be dedicated hacking, refined over time, it would likely be on someone's dime, or using someone's heavy-duty business connection. That meant it was likely either to be institutional—at a workplace of some kind—or to have a sponsor. The top-down analysis seems reasonable on those terms.

Only now, and very suddenly, the rules had changed. Milošević's remainder Yugoslav state of Serbia and Montenegro remains the only nation ever to make free internet a right of citizenship.

It is nearly impossible, in this day of unlimited internet access, free Wi-Fi, high-speed broadband, and ubiquitous hot spots, to conceive of just what a radical move the liberation of online time was—or how this early experiment in internet access changed all our lives when it succeeded. This former Communist buffer state had fired the starting gun on an experiment that was not just national, but global, one with the sole aim of turning its online teens into weapons aimed at the United States and its allies.

At a stroke, it had become the world's first permanently online society, and provided a case study for Silicon Valley and Wall Street.

If the dial-up model was the key break to hacking as leisure activity, the sudden explosion of time spent online, and the cycles of invention and refinement it achieved, was proof of concept for e-commerce giants in the West. It soon became clear that new, hungry and US military- or intelligence community–funded start-ups such as Google, and older names looking to pivot (Microsoft would launch Xbox Gaming in the wake of the conflict in March 2000), were watching closely. War has always been a crucible of technological innovation. In this war, it was the smaller belligerent, and not NATO's cruising heavyweight, who had been forced into it.

The first effect was to turn Serbia's young into internet junkies overnight. Suddenly, it mattered what people elsewhere in the world were seeing, and it mattered what they thought about the war. One of the first operations carried out by the security services was to encourage swarms online to write comments to Western websites. Polls and comment sections on the BBC, CNN, and others suddenly exploded with unsourced claims of NATO brutality, US arrogance, and otherwise unreported casualties, as well as diplomatic appeals, cryptic warnings of "the Albanian threat to Europe," and oaths of vengeance against NATO members. They prefigure today's social media explosion. Only in a society where being online constantly suddenly cost nothing could its population suddenly flood the available forums with their thoughts, experiences, and posts. No wonder the US representative to NATO's cyber defense HQ in Estonia, former NSA officer Kenneth Geers, observed that it was "the first internet war." The internet was not just a citizen cyber weapon; it became the first 24/7 channel for live citizen commentary and information warfare too.

The second effect was to flip the switch that turned a generation of hacker-minded kids into a nation of cyber warriors. "The young took the lead," recalled Mirjana Drakulic. "Hundreds of them were online day and night."

First, in quick succession, came hits against NATO and American targets. The US Navy's website and digital communications went down. Then NATO's email servers vanished, having succumbed to a bombardment of its own, of more than twenty thousand emails, carrying a total of twenty-five different kinds of malware, every day.

As the first successes registered, someone within the Serbian authorities finally seemed to have cottoned on to the effectiveness of just whatever the hell the kids were up to. Darko Popovic, a seasoned broadcast news journalist who worked for the official state agency Tanjug, still dismissed teen hackers as a subculture, until a friend at work confided in him one evening. "Darko," the friend said, "I set my 16-year-old son up in the basement, just so he could go online all the time. Now he went on, and he's doing things online, against NATO because they're bombing us. What do you make of that, huh?"

The next day, he was talking to another acquaintance, the owner of a Serbian internet service provider. Bitsyu had strong links to the Milošević government and security services. It was the official internet provider of all connections to the Yugoslav government, security forces, and army. The acquaintance mentioned in passing that he had gotten his kid, and all his kid's friends, to sit at their computers, and "counter anti-Serbia propaganda from NATO." Popovic asked, half jesting, if that was a company-wide thing everyone was doing. The man looked at him. Yes, he said. It was.

Bandit groups popped up, claiming responsibility for hacks against NATO. Lines of code appeared and proliferated, links and passwords, scraps and text files. The birth of modern internet file sharing was not Silicon Valley's. "It was basically Napster for NATO plans," said Sasa, one of many hackers who claimed in the 2000s to have played a more serious role in the initial wave of attacks. "The language helps. People in English-speaking countries just can't access us in the same way that we can access them! We all grow up copying American films, so we can be who we want, and online nobody knows. But there is no way they even, you know, figure out what we're making, not easily."

Another teenage hacker saw it as a time when they could say what they liked, and do whatever they felt they needed to do. Illegal or legal didn't matter. It was a new dimension, where none of that applied. It was a great, golden age of what-if-we-try-this.

The disorganized nature of the hacker wave, the impossibility of pinning any one goal or motivation to it, made it almost impossible to predict, stop, mitigate, or even strategize effectively.

There were copy-paste jobs from kids as young as six years old, the seasoned hackers' ranks swollen by parents, kid siblings, teachers, workplace colleagues, army, intelligence, by diaspora members everywhere, from the United States to New Zealand and Austria to Argentina, who happened to want to give America a nosebleed. Yet these waves of script kiddies were undeniably effective—they were the gleeful, mischievous gremlins in the smooth US-made machinery of the internet.

In the United States, these gremlins made the White House itself vanish from the internet entirely on Sunday, March 28, 1999, through Monday, March 29. "It is unclear," reported the BBC, "whether the attacks are state-sponsored or the work of individual groups of hackers." The Secret Service was scrambled to investigate the cause of its sudden vanishing. The operatives' briefing for the job struck a curious note for the time. They were instructed to look specifically for any evidence—in any code or signs of location and origin—that suggested the young Belgrade hackers who were prime suspects in its disappearance had support from Russia.

The White House's servers had gone down under a twin attack. A bombardment of incoming messages had paralyzed the system; those emails that had gotten through were infected with a macro virus called Happy 1999. The virus made alterations to its host computer's interface, disabling its connections to the internet. Having done so, it launched a .exe file that displayed spectacular fireworks while the machine itself crashed.

All this time, I was haunting some of the publicly accessible chats, following as well as I could using a printer, translating dictionaries, so-so Russian, and a smattering of Serbo-Croat. The real-time way rumors and ideas and plans were shared—still more or less openly, with an amazing naïveté that still hadn't begun to be bothered (or paranoid) enough to speak in code—was thrilling beyond words, partly for the sheer excitement they took, partly for the way it seemed to show a way forward and back: back to the early spirit of the internet, as an ideas exchange for academics and military...but exploded out into the world of teenagers, agitators, activists, and others, and forward, into the unknown.

Not every special operation this army of kids with keyboards tried during the Kosovo war was a success. The unregulated, word-of-mouth way in which know-how spread among this ad hoc cyber army was as prone to dangerous errors as it was to pooling hacker technique. At one point, a rumor from one of the university boards took hold among Serbian forces that NATO-deployed rockets looked for, and locked onto, Serb radar systems to find their targets—and that these radar systems worked similar frequencies as standard kitchen microwave ovens.

Such was the joy of this discovery that it swept the front line immediately. All the units on the ground had to do was to turn off their own radar at a critical point, and switch on microwave ovens somewhere wide of the target, and the rockets would lock into and destroy the kitchen appliances—which were left running off the motors of beat-up Opel and VW cars fitted with cardboard "wings" in neighboring fields—and not into the Serb unit. There were stories of soldiers volunteering to do the risky job of setting off the microwave ovens, waving good-bye to their comrades, and driving off in a beat-up Opel Astra with cheap microwaves humming off the battery in the passenger seat, to what they thought could well be the site of their self-sacrifice—only to watch on helplessly as the rockets sped past to their targets.

This was not just cyber war; it was war as hackathon, a whole nation of digital electronics hams, brainstorming, rigging up, and hacking together ways—from the speculative to the ingenious—in which to combat a vastly superior force. Like an episode of *Stranger Things*, the teens online believed that the sinister powers invading their skies could be outwitted by a bunch of kids and their lab-reared superpowers.

Some argued for peace and tried to share accurate information instead of joining the offensive. One group calling themselves Serbian Angels (their calling-card tagline: "We wish everyone a peaceful sky and solid bridges") coalesced around the concept not simply of technological hacking, but of attention hacking too, in order to bear witness to the realities of the bombardment.

The brainchild of the Belgrade University group, they formed as the bombing started. While their colleagues focused on so-called ping-of-death attacks to saturate servers, malware insertions, and the information war, the Angels brought some of the same infowar techniques to bear in their live, on-the-ground citizen-reporting initiative.

Crucial to their strategy was something called "infobombing." They explained it as "a benevolent cyberattack for information war purposes."

Serbian Angels' hackers would gain access to and deface high-traffic web properties in the United States or elsewhere. Only instead of defacing it with obscenities, they would replace the hacked site's highest-traffic pages with photographic evidence of things—bomb damage, casualties, locations under attack—that NATO's spokespeople denied.

They maintained several identical (and often shifting) websites of their own, on different servers and in different locations. These websites operated as independently as possible—defensive measures, in much the same way as sites like Pirate Bay will mirror themselves today in case one is taken down by the authorities. Again, they would use hacks to traffic attention to these sites, often by diverting links in news organizations' or governments' websites so that they led to a Serbian Angels report. Reports from the field on civilian casualties and updates on bombings were typically updated every five minutes.

Crucially, such actions are only effective as asymmetric measures; the media hegemony of US and Western channels was, in this case, their opportunity. Large, global audiences could be reached and influenced through extremely limited hacks, and with almost no means. In deploying both techniques, they were the forerunners of practices that are now commonplace.

As the bombing wore on, they refined their approach, learning in a live-fire cyber-war exercise, testing posts and techniques simultaneously to audiences around the world in different languages. Soon, they had a clearer idea of what worked. They took to replacing the home page of American, European, and Asian news websites with meme images instead—the meme's first deployment in the arena of warfare.

An early meme featured an adapted version of Microsoft's Windows 95 logo, restyled "Windows 99—Yugoslav Version," in which each of the boxes of the logo's Windows grid now featured a thumbnail scene of a real broken or charred-out window in Serbia, destroyed by NATO's bombing campaign. At the bottom, the small print said, "Russian, Belarus and all other versions available soon." Before the fledgling Wikileaks, they brought opening up the gap between official statements from governments—such as NATO's claim to have executed only "surgical strikes" that killed no civilians—and the reality. They believed that information about the realities of war was the best argument against continued hostilities.

The infobombers of Serbian Angels were careful not to get mixed up with the hackers who dealt in offensive defacements or malware. They made it a point of pride to be careful with the content of the sites they took over—neither deleting or crippling the servers nor damaging content. This approach saw the organization doing far deeper work on the ethics of hacking than anyone at NATO had been able to muster. While the United States and its allies remained unclear on just what cyberspace even was or what status civilians enjoyed while they were in it, Serbian Angels created, published, and established a set of commandments and standards for its hackers—a Geneva Convention for cyber war. In the process, the students of Serbian Angels have a good claim to being the first truly global ethical hacktivist organization, and they were in front of the Pentagon in tackling questions of what it meant to hack civilian targets and a taste of what was to come in this sudden new world of crowdsourced digital war.

Then, just one week into NATO's air offensive, something seemingly inexplicable happened.

It seemed at least one of the hackers' kitchen-sink attempts at breaking into NATO's communications had borne fruit.

Chapter 5

Black Jet Down

As night fell, the sky over Belgrade was cloudy and overcast. Saturday, March 27, 1999, was another evening of sorties for the United States and its allies over the Balkans. The black clouds glowed orange with the city's fire and flickered with reflected emergency light. Visibility was poor, but neither side trusted its eyes. The Serbs' 250th Air Defense Missile Brigade had been switching its air-detection systems on and off, looking in extended blinks of a few seconds at a time to avoid being detected itself by NATO's own anti-air-suppression systems. At around 8:15 p.m., almost the full seventeen seconds into the blink, the battery detected a US Air Force Lockheed F-117a Nighthawk stealth attack aircraft about fourteen miles off.

The first operational aircraft in history to be designed specifically around stealth technology, the Nighthawk was code-named the Black Jet. Its exterior was composed of flat panels at angles that would "scatter" more than 99 percent of radar-signal energy. Its stealth missions had won it fame over Iraq and Kuwait during Operation Desert Storm in 1991. Its very existence had been classified throughout its development; it was admitted by the USAF and US government only in 1988. Nevertheless, the F-117 had been the subject of heavy speculation during its black-ops development through the 1980s, earning it comparisons to—and even seeing it jokingly nicknamed after—the fictional MiG-31 of Clint Eastwood's

1982 movie *Firefox*. It was vaunted by Lockheed and, over the years of deployment, by the USAF itself as "invisible."

Yet there it was, blinking in the darkness of the ground-to-air missile battery's screens.

Inside this F-117—Air Force serial number 82-0806—Operation Desert Storm veteran Lieutenant Colonel Darrell Patrick "Dale" Zelko saw two antiaircraft missiles zip upward through the low, black cloud cover, coming free and up, through clear sky, and toward him.

The first passed him, buffeting the Nighthawk, then whizzing off into the darkness beyond. The second would be closer. Too close. When it exploded just feet away—its flash bright enough to be spotted by US airborne patrols over Bosnia—its shock wave and shrapnel tore into the Nighthawk, smashing it sideways and perforating the F-117's metal body and wings. The wave of white-hot metal and impact sent the plane into a uncontrolled earthward lurch that jarred Zelko so violently that his vision blackened for a moment. The pilot was pinned into the cockpit by intense g-forces. As the plane spun more and more wildly, and the seconds passed, he found it impossible to maneuver into position to activate his ejector seat. In an act of desperation, he pulled, and as the night exploded around him he was out, stunned, and shooting through the roaring night. But alive. As he recovered his composure, Zelko realized quickly the seriousness of his situation. This was enemy territory. The explosion that had downed him would have pricked ears everywhere. And any second, there would be an almighty explosion from the ground, as his plane hit a road, or a tower block, or just hills and fields below. But the expected explosion didn't come.

Disorientated but thinking fast, Zelko managed to radio his distress call as he fell—against protocol for supposedly secret flights. His luck looked in, as he was able to steer his descent toward a field outside what he later learned was the village of Ruma, about halfway between Belgrade and the country's second city, Novi Sad.

The location might have saved him. Bruised by a hard landing but running high on adrenaline alert, he slipped his parachute and ran low, across dirt and uneven furrows toward the ditches at the perimeter of the fields. Once there, he smeared himself with earth and foliage, conscious that the search parties with dogs would be just minutes away, combing the area for him, and he waited, rattled every few seconds by shock waves from the bombs of US Air Force B-2s in action that night. Successive Serbian foot patrols—dogs, police, army, irregulars, and villagers—all narrowly missed his hideout. As the minutes ticked toward midnight, one police patrol turned toward the area where he was hiding. He would later learn that he was, in all probability, minutes from being captured that night. But if the patrols were working in the dark, NATO, with its military communications and air dominance, was not. A KC-135 Stratotanker aircraft refueling peacekeeping patrols over the mountains of Bosnia that had seen the flash of the distant missile exploding had picked up his descending distress call. NATO rescue units were scrambled. After some eight hours of Zelko crouching in the cold ditch, the USAF combat search-and-rescue team in a Sikorsky MH-53 "Super Jolly Green Giant" helicopter gunship descended on the field in the early hours of Sunday morning. If that let slip to the local patrols where the downed pilot was hiding, it was too late. The crew trained their night vision and machine guns to cover all approaches, cleared the area, and pulled the exhausted Zelko to safety.

That just left the invisible plane.

The flat, dark delta had pitched away into its death spiral as Zelko ejected. The airman, descending through the night toward the fields, had watched for an explosion below. But it never came. It was as if, having flickered into visibility for the enemy, it had vanished from view to its own pilot. The sea of blackness below had simply opened up and swallowed it. And this is where the secret jet crossed over, became something else entirely.

The stricken Nighthawk had hit the fields in an inverted position, slamming into the ground with incredible force as it spun faster and faster in its own inexorable fall. Yet even laden with fuel and ammunition as it was, somehow it had failed to explode into a fireball on impact. Instead, it had simply plowed into the ground, parts detaching, with a crump so deep that residents for miles around associated it with the possibility of some underground explosion. It came to rest—damaged, perforated, ripped, but remarkably intact—lying at a melancholy, flipped angle. By dawn, the wreck was crawling with people. The police cordon had been breached, and locals were inspecting it. The United States decided early on against a retrieval mission on the basis that the F-117's technology was an open secret in China and Russia anyway by this point. Nevertheless, parts were removed by the Serbian army and shipped to both China and Russia for evaluation.

The internet was alight with the news that the "Crni Bombarder" (Black Bomber) was "not so invisible"—at least to someone. But to whom?

The bright Sunday morning brought swarms of locals running to the crash site—and photos would show old ladies, dapper young delinquents, teenage boys, sturdy farmers, civilian militia, and soldiers in fatigues dancing with joyous abandon atop the battered wing, grinding their shoes on its white USAF decal, and milling around the wreck in euphoric disbelief. As they climbed and sang defiant chants on the cooling metal, the Serbian news media was running with the first clues that something very unusual had happened. While Radio Belgrade and B92 alike were speculating how it had happened that a Cold War–era battery had located and shot an invisible stealth plane, the antiregime *Glas Javnosti* (Voice of the Public) hit the stands with the headline "HACKER WAR—TO THE DEATH."

There was no doubt whatsoever inside Serbia's military, intelligence, and tech communities—let alone its young hackers—as to how the plane had been downed.

The story beneath the headline gave a very clear hint that the plane had been detected with the help of Serbia's teenage hackers, tying the Black Jet's detection to the simultaneous infiltration of US military and government systems by Serbia's youth army of hackers. "This is the F-117, one of which was shot down by the Yugoslav anti-aircraft defense last night.... The central computer of the American Navy also fell victim, but most of the official websites of the governments of the aggressor Western states woke up in the morning particularly affected." Then, any sense of humility disappeared: "Yugoslav hackers are once again in control.... Our country

Tyler Clemons, *Sorry We Didn't Know It Was Invisible* re-creation, 2021. Used by kind permission.

is under attack. And that means we're all under attack. If ever they truly existed, now all ideological differences have ceased for good. Now, it can be revealed how elite the Serbian hackers can be....In the shadow of this unprecedented aggression, the other war—the virtual war—is going well. For now, we are winning this battle."

Almost immediately, an early meme spread across the American internet, as well as posters, flags, and placards across Serbia. The text was often longer, with some Serbian among the English. The completely black silhouette drawing of the F-117a and the punch lines in English bold capital letters left no doubt—in the minds of members of the public on Yahoo! groups or AOL chat rooms, Serbs themselves, or US and other intelligence agencies—that something extraordinary had happened:

Underneath it were a number of lines:

"Sorry, your plane is on fire"
"Mine is visible, but at least it doesn't crash"
"Airplane junkyard: 'We have F-117 parts!'"
"The ground suddenly got in his way"
"You missed Surĉin Airport"
"Look, Dad, no hands!"
"Give us another one...I need a roof for my pig pen."
"What's going to happen to the White House? I'm
     going to set it on fire."

Another popped up almost immediately. It showed the F-117 flying above the sea, toward what looked like the Montenegrin coastline. Over the USAF stealth plane, the universally dreaded Microsoft Windows 95 error pop-up appears: *This Airplane has performed an illegal operation and will be shut down. If the problem persists, contact the plane vendor.*

They were near-perfect infobombs: in a viral manner, they pointed out a genuine disjunction between what the United States had claimed about its aircraft on its TV networks and in its press briefings, and what was now undeniably and demonstrably true. It was also very funny. Total War had thrown up the first example of a new phenomenon: memetic warfare.

Memetic warfare is now a recognized branch of information and psychological warfare. But its approach embraces humor and irreverence, using internet memes to spread information (or disinformation) as highly shareable jokes and graphics. In this way, they spread online between closed communities of users before monitors have the chance to intervene, turning their content directly into street-level "folk knowledge" immune to gatekeeping or factcheckers. The US military had not begun to study this new front—memetic warfare became a field of inquiry only after the conflict was over—and, indeed, only found traction in terms of funding for research in the post-9/11 mobilization of media as part of the War on Terror. It would be 2005 before Major Michael B. Prosser of the US Marine Corps would produce the first development study proposing the US military take a proactive role in memetic conflict.

And even then, six years after the Kosovo conflict, the definition of cyber war in the US military and intel communities remained, argued Prosser, frustratingly narrow. "Tomorrow's US military must approach war fighting with an alternate mindset," he argued, "that is prepared to leverage all elements of national power to influence the ideological spheres of future enemies by engaging them with alternate means—memes—to gain advantage."

Yet the Yugoslav deployment of memes undermining the US and its allies' information operation—at the same time Yugoslav hackers were seeking to undermine its technological superiority—was undeniably effective as far back as 1999. It was estimated to have captured more attention online globally than *the entire series of official NATO briefings*. The very credible idea these memes contained spread across the world at the speed of digital transmission: US claims about the conflict were not to be trusted.

Cornered, the USAF tried to walk back the Nighthawk's much-trumpeted superpower. The aircraft had never been genuinely "invisible" to radar, commanders explained. That had just been a manner of speaking, a shorthand, hype from the US Air Force. And when others had taken it up, it was publicity. It was merely an aircraft of a "very low-visibility" nature.

But the damage had been done. Engagement with Serbian Angels' work rose that week to unprecedented levels, as people around the world sought to find out "what was *really* going on"—a phrase that haunts the West today in online discourse around everything from QAnon conspiracy theories to COVID-19. The US military was in a double bind. Either an invisible aircraft had been located and shot down somehow, which meant the hackers were running riot inside their systems, or they had been using disinformation—propaganda—and been caught out.

Where militaries move slowly, hackers move fast.

In Belgrade, the leading gangs of teenage hackers were already street-level heroes—the words "Crna Ruka" and "Serbian Angels" were already scrawled in spray paint on subway walls and station yards as the clouds of bombardment gathered in 1998. Kids in schools would claim to be part of them, or know someone in them, in the same way that kids claim to have girlfriends "who go to a different school."

These youths had seen their futures truncated. Left behind by a political scene that had seen the urban, the outward looking, the Westward facing shut down by a former Communist Party apparatchik and his right-wing cronies, they had been impoverished, brutalized, and turned into global pariahs by their own government. Now they were being bombed for the privilege. And they had had just about enough. A group of teenage and student-age hackers calling themselves simply the Belgrade Hackers (the city crew name was a pointed snub to the nationalists; an educated, thoroughly modern city, Belgrade had always been more liberal and staunchly antiwar than the rest of the country) began taking over sites across the world by the dozen, from the US Navy to media organizations, replacing each home page with the legend, "Stop NATO attack on Yugoslavia," and beneath it "WE ARE ALL TARGETS." The phrase spread. It became a sign-off for messages, emails, and blog posts. A T-shirt.

Forces, companies, and individuals perceived to be working with America and its allies were attacked and compromised. They ranged from political parties across Europe to US shipping and transport infrastructure and to one German telecommunications and transport-parts manufacturing company that was merely suspected of being a supplier. By the end of classes that same day, the systems of NATO and its partner nations, from Washington, DC, to Brussels, and from London to Prague, had been infiltrated. By Tuesday, they were crawling with malware. On Wednesday, May 31, amid widespread alarm and media reports that NATO and the US government were at the mercy of a bunch of kids from Belgrade, NATO had no choice.

"We have looked at this very carefully," croaked Jamie Shea, with the demeanor of a head waiter bearing bad news about the main course. "It seems we have been dealing with some hackers in Belgrade who have hacked into our website and caused saturation of the server by using a ping bombardment strategy. It has also been saturated by one individual who is currently sending us 2,000 emails a day. And we are dealing with macro viruses from Yugoslavia into our email system."

NATO was consistent on one point. Nothing, it insisted both publicly and to press contacts both on and off the record, had been compromised. There had, we were assured, been absolutely no access to classified or sensitive material of any kind. In short, there was nothing to see here. This was a lie. Privately, its command was rattled. They knew they had indeed been compromised. What they did not know was how, or to what extent, or even whether they were now clear and their information or attack systems secure.

Even later, not one person I spoke with seemed certain exactly what had been going on.

There had been attacks. They had recovered the service. They knew the volumes of the ping that caused the DDoS, or denial of service, effectively clogging the servers. Those were the easy bits. As for what else had happened, they simply did not know. What had been compromised? Nobody at all was sure. A new term began to gain currency among those at the briefings, and in the wider military and media. NATO now called the current conflict not simply a military engagement but an "infowar."

It was an odd moment in which the military was getting on board with a piece of conflict jargon, not creating it. For almost everyone in the US military, information war was traditional propaganda and had nothing really new or essentially cyber about it. Some things that *did* rely on the internet, such as hacker activity, were far too limited in coverage of either attackers or targets to be of use as information war. There was, simply, too little public internet for info-jamming or signal hijacking to matter. So when the US military anticipated and prepared for cyber war—even founding the 609th Information War Squadron (motto: "Anticipate or Perish") under former fighter pilot Lieutenant Colonel Walter "Dusty" Rhoads—it was forced to do so within the constraints of what cyber meant at its conception. And that meant needle-sharp, strategic incursions. State-on-state attacks, cogent chains of command. Specific actors. Specific targets.

That failure to anticipate was ever stranger for the fact that the United States had been using network-jamming techniques pre-internet. The roots of the squadron lay in Haiti two years previously. Rhoads was commanding the US Air Force's electronic signals team. As a pilot, he'd seen firsthand the importance of signal scrambling and diversions to provide cover for air operations, and it was with this interest in mind that Air Combat Command called on him in 1994.

Rhoads was tasked with planning operations in support of a possible US military action called Operation Uphold Democracy. The operation was a campaign to reinstall democratically elected Haitian president Jean-Bertrand Aristide, putting pressure on the junta installed by the 1991 coup that had overthrown him, and that President Clinton was beginning to maneuver behind. The threat of military invasion had to be real enough that if the US diplomats' bluff was called, US forces would take Haiti as bloodlessly as possible, and in a way that minimized US casualties and other telegenic opinion dampers foremost.

Rhoads soon identified a junior officer who had come forward with his experience in civilian life of being a "phreaker"—an early subculture of technologically curious kids who hacked telephone networks to get free long-distance calls and could break into message centers and set up bogus chains of communication, either by reverse-engineering dialing tones or, from the mid-1980s onward, through manually dialing businesses or voice exchanges and identifying faulty diverters, which they could use as their own personal exchange to place and receive calls. Phreakers—sometimes known in the United States as demon dialers—had their own radio shows, their own newsletters, and sometimes even their own organizations, operating like quasi-legitimate businesses and subletting lines for a fee to whoever wanted them, often immigrants who needed to call relatives back home. By the mid-1990s, this junior officer was in good company—Rop Gonggrijp and Felipe Rodriguez were the lords of European telecoms hacking, while Apple's Steve Wozniak made no secret of his own background in the art. If you ever used one of the short-lived cheap call services that proliferated in the 1990s, their numbers often handed out as fliers at subway stations in New York, there's a fair chance that you were a phreaker too, albeit unwittingly.

The junior officer explained to Rhoads that he knew from his phreaking days how US Air Force Command might easily hack into the Haitian civilian telecoms exchanges and jam all the phone lines in Haiti simultaneously. Any attempt to use the network for as long as the US intrusion lasted would simply get the "line busy" tone. He further explained that since the Haitian defense systems used the telephone network for their signals, doing so would not only cut the Haitian command's communications, but also effectively ground its defenses, allowing the US Air Force an undefended sky. Within minutes, Rhoads had put a call in to General Kenneth Minihan, who took it to the president. President Clinton approved the plan.

The invasion never happened, nor did the phreaking attack; the threat of US military intervention did its job. Yet that junior officer's presence in the military machine was a quantum moment, one that held within its superposition two future worlds.

In one of them, his commanders recognized not only his idea, but the value of his experience. He had come from a background trying to break into systems, to hack them—not as a government employee, but as a criminal. In this universe, the United States and its Western allies might have developed military and civilian infrastructure capability that encompassed the thinking of those whose experience was in hacking them. The United States might have been cured of its hegemonic blind spot. The Western internet could have anticipated this new, wilder Eastern variant.

In the other, the military took the specifics of the plan and moved on. While it would engage with the idea of asymmetric information warfare and cyberattacks—General Kenneth Minihan was the man behind Eligible Receiver '97—it would be late in sufficiently recognizing the capability of criminals, outsiders, and citizen hackers to define conflict on a wider scale than military incursions.

The term "cyber war" had been circulating in military communities informally since at least 1996, when the US Air Force had floated a trial balloon by forming the experimental 609th Information Warfare Squadron operating from Shaw AFB in South

Carolina. Yet even the best efforts of the 609th had been spent fighting off traditional, needle-sharp cyberattacks. As head of US Air Force intelligence Major General John Casciano had put it, "A lot of the targets and a lot of the things we would want to affect—command and control nodes and the adversary's integrated air defense system—are things the Air Force worries about on the battlefield."

The American view of cyber war was very much like its view of actual war. Strength, strategy, and top-down structures would prevail. Yet the internet's proliferation and the dot-com explosion had already outpaced it. By the time 1995's annus mirabilis for internet growth in the United States was over, there were 342,081 websites online. By the bursting of the dot-com bubble in the summer of 2000, that number was 20 million.

Yet, to a large degree, the American military *was not prepared* for the new form of cyber war it was facing in Kosovo. It had practiced endlessly. It had scenario-planned. It had invested. It had carried out maneuvers. It had simply failed to anticipate the form it would take—not just over Serbia, but for the coming decades. Cyber war, when it came, simply did not resemble the top-down, military-out command structure that everybody in the US military, government, and corporate giants was capable of imagining. It was conflict rich in tactics, but utterly without strategy, and if its methods were many, its vectors appeared infinite, taking in civilian populations way beyond the belligerent countries, military and government, businesses everywhere, and the autonomous intelligences of the hijacked PC and hard drives of unsuspecting internet users, as well as the minds of NATO's own civilian populations. This was Total War. And nobody had a clue how to see it, define it, or address it, let alone fight it.

This is not to say that exercises like Eligible Receiver '97 had not been valuable. The team tracking the Moonlight Maze too had done exceptional work, and both undoubtedly protected America as far as they could. Yet they were limited by the very nature of the exercises: carried out by the military, envisaging an attack of very specific kinds at specific times, staffing up, and reacting accordingly. This was ultimately a very "un-internet" way of thinking. In a sense, the military's "command" approach to the exercise proved that, while the exercise itself had revealed much, the very framing of Eligible Receiver '97 and the structures that conducted it fell into the same trap of assumptions that had frustrated Soviet attempts to create cyber networks.

Yet this new form of warfare arrived as the idiot-savant sibling of cyber war. In the words of Mark Twain, in *A Connecticut Yankee in King Arthur's Court*, "There are some things that can beat smartness and foresight. Awkwardness and stupidity can. The best swordsman in the world doesn't need to fear the second-best swordsman in the world; no, the person for him to be afraid of is some ignorant antagonist who has never had a sword in his hand before; he doesn't do the thing he ought to do, and so the expert isn't prepared for him."

This strange, unforeseen take on cyber war was not defendable by even the world's best-equipped sword fighters, the US military. It would be something too nebulous to identify, let alone fight back against or defend: a continuing, unpredictable push for advantage, attrition, and damage—not as commanded by a strategic center, but in a way that was almost viral. Decentralized, low in risk and cost, high in effect, and unpredictable because even those carrying out the attacks were often unaware of their chances of success or rationale behind their methods.

While limited DDoS attacks has been tried before in the United States—recurring since 1996, with individuals hitting shopping malls in Vegas and tech companies for short periods—the Kosovo method was new. Rather than an attack from one vector, this could come from anywhere, or everywhere at once. And none of it need have anything to do with your ostensible opponent, or their strategic goals. The email attacks represented what Dan Kuehl, a professor at the School of Information Warfare and Strategy at the National Defense University, called "a step up the [food] chain" for hacking.

"If someone gets into the logistics control network," he told *Federal Computer Weekly* in May, "that would be a third step up the ladder, because in this era of just-in-time supply you might be able to directly impact ongoing operations." In other words, while sloganeering on the White House home page was a high-visibility way to proclaim your presence, email attacks could bring your opponent's comms, logistical, command, and perhaps even operational capability to a halt and sow chaos.

They were also potentially almost infinite in scale.

The bombardments of incoming data—dubbed the "pings of death" by security workers in Washington, DC, in recognition of their potential—were scalable in a way that defacement ops hadn't been. You could use any number of allied accounts to send traffic from, either by enlisting more people or simply by taking over their machines with a simple virus. A Trojan like Anti-Smyser-1, perhaps, embedded in something ubiquitous like the macros in Microsoft Windows.

It was simple—almost ridiculously so. Once you knew what it was, and that it could be done, there was almost no bar to entry and, for the target, no way of preventing them from trying. It quickly became a reductive game of numbers. Targets had to keep capacity higher than the potential influx. Attackers simply had to go around increasing the size of their ping network. It was an arms race—and NATO was losing one that took an operational toll on the defenders way out of proportion to the trouble or expense incurred by the attackers.

As early as April 4, NATO was forced to disable all its online services—including live collaboration in the field, global communications, and all broadcasts—with the exceptions of basic http access and email. Then email was crippled too. NATO—and governments everywhere—learned two lessons from these attacks. First, they had to invest much more in security, and, second, as Chris Scheurweghs, head of NATO's integrated data service, said, "The internet is no longer a side issue."

Yet this viral form of citizen cyber war seemed immune to traditional security. Its ammunition was inexhaustible—it harnessed the attack energy out there, stored in thousands, perhaps millions, of human minds, lives, and connections across the globe, and could quickly convert more.

The energy surge was the result of a perfect storm. The engine of their new cyber-war machine could be powered by anything from giant defense budgets and sophisticated botnets to teenagers, students, grudges, and lulz on a global scale. It ran on the fear and desperation of networked teens under bombardment in Belgrade; on the wounds and '90s blowback of humiliated and impoverished Russian political, military, and technological workers; on alienated kids worldwide; on anyone with an ax to grind against the United States and its allies; on what World Bank chair Joseph Stiglitz called the "discontents of globalization"; on conspiracy theories; on simple mischief. And it ran on a ubiquitous, free citizen internet.

It's not just that all these things were cresting and they happened. It's that Kosovo was the perfect high-water mark for *all* of this, the moment where all these different historical and technological forces collided. You couldn't have invented a better moment in a lab to begin cyber war.

There were more things in heaven and earth than are dreamed of in the philosophy of even the most talented group of somewhat homogeneous US service people.

And to bring information warfare about in anything like a realistic way, sensible people working to command would need a little of that chaos.

Chapter 6

Chaos Particle

In the seed of it, in its secret roots and its dark runners, the Eastern internet was an outsider. It was an insurgent in the fight for American-dominated cyberspace. And so were its users.

They say that to a tyrant the whole world smells of fresh paint, but in this case it glowed with state-of-the-art tech and smelled of fresh flowers in vases. The Milošević regime's foot soldiers got to work, starting with the proregime news organization Politika. Within days of the bombardment starting, men in dark overalls arrived. Floors were cleared, computers brought in, connections rerouted. The result was one of two almost entirely regime-controlled epicenters of anti-NATO cyber war, in a location that they rightly judged to be untouchable.

Editor in chief Hadži Dragan Antić boasted that his office had more internet connections for the work than anywhere else in town, "including Parliament, including the army, the university, including [state robotics and weapons manufacturer] Ivo Lola Ribar, you name it." Slobodan Milošević's wife, Mira Markovic, was a constant presence in the offices; she saw it as her plaything and the banks of computers opened to computer clubs as a success for which she could take credit. Politika was her vanity project. She imagined herself a power player on the global stage, just as her son, Marko, imagined himself a street-cool hacker. Having the terminals inside Politika run hot was, she declared, "in the national interest." This conclusion set the army bosses thinking about the other untouchable spaces they could set up as more formal operations centers.

Belgrade University's faculties throughout the city were already hosting twenty-four-hour hackathons targeting American cyberspace. The campuses and broadcast offices were soon joined by the towering silhouette of the looming Beograđanka skyscraper in the commercial district. They became improvised Hogwarts-style playgrounds for the imagination—somewhere the young, the angry, the technically skilled, and the regime sponsored could learn powerful secret formulas that could make American planes shoot the wrong targets, objects fall from the sky, White Houses vanish. The experienced hackers, together with Mirjana Drakulic, Ratimir Drakulic, and their colleagues, were their mentors. This was cyber war not as a dark and lonely pursuit by the specialists of Moonlight Maze, or the military minds of Eligible Receiver '97, but as an impromptu online academy.

Their exploits were now a national spectacle. TV bulletins, magazines, and newspapers celebrated them. Classrooms and cafés buzzed with them. Lampposts fluttered with flyers advertising a recent triumph or trumpeting a future raid on American cyberspace; the lower edge was cut into strips, easy to tear off, on which would be written an email address or URL.

All these stories focused on spontaneous hackers coalescing around the machines in two tech faculties: Electrical Engineering and Organizational Sciences. But unknown even to the university's staff, there was another part of the university in which a third, altogether more serious, group of hackers had been installed.

Mirjana Drakulic was gathering material for her Alternative Academic Network stint one hot, late afternoon in spring 1999 when the phone rang. The voice that greeted her belonged to the Milošević government's information tech mandarin, Nikola Markovic.

Markovic was already the elder statesman of information tech in government and was known as one of the toughest of regime hard-liners. Now fifty, a slender, serious ghost of a man with high cheekbones and deep eyes, he was a data fiend, crunching numbers endlessly in his office. But he was no isolated expert. Markovic was something of a gray cardinal, with his hand firmly on the wheel of government. He'd been in charge of development and strategy of major IT projects in Serbia since 1980 and was known as the Balkan king of gerrymandering, fixing electoral boundaries in ingenious and increasingly tortured ways, so that results clearly favored Milošević's Socialist Party.

Yet his canniness and ability to manipulate to his advantage anything from data to people was respected even by his enemies.

Mirjana Drakulic was always careful around him. Though they disagreed on much, she had collaborated with the older man well over the years. Markovic, for his part, knew only too well that Drakulic was against Milošević and his regime, but the two managed to skate along on the surface when they worked together, Mirjana almost grateful that the political operator respected the unspoken boundaries between them. They contrived, over the years, to talk in a carefully coded way, so as to gauge each other's stance on certain issues without ever making the other one say anything outright that might change things between them irrevocably. It was a subtle dance familiar to anyone who had grown up under Communism and now had to negotiate an arcane patchwork of loyalties—ethnic, religious, political—as a matter of survival. You could be damned by what you let someone tell you, just as much as what you said.

Yet that day, over the phone line, she sensed a change in his voice. He sounded tense. Drakulic asked what was wrong. He just said, "We have a huge problem."

The older man seemed hesitant with Drakulic. He asked her whether she had seen the previous night's humiliations that had

been inflicted upon America and its allies using the internet—
NATO's systems seizing up, transport networks dropping off the
grid.

"Sure, yes," replied Drakulic. Her mind was working frantically, wondering if he was talking about her own students' activities. The university had a sitting administrator who worked for the
government, and who would read emails sent and received for anything that might displease the party bosses. Staff could have their
email access revoked at any minute. Looking over her shoulder had
become second nature. But that wasn't what Markovic wanted to
say. Instead, he seemed to come to a mental decision. He simply
said, "Well, we've made a secret group. And I'd like to talk to you
both about joining."

The Drakulices were curious. On the one hand, they were
antiregime. On the other, says Ratimir, "the bombing had changed
that. This was now about us being bombed by NATO. That brought
people together against that, where before we were against our own
government." Both told the regime's tech czar that they were in.

The following morning, they were summoned to a meeting at
one of the faculties in the center of town. There, they were introduced to the others in the group. Some of the faces were familiar to
them from the university. Others, they knew only from the news.
Still more, in uniform, were new to them. "There were two delegates there from the main internet service providers," says Mirjana. "Another from the army. One from the police. Two university
staff from our faculty—one political appointee, and one from
philosophy."

They were, Markovic explained, going to become the country's
internet monitors and strategists for a whole new phase of warfare.
One of the soldiers began the briefing. The role of the group was
going to be to monitor hacks and online activity hostile to NATO
and help the government and the army to understand what was
going on, who was doing it, and what it was achieving in terms

of actual damage and real-world impacts, in something like real time. They would then propose—not to the hackers directly, but to their committee handler—how the attacks could be sharpened and made more effective or what decisive new forms they might take with a little work. As for what happened to it then? They were told simply that it was classified. They were all government employees, one way or another, and as of now this work was their only priority. They started that night.

At the third such meeting came a surprise. One of the government delegates, a suited, unsmiling figure who'd remained silent throughout, stood and announced that those around the table had worked hard and well. He apologized that, so far, they had not been kept fully in the picture, but that could change. They were now invited to see the glorious result of all the mission-critical information they had been feeding in. They were now going to see the secret operations center. "We had to guard it closely while we knew what form this group would take," he said. Then he motioned toward the uniformed guards at the door, and smiled. "Shall we go?"

The group filed out into the street, where cars were waiting. The university itself is a body of thirty-two different locations across Belgrade. To their great surprise, the mysterious invitation was to another one of their own university's faculty buildings across town. They were met by Markovic, who conducted them through the faculty's corridors and staircases, until they arrived at a guarded door. "This is where we keep the secret weapons," he winked. The sentries conducted them inside. In that hall were between fifty and a hundred young people, typing frantically away at machines, smoking, talking in low murmurs in groups. This was the evening shift. The room smelled stuffy. It was unbearably hot, the air fugged with stale cigarettes, stale sweat, and beer. These shifts, Markovic murmured to them, were working around the clock. Why didn't they wander around, see for themselves?

Walking among the massed machines, packs of chips, and

Coke cans everywhere, the babble of languages was intense—
Serbian, Chinese, Russian, American-accented English, German,
Italian, Japanese. The group was encouraged to stop and chat with
the youths. Around half were diaspora members, educated outside
Serbia. Like combatants in Syria and Iraq, they had returned, making their way from America or Australia, Italy, Germany, Britain,
or South Africa. Others were "seconded"—Russian and Chinese,
they were part of the student base in Belgrade, a traditional link
between Communist countries that had never lapsed—or they
were on diplomatically arranged trips, solely for this project.

The group was part endless hackathon with NATO as its objective. They covered all disciplines. At the heart were dozens of
seasoned Black Hand hackers; around them were cryptographers
and coders, front-end and back-end website developers. But where
hackers tended to be technical—in their methods, educational
backgrounds, interests, and mind-sets—the group was founded on
the principle that there was no divide between hacking computers
and hacking minds.

It was also, Mirjana and Ratimir agreed, a part real-time "content machine." Accompanying each hacker was a huddle of at least
three writers, behind them translators and designers. Their job
was to post to boards and comment on news websites and blogs,
with the aim of creating doubt about the NATO mission by exposing the hypocrisy and falsehoods that Serbia saw behind the treaty's
announcements and actions. They also ran messaging and mailing
groups, so that anything from evidence of NATO's falsehoods to
memes and Trojans and other viruses could be distributed globally
in coordinated fashion.

Also present were specialists from one of the state security service's covert infowar divisions, the Department of Chaos. Composed
of members of the security services who'd shown aptitude in journalism, performing arts, propaganda, or advertising, its job was,
according to its former commander Bozidar "the Weasel" Spasic,

"simply, to fuck people. Really *fuck* them, in the most elegant way, so that it became not disinformation, but *art*."

But if they could ease the path for hacks—supplying lists of targets, helping with cryptography—they were at least as keen to learn from the hackers.

The kids brought the science of digital attribution—figuring out what was happening, and why. Content and creative—the design of viral visuals, the most effective subject lines and calls for action, appeal text—were tested, optimized, launched, and retested with a ruthless, real-time A/B approach familiar to hackers worldwide when they're trying to crack a password or other security measure, but at the time completely alien to anything else, let alone the global news cycle. The graphics of the downed Nighthawk, of Windows 99, and hundreds more iconic pieces came from this room. They would simply seek to open up space between the official US and Western European narrative and public perception. The world was witnessing the birth of global networks of citizen journalism and the start of its own ongoing negotiation with information war as the regime's hackers, white-hat reporting projects, intelligence agencies, and diaspora extremists all hit the direct-to-audience trail.

Among the elite hacking team, most seemed to be enthusiastic amateurs—unpaid, and working for kicks, kudos, and clout. Yet there were a few who had formalized their relationship with the security services and accepted paid work. Once schoolkids hacking into Croatian and Albanian news sites, their online boasting about Black Hand or C1337ORG affiliation had become a beacon to those tracking them in Belgrade. The security services had approached them either online or by threatening them with arrest on the street. At that point, the leverage was theirs. Accept some paid work for the Ministry of Information, earn privileges as if you were in the army, or we'll bust you. Once they were through that door, they called themselves cybersoldiers.

The Serbian kids from the Western diaspora were harder to

fathom. They were tired of being seen "back home" in Wisconsin or Illinois, Toronto or Vienna, as "baddies," constantly asked about the Bosnian wars, the ethnic cleansing, then Kosovo. Made to bear shame for something they had no part in, they had found themselves wondering what they weren't being told and had resolved to find out—online at first, before being groomed into service in Serbia. It was a dynamic that prefigured the flood of angry, alienated kids to the Islamic state in the 2010s—not just to Syria and Iraq, but as online jihadis in an ongoing war of information. They were angrier, and often worryingly careless about operational security. They flashed with hatred in their comments against America, fought hard to make hacks as destructive as they could. The Belgrade kids in the group called this group the cyber mercenaries.

Then there were the Russian and Chinese hackers. They had a very specific job. They would cultivate the small but growing communities of internet users in Russia and China and turn some of the viruses being devised into packages that could be understood and deployed from there, but they were also liaisons with the government and press there.

For Drakulic, entering the room felt like the reveal of a Bond villain's operation; so well had the secret been kept, so complete and lavish was it. Yet to the guests, as they were guided through it, it was more than met the eye. They saw in it the kind of big spending that they had all gotten used to thinking simply wasn't possible anymore. They were organized into teams that ate together, worked together—everything as a team, as if they were in the army. "The hackers had clearly become good friends," remembers Drakulic. "You could see them laughing and chatting, even as they were working hard."

It was clear that this was not an operation born of careful and thorough advanced planning, but one of agility and reactivity. The reports of Mirjana's committee had functioned as briefs. They had reported traction among Russian and Chinese hackers and internet users; now here were desks of Russian- and Chinese-speaking hackers inside the building, to target and amplify those movements. The reports had remarked on the success of ping attacks. The government suit showed them groups who were creating automated ways to generate them by taking over unsuspecting machines. They had floated the success of highlighting the differences between the official NATO account of casualties and bombing policies; now here was a group working with sympathetic hackers worldwide to crowdsource Trojans that could infect, search, and open up NATO files for the world to see.

This was not a cyber-war bunker like any before it. Where the United States and its allied armies spent millions on undetected incursions by highly trained military-technical specialist teams, and Russia did the same, here was as team of coordinators, among them not one military employee. Nor were they all that bothered about remaining undetected, or about being technically superior to whatever DARPA could create.

It would not be until 2006 that Major Michael Prosser's study on memetic warfare argued for the idea of a US military Meme Warfare Center. Yet seven years earlier, memetic warfare was already part of the hacker group's work inside Belgrade University.

But while the political and military members of the committee were overjoyed at the tour of the operations center, some of the lecturers sounded a note of alarm.

The committee members had been observing the methods of hackers, some of them playing alongside the amateur hacker militias, for some time. They recognized the telltale sign of the networks of loyalty and allegiance that developed between the hackers as they worked. They also knew that those loyalties tend to go further than any others—to corporations, countries, or paymasters. When they surveyed the room, they saw not a hall full of kids, but a hall full of Frankenstein's monsters.

The group took the suited mastermind from the Ministry of

Information aside and confronted him. What, they asked, did he think he was doing? Didn't the ministry or the army care that using an educational building for any kind of attacks during a time of war was against all manner of conventions? That they were putting the kids in danger? What exactly did the government man think would happen if the Americans worked out that this was one of the hot spots for attacks on its systems? He attempted to calm the group. They would be careful, he said. But how careful could you be with a bunch of kids?

The group fell silent. Then Mirjana spoke the words that were on everyone's mind. "Well, I really hope you've got a plan for all these people."

The man turned away, but she continued. "Just what do you think is going to happen to these kids once the bombing is finished? They're doing what you want now, but you're giving them all this experience, and bringing them together as a network. Have you even *considered* what that puts into the world? They're your hacker army today; they could just as easily become hackers for anyone else when all this is done. What if it's for a less government-approved motivation? Because they're connected now, and they're trained, and they're angry. You've *made* them. Now what?"

The man from the party shook his head, raised his hands. "That's ridiculous," he said. "They are just kids. They are here from their universities abroad, their lives elsewhere, or school in Belgrade. Afterwards, they will go back to whatever they were doing. You know what will happen after this? *Nothing.*"

They weren't government employees, argued the group. Many of them weren't even nationals. The Black Hand hackers were already part of a criminal underworld. This was like some cyber-mercenary convention—members from all over the world, brought here to learn how to fuck with superpowers.

The man from the government shrugged. If that was true, he reasoned, then Serbia had finally gotten something that would make the big boys listen. He boasted that just one virus that the kids in there had prepared would automatically scramble the text in emails sent from any infected system, adding strings of anti-NATO polemic to whatever anyone was sending out. "Imagine what that will do when it hits the United States!" he breathed. Then: "This is the start. We can make people say anything we want them to."

In fact, the chaos Drakulic was so afraid of was just as much part of the Serbian authorities' strategy as the group itself. The logic of the situation—they were outnumbered, outgunned, and playing internet catch-up with America and its allies—meant that to really cause the United States problems, asymmetric cyber war itself would have to be replicated and spread in the wild, both at home and abroad. It meant leveraging neutral citizens worldwide, and the machines of unsuspecting millions, starting in Serbia itself.

That week, the main television channel of the national broadcaster took to sporting a screen showing a list of "target websites" the public at home and in the diaspora were invited to hack, flood with comments, or inundate on behalf of the country. "Please send as many emails as possible" was the message on-screen. If they could, they would deluge the target servers with emails, causing them to shut down.

Simultaneous email campaigns went out across the population of Serbia and sympathetic internet users overseas. A flood of directions hit you in your in-box each morning, instructing you how to make your computer count in attacks on NATO. "Everyone who receives this email," they started. Then came the instructions— websites to hit, ECE or PDF files with malware in them to forward to everyone they could in the United States. They would be ranked, templated. "This one is a national emergency, of primary importance for your country. Send. This one is of secondary importance. Send."

The military-groomed university group's next innovation still feels shocking today. They turned almost the entire online population of the country and its diasporas into a voluntary botnet of cyber warriors. One morning, the messages that pinged into email in-boxes directed users to a site. On that site was a small program they asked users to install for the greater good. "Just one click to install this program, and your computer too will become one of the ones making automated attacks against NATO," it read.

Not only did the program work. It proved irresistible—perhaps the internet's first genuinely global viral event. From the Balkans to China and Russia and the United States, hundreds of thousands of computer users willingly turned their machines over. Countless others exploring online downloads and opening attachments out of curiosity unwittingly swelled the attacker networks too. The classified documents circulating worldwide that made their way to me had started with a piece of malware devised by the hacker group and first sent from a computer in one of the Serbian enclaves in Kosovo. By the end of the war, the servers of NATO and its constituent member militaries had been penetrated with at least twenty-five strains of virus-infected email.

That is an incredible statistic. It meant the systems of the Western military alliance—an alliance led by the very inventors of the internet, at the peak of its power—had been penetrated with enemy malware more than once every three days.

It would become clear later that the true cost had not been in the attacks themselves, or the malware that had escaped into the wild. It had been in the very idea of a new civilian-military breed of Total Warfare that had gotten out into the world.

And in the hands of more powerful foes than Serbia, it would come back to haunt the United States.

Chapter 7

The Birth of a Global Brand

The Serbian authorities were canny enough to see that they had been led into a promising new area by kids over whom they had zero control. Now, as early May cooked the streets of Belgrade, they looked to brand it for the military.

A website appeared on the old Tripod free-website service popular at the time. The site was recruiting hackers for something called the Serbian Internet Army and was covered in Serbian flags and military regalia.

The Serbian Internet Army's founder identified himself as one Captain Dragan. It was the nickname of Dragan Vasiljković, an infamous forty-five-year-old Yugoslav Australian. Vasiljković was the former commander of the notorious Serb paramilitary unit the Knin Ninjas during the Bosnian wars. He was already wanted on war crimes charges in The Hague—his name was on the list of "high-value targets" covered by the scope of the hacked NATO documents that spat out onto my computer—but he remained walking the streets and partying at Marko Milošević's gangster- and government-packed Belgrade nightclub Madona as a free man and regime henchman in Belgrade. This newly announced Serbian Internet Army, affiliated with a high-ranking war criminal and using Tripod internet and a bunch of free webmail addresses, was stationed on a whole floor of office space in the iconic Beograđanka building, now one of the headquarters of the government-sponsored hacker army and housing desk after desk of shiny new PCs, glowing late into the night as they launched attacks on NATO.

"You will certainly remember the Knin Ninjas from the Bosnian war," he wrote on the website. "They were the elite and the pride of our forces. However, I believe that the coming wars will not be fought for physical space but FOR VIRTUAL SPACE." Anyone wanting to hack America in Serbia's name or that of the global push against the aggressor had, explained the site in a message from Captain Dragan, to swear to him "that I am ready to become a member of the SVI, which I prove by submitting my own email address."

But there was something deeper at play. The captain on the website referred to himself not just as a hacker, and a Knin Ninja, but as "regent"—a title not lost on Serb nationalists worldwide who looked forward to restoring the monarchy abolished by President Tito and his Communist Party after World War II.

This was a play specifically to the attention of émigré communities. The whole website was a deliberate exercise in the global branding of hacker activity. It targeted their primary pool of recruits, signal boosters, supporters, and hangers-on. The global diaspora, from Chicago to New York, Sydney, Toronto, Vienna, Berlin, Milan, and London. The flags and dog whistles were important marketing collateral for overseas hackers to join and swell the numbers. Groups of Serbs in Australia, Canada, and the United States joined up, motivated by the idea of becoming part of some kind of noble, anti-imperialist narrative, but so did non-Serbs, animated by the prospect of fighting back against the power of the United States, and drawn by the allure of excitement and notoriety.

Among the Black Hand's new recruits was a Serb from Australia whose nickname was Dr. Snake. He was in his thirties, drove a fast but fifteen-year-old Volkswagen, and failed to impress his fellow hackers, having the air of a real-life example of a small-time smuggler who would go to the *splav* bars on the river, barge pubs frequented by gangsters and flash wannabes, when he was in Belgrade. He was typical of most of the hackers who came from outside Serbia in that he had a very specific way of expressing his nationalism, which caused trouble with the native Serbs. The outsiders would encourage the natives to go to Kosovo and fight, to which the natives would say, "Okay, fine, why don't you come over from Australia and go fight if you want to, but don't tell me what I should do."

The Serbian Internet Army site was calibrated, targeted marketing for exactly these people. Young, alienated, and idealistic, these cyber warriors were not inside Serbia at all. They were in the United States, Canada, Germany, Italy, Britain. Captain Dragan was the figurehead, not because he was any good at hacking, but precisely because he was an Aussie Serb. The recruitment drive, with all its melodramatic postures, was a deliberate, targeted, and calibrated wooing of alienated Western diasporas and a conjuring of the ideal state that needed defending. It looked laughable to young Belgraders, but they were never its audience. It was a new kind of recruitment drive for the new age of mass internet access. It was less important what people on the ground (poor, low on resources, few in number, cynical) thought of the cause than what the global diaspora (wealthier, well resourced, numerous, idealistic) felt.

It was a calculated exercise in global branding we would witness in different forms over the coming decades, from Russia Today (RT) to the slick media appeals of the Islamic State to the alienated global *ummah* of a struggle to restore something that, just perhaps, had only ever existed in the echoing minds of disaffected idealists. It was the great promise of internet connectivity brought to life in a way that its creators had failed to envisage. People all over the globe were suddenly able to connect in a way they never had before. The people who were connecting were tech savvy and young, idealistic and frustrated. They were right in the sweet spot for the Serb recruiters. Their audience was an army, out there waiting for them.

All the Belgrade University team and its cells across the city needed to do was activate them.

In this attempt to internationalize the struggle for an idealized state—casting a war criminal as the regent, holding it for the return of the perfected rule—it would prefigure the Islamic State's use, in the middle of civil war in Syria and failing post-US governance in Iraq, of social media, YouTube, and publicity stunts to attract youths worldwide to its promise of a perfect, idealized caliphate.

A new kind of war was announcing itself—one on which citizens across the world would be turned, would become either agents for the cause, or fighters, or simple counters, spreading the word and amplifying the message. Again, the United States and its allies failed to heed the warning, or to engage with them in any way.

The realization that people and internet terminals around the world could become not just attackers but vectors through which Serbian attacks could spread struck Serbian intelligence and hackers with a wave of euphoria. Perhaps, after all, the fight was less unequal than it seemed. The groups began looking in earnest at the possibilities for disruptive communications—in effect, trying to create more "viral" events that could spread through the internet in ways that would hinder NATO.

The Belgrade University group had seen how well memes performed across cyberspace, how they spread faster than news bulletins, and used wiseguy humor, irreverence, and online slang to reach further, and to "educate" their recipients to resist what they might later see from official NATO sources. Yet as Serbian intelligence worked through the reports from Drakulic's group, they realized they had something potentially far more powerful.

The reports showed that as an emotional payoff, humor and anger were both powerful tools in getting people to spread the group's messaging. But perhaps other powerful emotional payoffs might work equally well? The feeling of being clever, for example. Or being one of the chosen few to see something clearly.

Their next step was to test this new emotional fuel and harness the power of online conspiracy theories for the first time in modern warfare. And they knew just the man to draft in to help them do it.

Colonel Svetozar Radišić was slim and wiry, in his fifties with cropped gray hair, glittering eyes, and a mustache. Radišić had been the Serbian forces' press spokesman during the Bosnian wars. The issue then was that he was widely regarded as insane. He considered himself the founder of something called Neocortical War, in which Serbian mind power could be used, Yuri Geller style, to make enemy forces explode or cause mysterious heart attacks or medical disasters for enemy leaders. This had made his briefings during Bosnia the stuff of unintentional comedy and Radišić himself an embarrassment to the army, among whom he earned the nickname Agent Mulder. After one too many outlandish claims, he was unceremoniously kicked from the job and demoted to a backroom role where the public wouldn't see him. Now, he was back, feeding news into the email groups sent by the university hacker group to a global audience.

Dr. Jovan Byford of the Open University is the world's leading researcher on conspiracy theories in the Balkans. He tracked Radišić's odd internet-powered second coming.

The mystery was that this very same man, who was moved off to a less public role after the Bosnian wars, is suddenly pushed very forcefully and suddenly back into the spotlight in 1999. Very suddenly he's not just back, but the *official face* of the Yugoslav army during the bombing. And not only *that*—he's online, webchats, emails chat shows, being trumpeted there as credible—as the Editor of the main military publication; he's publishing a book on neocortical warfare, promoting it across Serbia. He's been rebranded as an "international expert"—in fact a *star*. Something happened in that short period of time, a shift in the idea of what he was useful for, that allowed Radišić, with his conspiracy

theories to suddenly become marketed as an expert on geopolitics and contemporary warfare again.

For a couple of years now, Radišić had headed up an informal group within the Serb military called Group 69. Its remit was
"parapsychological" or neocortical warfare, and Radišić was its
conspiracy theorist in chief. Among its officers were TV astrolo-
ger Milja Vujanović-Regulus (who adopted the hyphenated name
on the occasion of her marriage to the star Regulus, part of the
constellation of Leo and seventy-nine light-years from the sun), a
necromancer, several high-ranking army officers, and a few radical philosophers. It had become a think tank for kooks, loved by
the queen kook, Milošević's first lady, Mira Markovic, mocked
and barely tolerated by army colleagues. Now, Serbian officials
considered this word-drunk, heady, and often incoherent cocktail
of conspiracy theories, nationalist fantasy, inflammatory rhetoric, pseudoscience, and mythopoeic ramblings in a new light. If
they were annoying distractions to those who met them in person, imagine the damage these could do piped into the in-boxes,
blogs, and news media of every new internet user in America. If the
world thought it knew why NATO was bombing Serbia, let them
try to engage with this! Trials on message boards and chat rooms
showed that they immediately outperformed the dryer, more fac-
tual reports and quickly found a way out into the global media,
feeding the sudden explosion of "News of the Weird" content not
just online, but in printed daily newspapers, TV, and radio reports.
The result was quietly astonishing, with anti-NATO content rising
steadily in every country targeted, even when based on the most
feverish, fabricated claims about how the stars' alignment had sent
President Clinton insane, that papers had been discovered revealing the bombing of Serbia was part of the plans for a New World
Order commanded by George Soros, or that magical revelations in
Orthodox churches showed Slobodan as a Christ figure, resisting

great evil once again. Even more astonishing was that these stories were being shared more readily and reaching wider circulation not just in Russia but in the United States and Western Europe too than most of NATO's own communiqués.

These kooks and conspiracists, psychics and experimentalists of Group 69's leadership were joined by a team of army "technologists" who would liaise with both the Belgrade University network and the Serbian Internet Army. The result was the world's first state-funded cyber-disinformation unit.

Their job was to leverage this explosion in online protest, hacking, and general chaos in order to introduce uncertainty into the minds of internet users worldwide about the mission, and into NATO's own forces from the US Air Force and central command, about what exactly the Serb hackers had found out about their plans, or done to their computers, or indeed their equipment and personnel, methods that would be used by QAnon twenty years later. Suddenly, hacker defacements were awash with warnings. Comment threads and instant messages, email chain letters, bulletin boards, and even lines of code left inside NATO computers themselves were awash with ominous warnings, breadcrumbs, and "drops." Something terrible was about to happen to America.

It was imminent. There were those with inside knowledge who reported that its technology was about to cause a horrible malfunction. Geologists—in fact, Group 69's cranks—had discovered that a US supervolcano under Yellowstone Park was expected to erupt imminently, causing terrible devastation. Politika and TV stations picked up the digital output and reported that "some great misfortune" was looming and that "secret forces within the US [were] at work behind the scenes." A plan was working, slowly. Watch this space. Civil unrest had been reported in America, but was now being covered up by the mainstream US media and global networks. A nuclear accident in a US nuclear facility had been reported; that was now also being covered up by a mainstream news blackout in America. The nuclear accident's origins lay in a mysterious computer outage that they could now reveal was the work of none other than the hacker kids of Belgrade.

These messages began to gain traction.

They spread not just in the fringe email groups and underground collectives, but into Russian and Chinese state media. From there, they made their way into normally sober US commentators' briefings. My own publishing company received emergency warnings to be alert for anything suggesting more information around these events from its owner, the US media giant Omnicom, Inc., on Madison Avenue.

Incredibly, they were then amplified inside NATO itself. The story that a spy or spies at a high level inside NATO forces, either in DC, Brussels, or London, had been spreading secrets to the Serbs, started here. NATO itself not only could not discount it but began investigating, spending time and resources going off down false trails.

Like QAnon, it was maddeningly suggestive. Every new event seemed to become a sign. American and European monitoring stations were confused in their impressions. Did they mean something concrete? Did they have information? Was it crankery? Were all these bizarro stories coded references to something else, being sent to the field? This wasn't an infowar in the sense that it was a war fought *with* information; it was a war *on* information itself.

Yet the defects in this new phenomenon were there at birth. The government's cultivation of conspiracy theories and fake news as the essential, viral part of its high-volume 24/7 content production and amplification program meant that the hackers committed to honest reporting—even when it showed up disparity in the NATO briefings coming from America and Britain—were simply drowned out by more outrageous, fabricated claims to truth from their own hacker colleagues.

The flooding of timelines, in-boxes, messenger services, TV screens, and websites with claims of cover-ups and "what the global media won't show" was deliberate. And it is a tactic that laid the foundations for today's fringe media in the chase for clicks, hearts, and minds.

The Serbian state had set out, using its own media and globally online, to inoculate people against crediting the truth in real news from elsewhere. Their goal was to persuade people to buy into the idea that what they were seeing from every other news source was faked somehow, part of a global media conspiracy, so that Serbs themselves would then not believe the reports were coming through about what their paramilitaries or government had done. It was, in effect, a preemptive strike against the truth. And the more plausible CNN or the BBC reports were, the more that "proved" they were part of a disinformation campaign planned by the West, and the more confidently and easily these reports could be discarded.

It was a recipe that would quickly find itself adopted wholesale from St. Petersburg's Internet Research Agency troll farm to the viral content models of Fox News, RT, and OneAmerica, the "drops" of QAnon boards and the Twitter and Facebook posts about everything from vote rigging to ivermectin in the years to come. As the title of Peter Pomerantsev's 2014 book on working in Russian TV through the 2000s put it, this was a world where *Nothing Is True and Everything Is Possible.*

For Serbs and those around the world exposed to this first industrial crack hit of internet disinformation, the result was giddy and paranoid disorientation. The fuzzy sea of conflicting truths and counterclaims, conspiracy theories, and unlikely reports held all possibilities inside it. The Serbian Internet Army had been recruiting. The hackers were turning the tide. In supposedly "intercepted" messages in code and mocked up in Russian, Russia's army had signaled that it would intervene, defending its fellow Slav nation. George Soros was behind the bombing because Milošević would not let his paid armies of troublemakers rig the Serbian election.

The footage of columns of survivors from Kosovo being rescued was faked, or it was from a Serb town menaced in Bosnia years before. Leakers were running riot inside the Pentagon. NATO was finished, being sabotaged from the inside by thousands of righteous hackers. Even NATO itself was investigating its own people, who were turning against it. The American war machine was all about to collapse. President Clinton had already been assassinated. Yosemite had already blown up; there had been hundreds of thousands of deaths. This bombardment was just the distraction to prevent TV news crews from traveling to California. There were hints everywhere if you looked. The omens were everywhere. Something big was coming.

And then, on the sweltering night of May 7, 1999, a month and a half into the bombardment, it came.

Chapter 8

Horror Show

"...this morning, and NATO has a lot of explaining to do!"

The voice jolted me awake. After an evening and night haunting message boards and chasing exchanges in a half-dozen foreign languages, I had fallen asleep. Now I was wide awake, the early-morning sun lighting the room, trying to make sense of the peppy British news anchor's urgency.

While I had been chasing hackers, two American B-2 Spirit stealth bombers had been dispatched from Whiteman Air Force Base, just east of Kansas City, Missouri.

NATO's nighttime bombing missions had been taking off from airbases such as Aviano, far closer to the Balkans in NATO-member Italy. But as the bombardment had settled into its nightly rhythm of mayhem, it became part of a channel of real-time underground communication along new internet and long-standing shortwave radio hacker networks too. "Many users from Slovenia, Bosnia and Herzegovina, Croatia, Hungary, the Czech Republic, Slovakia, Bulgaria, Macedonia, Greece and Italy send information about the take-off of NATO planes," said a report compiled by Ratimir and Mirjana Drakulic. As they heard the roar of warplanes soaring overhead, internet relay chat and shortwave radio users on the flight path would often relay the planes' location and path to their networks of users in Belgrade and elsewhere in Serbia and Kosovo, who would then relay the signal within their own networks, or amplify them through command centers such as the hacker operation inside Belgrade University, with connections to state forces.

That was good news for citizens of the towns. For America and its NATO allies, however, it was a blow to the prospects for any air mission that depended on secrecy, or the ability to catch an antagonist in the act—for example, listening for its signals, or attempting to fix on its radar—before firing its missiles. It had also added to NATO and US unease about its operational security amid the flood of rumors about spies and hacker incursions.

The upshot was extreme secrecy even inside NATO. If it wanted to come in and evade the warning grapevine, it would have to come in high. And it would have to be a rogue operation run on a need-to-know basis.

These low-visibility B2s of USAF 509th Bomb Wing had crossed the Atlantic in fair weather, with the orange sun chasing them and the deepening blue ahead. Their flat, matte-black triangles cut into rushing darkness toward Belgrade. Shortly before midnight local time, the Spirits' navigators had locked onto the precise coordinates of their target, a grand building on the jutting corner of New Belgrade outlined from above by the flat black ribbons of the Danube and Sava Rivers. This was a target that had not been selected by NATO. Nor was this a NATO mission. This flight had been commissioned by the CIA, and under conditions of utmost secrecy. Not even NATO's own airborne or command forces had been informed of its existence, let alone its mission.

The roar above the buildings intensified for a moment, then exploded as the Spirits' five US GPS-guided JDAM missiles slammed into the compound of the Chinese embassy in Belgrade. Four hit the embassy, killing four Chinese nationals inside what had been considered a protected space, and injuring twenty-seven. The fifth bomb smashed through the roof of the ambassador's residence next door, failing to explode. Above the screams, sirens blared. There had been an electricity blackout in town, but now flashing lights turned thick smoke, emergency responders, cries, and panic into a stroboscopic horror show.

In Brussels, Jamie Shea jolted awake. The phone at his bedside was ringing. Mere moments after the strike, he picked it up. The voice must have felt unreal in those first few seconds, briefing him and telling him that he would need to face the world's press at the morning briefing and offer some explanation. Shea was given little more that he could share at that stage, but when he spoke to the world's press cameras on Saturday morning, he was clear about one thing: the bombs had "struck the wrong building."

Ratimir Drakulic encountered a morning of clearing smoke, in which the dust of rubble clung to the tongue, making speech thick and labored. The lecturer-hackers lived not far from the embassy and had been shaken by the explosions. As morning broke, they set off on foot together for work at the university. The first sight was the rubble—the familiar shape of the corner had vanished. Then the blood. So much of it, all over the rubble. Then the bursting of pipes, and the street flooding.

CIA chief George Tenet explained the strike as an error, claiming that the United States had used an outdated map and that satellite images of the compound gave no indication the target was an embassy—"no flags, no seals, no clear markings." (In fact, all three were clearly visible.) The intention had been, NATO said, to strike another building—the Yugoslav Federal Directorate for Supply and Procurement, some 380 yards away, across a wide street and past more buildings. The guidance systems, he said, were so imprecise they should never have been used. However, Tenet also told a congressional committee that this was the only bombing of the entire campaign organized and directed not by NATO at all, but by the CIA alone.

China was outraged, declaring the error story to be "unconvincing." By evening, US and British embassies in China from Beijing to Chengdu came under siege as massive crowds not seen since the Tiananmen Square protests swarmed around the compounds, demanding revenge strikes.

As the dust settled and the two narratives solidified, the British *Observer* and Danish *Politiken* newspapers investigated; Jens Helsoe and John Sweeney's eventual report was that not only was the strike deliberate, but it was based on CIA intel to the effect that the Chinese embassy was being used as a rebroadcast station by Serb forces as their own comms had fallen and that accordingly the CIA had removed it from the prohibited-targets list.

A Serbian humanitarian activist would later testify that on the morning of the day of the bombing, Chinese military attaché Ren Baokai had spoken openly of the embassy being used to track NATO military aircraft and spy on US operations—in a quid pro quo, perhaps, or China receiving parts of the intact downed F-117 for analysis and inspection. Serbian witnesses claimed to me that the Chinese embassy itself was in close collaboration with the China contingent within the Belgrade hacker group. It had been, they said, their employer and manager in the project.

So concerned were the US Air Force and CIA about whether Serbian, Chinese, or Russian hackers—or even flesh-and-blood spies, as the Serb-sponsored conspiracy newswires had it—were already far more embedded inside their systems that the need-to-know comms around the raid had indeed kept NATO chiefs and the president himself out of the loop. It would also later emerge that in the days leading up to the attack, the CIA had created an authorization folder named "Belgrade Warehouse 1," describing the target as a warehouse from which the Serbian military was organizing weapons distribution, and that it was in this form that authorization had been handed back down to the CIA by President Clinton himself.

These contesting claims are not mutually exclusive. NATO may have regarded it as a mistake; the CIA, concerned with intelligence and desperately worried about the possibility that the Chinese embassy was becoming the key relay point for bringing the

Serbian hackers into touch with the Chinese government, may have made the unilateral and deliberate decision to strike. China's outrage was sincere, while its activities in the compound also seem to have been in support of Serb hacker groups and units' military communications. As *Observer* reporter John Sweeney told the BBC: "This was, and always will be, a murky story."

Agent Mulder and Group 69's carnival parade of conspiracy theorists, experimental thinkers, fringe academics—and now hackers too—was suddenly in an interesting position. Globally, their cachet had suddenly shot up. Every single wild claim—about China and Russia planning to join forces on the side of the Serbs, about spies within NATO, about hackers who had been inside the US Air Force's systems sabotaging their communications and forcing them to hit the wrong targets, about neocortical mumbo jumbo—suddenly wore the glamour of prophecy.

"It helped like Pearl Harbor helped," said one member of the Belgrade hacker community, comparing America being brought into World War II to China joining the Serbs' cyber war against America. The same hacker said thousands of their community had been trying to achieve something like this for weeks. They had been inside American military and NATO computer systems all through the bombardment, attempting to feed false intelligence into the system in a way that would generate confusion and disaster. Now they felt the job had been done for them.

In the following days, the hacker groups in the university faculty and Beograđanka hit a new gear, reaching out with renewed intensity in Chinese and Russian, and working together with the small cadres of hackers and state technicians in Moscow, St. Petersburg, Shanghai, Shenzhen, Beijing, and Hong Kong to maximize their impact.

For the first time since the start of the engagement, Chinese hackers began to initiate massive attacks on NATO's communications channels and digital capabilities in earnest themselves, rather than just joining Serbian hackers' attempts.

The White House went offline, its website replaced with the message from Chinese hackers that said, "Protest USA's Nazi action! Protest NATO's brutal action!" In a bizarre piece of political tap dancing with the press corps, at one point White House spokesperson Barry Toiv refused to say in the press room whether the White House website had actually been hacked at all, despite the messages with which it was defaced, and the note that accompanied the hacks: "Stop all war. Consintrate [*sic*] on your problems. Nothing was damaged, but we are not telling how we got in."

In the three days the White House site was down, the US Departments of Energy and the Interior also vanished from the internet—the first sign that even if civilian infrastructure had been off the menu for NATO since Operation Uphold Democracy's phreaker attacks were shelved in Haiti in 1994, the embassy bombing had ushered in an era in which superpowers would now consider each other's civilian utilities fair game.

Even the National Park Service's electronic services went offline, also at the hands of intruders from the People's Republic of China. "We are Chinese hackers who take no care about politics," wrote one of the hackers, called Rocky. "You have owed Chinese people a bloody debt which you must pay for! We will not stop attacking until the war stops!"

This was a chilling development for the United States, and one that would echo down to today. China's burgeoning economic muscle and military might make it a different beast than Russia. But in the rush to de-escalate diplomatic tension, the sudden phenomenon of this Chinese iteration of the Black Hand—for that is precisely what it was, with coaching and direction from the hacker group inside Belgrade University—was missed almost entirely. While the diplomatic storm would be calmed, this emergence would be its most enduring legacy.

Where had this sudden explosion of hackers come from, in a country regarded as so behind the curve on the developing internet?

Rocky and his fellow raiders claimed affiliation with an organization called Whampoa Military Academy (WMA) in China, others with something called the Green Army. This represented a huge red flag for China watchers. The very idea that the Chinese military might be involved in getting inside NATO members' government systems—America's energy grid, no less—raised hair in the Pentagon.

The Green Army, a.k.a. Whampoa Military Academy, had been registered in 1997 in Shanghai. The original Whampoa Military Academy from which the group took its alias was one of the early training camps for elite specialist soldiers in China. Set up in 1927, it had led the creation of the Red Army's elite. It was, to Western consternation, funded by the Soviet Union as an act of Communist brotherhood. The site, it turned out, was not formally affiliated with the Chinese military, but its name would come to afford its founders a certain berth online, not to mention putting scares into NATO's top generals.

While Department of Energy teams would not say what had happened, they sent an urgent alert to US federal agencies and defense contractors. Sandy Spark, head of the agency's Computer Incident Advisory Capability, warned that a Chinese "tidal wave of e-mail with unresolvable IP addresses" was incoming to US government servers, in an attempt to overload them as the Serbian hackers had done to NATO. Staff across the country were put on alert for a likely incoming wave of mail bombings. In an unprecedented move, US officials prepared to put a nationwide block on all emails from China's .cn top-level domain.

Suddenly, Chinese hacker traffic was everywhere. Much of it was brutal, unsophisticated to start with, but Western observers watched in horrified fascination as it became more pointed, faster, better. The swelling of the numbers was bringing its own momentum, as the gathering crowds learned from each other's successes. For all that the past twenty years had put the spotlight on machine learning, here was a live human experiment, being performed at a global scale. This wasn't only about gaining admittance to servers or disrupting capacity; it was about picking targets. For a few tense weeks in the final fevered year before the millennium, it is no exaggeration to say that no major web presence in the West went unprobed.

The Black Hand and the Green Army were specters stalking the Western internet, testing doors and windows as they roamed, from air force bases to banks, government departments to hospitals. To this day, it is unknown just how many more they gained access to. The US military remains tight-lipped, and NATO's partner armies and governments closed ranks around the buried report. But some sense of scale can be grasped by the fact that in those few months in 1999 alone, their attacks are estimated to have cost private businesses in the United States alone $266 million—a figure unheard of at the time and close to half a billion dollars in 2022 money.

Whether taking down the White House again or raiding US military and government sites and stealing or deleting classified or function-critical data held on them, these Chinese attackers signed off as "honkers"—a name that puzzled NATO's admins at first. It didn't appear to have any military significance. It was some days before word came up the chain that it wasn't a military word at all—it was a translation. The Chinese term *heike*—a literal transliteration of the English sound "hacker"—becomes the conveniently appropriate Chinese word pairing, "dark/black visitor/guest." Rocky, LittleFish, and the other cyber warriors taking down US targets night after night referred to themselves online in English as honkers. The Westernized version of *hongke* was easily arrived at. Instead of *hei*—dark—these guests were very visible indeed. And they were *hongke*. Red Visitors.

This was alarming to NATO armed forces commander General Wesley Clark and its secretary-general, George Robertson, to say the least. More disturbing was that the Chinese authorities appeared to be covering for the hackers. The hackers had left a trail of chaos—including three thousand IDs for members of the Green Army alone, statements claiming responsibility for "more foreign websites than we can count," and open chatter online about their locations in Shanghai, Beijing, and Shenzhen. Yet despite the attackers from China leaving names, digital trails, and IP addresses all over their work, the Chinese government and military denied knowledge of the perpetrators carrying out attacks in its name.

In fact, the Chinese authorities had been as pleasantly surprised as the Americans were horrified. As the Yugoslav government had initially been, the Chinese government too was blind to the far wider Total War potential of cyber war until its young showed them what it could do. At this point, both had shown enough awareness and fleetness of foot to take an entrepreneurial approach, sit back, and supply the requisite amount of punch.

Throughout the 1990s, China had exploded with growth. The Chinese internet had exploded in tandem. From just 3,000 users in the beginning of 1995, it had leaped to 40,000 by the year's end. By 1997, that number was 675,000, the following year 2.1 million. By the early summer of 1999, in just three and a half years, that number had grown a hundredfold, to 4 million. Yet its user base was largely restricted to professional, government, and military usage, regarded more as a business and banking tool than anything else.

Outward-looking urban youths had internet access all right, but their plight was the polar opposite of the young Belgraders. In Serbia, a population of hackers by instinct and training, who were already able to strip down, break apart, and remake everything from machines to code, awaited only the touch paper of internet access to swarm online and cause chaos. In China, the young urbanites may have had machines, but they lacked hacker tools. Furthermore, in the information vacuum of a giant, still-Communist state, many of them also lacked the skills and experience of hacking.

One of the earliest websites for Chinese hackers had grown from a URL registered at the same time as the Green Army/Whampoa Military Academy one in 1997 called Chinawill—its owner, a young history nerd called Wan Tao, had wanted "to express positive stories from Chinese history." Over the next eighteen months, that lovably innocent goal would get a dark hacker-age reboot, and so would Wan Tao. By the Kosovo bombardment's end, he was regarded as the doyen of Chinese hackers, the website a one-stop resource of tools, code, proclamations of purpose, and tales of exploits.

Yet it too remained mostly dormant at first. The would-be Chinese hackers got their first taste of something like liberating information in 1998. Economic turmoil in Indonesia saw riots across the country, with blame for shortages falling unfairly on the sizable Chinese community of business and store owners. Nights of looting ended with several dead, their premises razed. While the Chinese government expressed its displeasure, however, it kept the news quiet at home. State news agencies simply did not mention the riots. Only through internet users sharing illicit communications did photos from the scene leak out inside China. It had been the first exposure to the power of the internet for early Chinese would-be hackers. The idea that it could open up knowledge that had been forbidden, or help Chinese people see the truth about themselves, struck a small group of users like a lightning bolt.

This was the moment that set things in motion, albeit gently. Before the riots, there was a sum total of seven websites in the whole of China devoted to content around internet hacking, and most of them were mere translations and lifts from content on American sites, as well as European organizations like Gonggrijp and Rodriguez's *Hack-Tic*. Actions were occasionally recorded, but they were sporadic and tiny in scale and weren't even created in China; they relied on email bombs purchased overseas. The majority of neophyte Chinese kids online simply had not yet acquired the skills to make them.

The Green Army's reincarnation of the WMA was no accident. Set up by a hacker going under the name Goodwill, it quickly attracted the cream of the curious among China's small online groups and became the training ground through which a generation of Chinese hacker talent would pass. It quickly established a core committee of admins going by the names Solo, LittleFish, Rocky, and Dspman (HeHe). Users from Beijing, Shenzhen, and Goodwill's home city of Shanghai flooded toward it for good reason: it was, for the bored and privileged urban youth of a country without opposition or much in the way of independent media or arts, as close to badass as they could get. Yet still, its constituency was small, in the hundreds.

Still, the kids could feel they—and China—were moving toward something powerful. A national resurgence had gathered pace; the evidence was everywhere, in the cars suddenly flooding the cities to the new entertainment complexes, and the sizes of the cities themselves. The moors and swamps on the outskirts were becoming roads and towers. The posters glorifying agricultural workers were slowly being replaced by images of urban achievement, even consumption. For most of them, the feeling of patriotism was far from the strange, nostalgic, or conservative feeling we associate it with in the West. They knew China was about to go warp speed. Being part of this light-speed transformation, this rising to the bright glow of a new morning bathed in technology and national purpose, was going to be *cool*.

By 1998, the Green Army had its first taste of Trojans like the Anti-Smyser-1 that gifted me NATO's battle plans. Ironically, it came from America, when US hacker collective the Cult of the Dead Cow made a splash with a new breed of Trojan called Back Orifice, releasing the program and its source code online. Cheap, scalable, and imbued with the spirit of opening up closed and secretive organizations to scrutiny by plundering their servers, Back Orifice was met with awe and excitement at the Whampoa Military Academy.

The issue was its applicability. As a foreign program, it wasn't easy for Chinese hackers to use, nor was it that effective working against Chinese-coded systems.

Shortly after, however, a Trojan did come to China. The CHH Virus used the simplified Chinese characters of the mainland, not the traditional sets used in Taiwan or Hong Kong, and ran riot through China's undefended online infrastructure, causing hundreds of millions of dollars in losses. The Chinese press quickly blamed Taiwan—it pointed the finger at "mentally unstable" Taiwanese military figures who aimed to strike blows against the motherland. For Chinese hackers, however, it was a wonderful exposure to the power and workings of the mighty Trojan.

The Chinese Communist Party itself had remained skeptical. Its embrace of the internet had up to then been as chaste—one might say as uptight and neurotic—as Russia's. With Tiananmen Square and its mass protests still fresh in the mind, it was not about to give the keys to any lateral, networked, unregulated communication protocol to its citizens without a significant upside.

Kosovo changed that stance within a few days of the first attack by the kids of Belgrade. To understand why, we need to reframe the very idea of success, to look at how the cyberattacks on the US military and government websites by the kids of Belgrade were perceived out in the world.

The first incursions against the US government and military websites were, by some US reckonings at the time, not really much of a problem. Had they caused loss of life? Permanent damage to human or mechanical forces? They had not. Did they present anything like mission-critical risk? Again, no. They were an inconvenience, a bad look at most. Of course, they represented a warning, but such was US technological dominance that it was not classified as urgent.

For American capitalism's discontents worldwide, though, they were a clarion call. The Chinese government quickly recognized that it had been presented with a once-in-a-lifetime opportunity. A completely risk-free, cost-neutral, life-fire maneuver on safely distant territory.

Night after night, honkers flooded the boards and messaging platforms—not just in Serbia or the English-speaking online world, but in China itself. Dormant sites such as Chinawill and Green Army exploded, becoming hives of activity and code almost wholly unmonitored by a complacent West. From nothing and nowhere, China developed a buzzing, fast-evolving, and massive hacker scene almost literally overnight; more than an exchange for existing code, by the engagement's end it had become the world's single biggest workshop for crowdsourcing attackware.

As the summer nights cooked with bombs and sizzling servers, yet another wave joined the attacks. This time, it was the Russians who were keen to invest their time. And it was an investment in the suddenly rocketing potential of crowdsourced and decentralized cyber warfare rather than in any resolution to the Kosovo conflict.

What was clear to the young hackers of Belgrade has only become clear to us in retrospect: Russia and China had both been presented with, and spotted, an opportunity to learn, at scale, in a live environment.

Incursions skyrocketed in early summer and then kept rising. There is no doubt that 1999's wave of Russian, Chinese, and diaspora hackers, information warriors, citizen vectors, and other cyber irregulars saw hacking itself leave the global side streets and go mainstream, a popular participation activity. Between 1994 and 1997, the number of denial-of-service attacks, for example, had been fairly stable—between 2,134 and 2,573 a year. The next year, 1998, saw a slow incremental rise, to some 3,734 known hacks. But the explosion spearheaded by the "pings of death" coming from Belgrade, Moscow, St. Petersburg, Shenzhen, Hong Kong, Beijing, and Shanghai saw that figure almost triple by the end of the summer of 1999, to 9,859.

The snowballing increase in scale itself made governments far more interested in the Total War model. It also made it easier to determine success. The increase in volume gave Russian government analysts and its small number of military-backed hackers and information warriors particularly an opportunity. At this scale, human power and connectivity filled the purpose of a machine-learning algorithm, the constant trolling, hacking, publishing, memetic posting, ping attacks, and more forming a live exercise. The giant field of directed actions meant that, by the conflict's end, Russia not only had settled on a strategy of online information war, but would embrace the flipping of populations into vectors with viral content, leading to Russia's Internet Research Agency and Russia's other troll farms of the 2000s and its networks of *kremleboty* (Kremlin bots).

This approach—get semideniable actors to try a lot of cheap and easy actions against the West online, and see what floated, what netted engagement, and what just faded away—was the antithesis of military-style thinking, East or West. Insofar as it represented a strategy at all, that strategy was simply to start fuzzy and refine. To engage in a massive campaign of tiny and continuous actions and to see where it led. The dominant business paradigm of the 2000s—strategic decisions guided in the moment by live-engagement metrics—may well have been claimed by Facebook's Menlo Park and Google's Mountain View. But it owes its first use at scale to Russia.

It is ironic that in the first full year that the CIA/NSA project Google operated, those attempting to get the most urgent fix on how quickly and under what conditions content spread on the internet were Russian and Chinese military intelligence. In this, they were the secret forerunners of everything Google, Facebook, and Twitter would by the end of the 2000s have established as the internet's primary business model.

In the wake of the Chinese invasion, the larger wave of Russian hackers set alarm bells ringing at last, as NATO realized that while its bombardment in Serbia and Kosovo was localized, the resulting cyber war was proliferating, becoming a global concern, and now pulling in not just a furious China, but a recidivist Russia.

NATO high command suddenly snapped to attention. Where the Serbian hackers had been ignored, the new wave of Russian hacks was immediately escalated by a face-to-face briefing between the tech teams and NATO supreme commander General Wesley Clark, at which they talked through a proposal to strike back and "nuke the Russian internet" for a limited period. The idea would be to take the country itself offline—there were still few-enough internet connections with Russia to achieve that. NATO would fight fire with fire. Or more accurately, with an American-generated bombardment of pings, "until things calm down." The proposal stayed on the table. Maybe they could ride it out without such drastic measures.

But things would not calm down.

Chapter 9

Alarms in Virginia

At least one group of US government employees focused on the problem of the hacks would have been horrified had they known that Clark was considering bringing down the entire Russian internet. They were a diligent group of FBI agents slowly working to unravel the webs of influence behind the rise and effectiveness of the hacker armies.

They had been trying to get a fix on the source of the Serbian intrusions behind the scenes since the very first attacks at the outset of the conflict, working in conditions of secrecy so tight that most of the NATO command—General Clark included—had no idea they even existed, let alone what they were discovering. They weren't concerned with stemming the attacks but with understanding them, and with tracing the webs of personal connections and hacker activity back toward their sources, in governments and private individuals.

One early problem for the group solved itself. By the end of the 1990s, US intelligence services were woefully underequipped with expertise and language skills to prepare them for activity across the rest of the globe. The Cold War having ended, the United States had engaged in an orgy of budget slashing for monitoring overseas. The view was simply that the Soviet Union was no longer a concern, and so nor were the strategic locations around the world where proxy wars had been played out. Angola, Guatemala, Vietnam,

Afghanistan all fell from the radar. It was a complacency and selective blindness that would come back to haunt it with 9/11. But even here, it was felt. Yugoslavia might have erupted into ethnic conflict through the 1990s. Diplomacy, and now military might, was applied. But its demands on the US intel community's language skills had been nil. Now American FBI agents found that they were required to pose as Serbian hackers online.

The Serbian Internet Army's outreach to disaffected hackers worldwide came to their rescue. Prevented from moving among the Belgrade kids in chat rooms as one of their own by barriers of language, and extremely specific street-level cultural reference points, the FBI instead posed as international hackers wanting to join the swelling of numbers in the aftermath of the Chinese embassy bombing.

This was not work for just anyone. On the orders of the Pentagon, the US Air Force Office of Special Investigations sent an experienced investigator in his thirties named Bill Swallow in to work with the FBI's Computer Crime Squad in Long Beach, California. Swallow, a USAF Air War College and San Diego University grad, had made a name for himself in the US military with some stunning work in the fledgling field of cyber forensics for the army's Criminal Investigations Department. On the back of a number of high-profile victories tracking fraudsters and crooked contractors through the army's systems, he opened the department's first office in San Diego and blazed through a mounting case load as the military's exposure to online fraud grew, recovering millions of dollars from defense contractors who'd been defrauding the US Army. But if his hot streak in tracking malfeasance through complex networks had made him a sought-after property, his focused, outgoing personality made him the obvious choice to turn to in solving the FBI's current headache with hacker prodigies from Eastern Europe.

An energetic, lugubrious presence with sandy hair and smiling blue eyes, Swallow seemed to relish moving from his management position to go undercover among the anti-NATO hackers who'd been winning against the United States and its allies. His brief was as open as it was simple: to do whatever necessary to identify and develop sources of information among the Belgrade hacker community and, through them, help investigators identify key figures—especially those behind the huge April ping attacks. In this case, "developing" them meant flipping them, by deception, threat, or reward. Once they were US assets, they would be put to use subverting and exposing further hacker connections.

Creating international hacker personae of his own, Swallow got down to business getting undercover and haunting the message boards. He wasted no time identifying and zoning in on prospective marks. Within days, Swallow was able to brief his superiors on a relationship he'd begun to develop with someone he believed to be one of the young Belgrade hackers. It was, he told them, a relationship he believed the United States could profitably exploit.

Based on interactions and information the anonymous hacker shared both openly on the boards and with Swallow in messages, he believed his mystery contact was someone not only embedded deep within Belgrade's youthful hacker underground, but also willing to help feed him genuine information.

But first, the bureau had to initiate a game of cat-and-mouse probing, cross-checking, and second-guessing. It wasn't enough to have someone online who talked a good game, after all—that could be a disinformation trap.

How, the bureau needed to know, could Swallow be sure he was talking to the genuine article and not some counterintelligence agent from the Serbian intelligence services or army, or even the Russians or Chinese? Or that this was someone of value and not just some loser, egging him on for kicks with the promise of information that would end up being duff? One of those would be a waste of time and resources. The other had the potential to be disastrous, for Americans to lose their lives, for the suffering in Kosovo and elsewhere to be prolonged, even for further escalation with China and Russia. The stakes were high. Swallow needed a way to be sure that he was cultivating an informant, and not being played.

Swallow's team escalated the checks to FBI headquarters in Washington, who put fresh orders out to its field offices across the United States, that investigating the source, provenance, and likely identities of the current crop of young hackers was to take priority in their work. As it turned out, one of the respondents with the richest info was a near-neighbor in Los Angeles.

Charles Neal was head of the FBI's Los Angeles field office, a tall white block just off a tree-lined stretch of Wilshire Boulevard in Westwood. Neal was a seasoned cyber investigator, well known inside and beyond the bureau for his role in catching the California teenage serial hacker Kevin Mitnick. A great number of the FBI's cybercrime investigatory techniques had been developed and introduced by Neal himself. He invited Swallow to his office, and together the two set about shaking out what they knew of "Kid X."

Neal asked Swallow about Kid X and then revealed what he'd been able to ascertain from his own investigations. Together, they were able to establish that they had not one, as they had assumed, but two different people acting as sources.

Their teenage mark was full of surprises. On closer examination, it turned out that their posts weren't originating from Serbia at all, but coming from inside the United States. Neal and Swallow were startled. Kid X was an American, with no previous record, a diaspora member, working closely with their young hacker colleagues in Belgrade, as well as the new arrivals from Russia and China, and others around the world.

This signaled a shift whose significance echoes down to us today, through its mark on Russian disinformation campaigns and election tampering, but went unremarked at the time. It meant that the campaigns by the Belgrade University hacker group and the

Serbian Internet Army had borne fruit and that while the United States and its allies were focused on cyberattacks originating overseas, the information warfare being waged could successfully flip US citizens to become domestic vectors of such attacks.

While the news was disquieting, it wasn't entirely surprising. On April 30, a US-centered hacker group calling itself Team Spl0it had joined in the mayhem, attacking the US government's domestic travel website recreation.gov and replacing it with the message "Kosovo (Stop the war)." The attackers, going by cellb10ck, jay, f0bic, and nostalg1c, opined that "NATO screwed up" and that Milošević didn't "give a damn about his people. He couldn't care less if they're dead or alive. . . . No more innocent people have to be sacrificed for a cause that is ineffective." They followed this up by coming to Swallow and Neal's own backyard, where they hacked the City of Los Angeles website and left the same notes.

That only served to drive home the point to Swallow that if they were connected in any way, then Kid X's US location could also be a gift from a jurisdictional point of view.

So how might Kid X cope with a little home visit from the FBI? What might we learn from Kid X's own contacts at that point? It was a question Neal and Swallow couldn't help but savor together. Even better was that the two officers quickly managed to identify a second potential source of information on the pro-Serbia hackers.

This one had seemed from online activity to be older. This source turned out through further comms to be not a kid at all, but a Serbian army officer. Moreover, he was already a decorated war veteran, and fairly senior, and he was currently working for Serbian military and intelligence services on its anti-NATO infowar. He was stationed not in Belgrade but in Kosovo itself, in the department working directly with their intelligence agencies on fomenting and promoting a multifront cyber war against NATO, taking

in technological attacks such as pings and malware as well as information warfare.

The two investigators were excited. If the army source was wit-
tingly or otherwise able to share information of value about other
hackers and government involvement, they had a route past the
script kiddies and yahoos and toward the highly skilled: the experts,
and perhaps handlers and instigators, of the anti-NATO hacks. A lot
of the murk could get easier. And given the sheer talent out there
right now focused on learning everything about the United States'
most up-to-date military systems and exploiting their vulnerabilities, this was one hell of a talent pool for the US military itself to
start recruiting.

As soon as they began cultivating the two sources, they realized they would need help to map their connections and try to penetrate the networks that they revealed. Back in 1999—at least inside
the FBI—help was hard to come by. There was one FBI agent who
had good form turning the hunters into the hunted, though. Special Agent Jill Knesek was a quick-witted star of the agency. A charismatic Texas A&M University alumna who'd impressed just about
everyone she'd worked with, bringing sharp people skills to a role
that had often attracted strictly heads-down types, Knesek's reputation was white-hot from her success in analyzing data to track
serial hacker Kevin Mitnick down through the wire and to nail him
convincingly before a non-internet-literate judge. Before that, she'd
been the programmer responsible for maintaining fifteen different
navigation and tracker satellites simultaneously for the US naval
Satellite Operations Center in the rugged, picturesque headland of
Point Mugu, off Highway 1 just north of Malibu. Before joining the
military, her lifelong fascination with law enforcement and coding
chops had seen her overseeing the online networks of the US Bank-
ruptcy Court in LA.

She also understood this world. She had a knack for deciphering (and writing) hacker scripts. Neal and Swallow knew that while they were cultivating the informants, nobody would be better than Knesek at seeing the patterns behind the data. Equally, while Swallow and Neal attempted to cultivate their hacker contacts, Knesek with her scripting skills would also be able to turn Neal and Swallow into convincing hackers themselves—the ultimate disguise in their bid to penetrate the pro-Serbia networks.

This was one part of going undercover with the Belgrade hacker underground that caused tension inside the FBI's higher-ups. In order to win the trust of the hackers, the team would not only have to talk a good game, nor was cyber forensics going to help them if they couldn't match actions with people. To do that, they would need to win the trust of some of the figures on the Serbian hacker underground, which meant they would likely have to join attacks against NATO or even Western civilian targets themselves.

But if FBI personnel were going to go around committing acts of cyber sabotage against US hacker targets just to go undercover and build trust with the real Belgrade hackers, they weren't going to do it without someone higher up signing off on it. And this is where a spanner threatened to insert itself into the works.

They say generals are always fighting the last war, and this cyber war proved no exception. As Eligible Receiver '97 had shown, their models were based on known unknowns. Many of NATO's top brass were still seemingly convinced that there was a command structure they could knock out or negotiate with. This made it easier for them to understand, perhaps. If commands were coming from someone high up—say, Russia—then it was a proxy war, just like Vietnam, Afghanistan, Korea, or any of the more obscure theaters of the Cold War in which small states became battlegrounds for shadow clashes between US and Soviet sponsors, from Nicaragua to Angola.

This was a loose, distributed network of actors, whose aggregate intentions were made manifest. Had NATO watched a little more carefully, it is possible they would have been more prepared for the new age in warfare in which this would be the antagonists' defining characteristic.

The obsession with command structures and seeing the world in their own military image would come back again to haunt them in dealing with al-Qaeda in a little more than two years' time.

Chapter 10

A Clash of Cyber Cultures

Swallow, Neal, and Knesek were champing at the bit to move more seriously among the pro-Serbia cyber-war underground and laying the groundwork to open up their two leading sources. In the meantime, without their knowing it, NATO's other options for stemming the cyberattacks were dwindling, and the FBI's LA office would soon be the last option standing.

By the end of the first week in May, NATO secretary-general George Robertson was among those running out of patience with the continuing attacks. After Robertson ordered his teams in Brussels to find a way to stop the hackers, he and President Clinton were allegedly presented with a plan that showed their tech directors' desperation. The proposal was to disconnect Serbia and Montenegro from the global internet completely—isolating them, and stopping the cyberattacks at a stroke.

Their methods read like something from a Bond movie, but it was almost breathtakingly simple. The proposal was simply to switch off the signal from a Loral Orion 1 satellite orbiting earth since 1995, owned and operated by Loral Space & Communications of Rockville, Maryland. Despite being the largest satellite internet provider for the entire Balkan region as well as much of northern Europe and the United States, the Delaware-registered internet provider has long been regarded as opaque in its dealings with governments.

On May 12, global news organizations and internet users began receiving this announcement from a Belgrade internet company called BeoNET:

US shuts down Yugoslav Internet—For immediate release
BELGRADE, MAY 12—We have reliable information that the US Government ordered shut down of satellite feeds for Internet customers in Yugoslavia, as a result of NATO air war against this country.... This is a flagrant violation of commercial contracts with Yugoslav ISPs, as well as an attack on freedom of the Internet. A Web site in protest of these actions should be up shortly. We will supply you with the URL. In the meantime, please be so kind to inform as many people as possible about this tragic event for the Internet community in Yugoslavia and Europe.

Two days after the BeoNET release, State Department spokesman James Rubin denied the story. "There is no truth to the allegation," he said, explaining, "Information and access to information are exempt" from embargoes or sanctions. But in fact, the idea of cutting the rump Yugoslavia of Serbia and Montenegro off from the global internet had been under heated discussion behind closed doors at NATO and inside the Pentagon for a number of weeks.

Clinton and Robertson themselves remained unconvinced. Both felt that it would represent a huge step and that it had the potential for consequences that were unpredictable, hard to hedge against, and potentially included irreparable long-term damage to the internet itself—the very engine of America's economic resurgence. Both expressed misgivings to senior officers and aides, fearing that America shutting off certain countries might prompt its strategic opponents—Russia and China, as well as Serbia—to develop their own internets.

These were still comparatively early days for the global

internet, and it was a reasonable assumption that America's exposure to attacks—way beyond that of any other country on earth—was merely a consequence of the fact that it was subject to more vectors and home to more targets because of its global dominance. Its investment and hoped-for global first-mover advantages over the global economy and geopolitical picture would be lost if it became a US-only tool.

Ultimately, that the plan never moved beyond the drawing board was a simple matter of timing. Cutting the former Yugoslavia off would do no good. Increasingly, the attacks were originating, or being joined from, beyond the Balkans—by government-sanctioned hackers in Russia and China and signal boosters among diaspora and antigovernment groups in the United States, Canada, Australia, and Western Europe.

In May 1999, while Swallow, Neal, and Knesek's plan made its way up the pipe, the Pentagon's own general counsel office sent the NATO secretary-general a report. The report was slim—it distilled the Pentagon's knowledge down to just a fifty-page briefing—but what it contained would define our world decades later. Its title sounded modest enough. Called *An Assessment of International Legal Issues in Information Operations*, it was an attempt by lawyers to map the fast-developing mass-participation cyber war to traditional frameworks for military engagement. They had mapped cyberspace to the realm of the physical, the better to determine whether cyberattacks on nonmilitary targets by the United States were—or were likely to become in the future—war crimes, in the same way that attacking them with bombs would be.

Overnight, this document became the US government's only guide in its attempt to negotiate a new nonmilitary form of cyber war.

It summarized the US military legal team's inquiry into, and verdict on, "offensive hacking." The team freely admitted that this was a tricky one to submit any guidance on, as this was new territory. Their guidance gave President Clinton, Lord Robertson, and General Wesley Clark pause, however. It found that although information-warfare ops may not legally be considered "weapons," traditional laws of war would apply to an attack, whether it was a military cyberattack or a physical one using missiles. This meant that any viruses, malware, ping attacks, or logic bombs the United States might use against nonmilitary targets in Serbia—say, the university faculties where students haunted the computer rooms through the night, hacking into US systems—could constitute nothing less than a war crime.

"Stock exchanges, banking systems, universities, and similar civilian infrastructures may not be attacked simply because a belligerent has the ability to do so," it concluded.

This was the stuff of metaphysics. Could cyberspace be mapped to real space, its properties count as if they were physical? And in any case, where did the damage to "cyber" stop and "physical" begin? Hardware? Real-world outcomes resulting from lost or amended data? It was the classic time traveler's dilemma from science fiction played out in the dual spaces of the present.

The Pentagon's legal team shrank from the brink. They applied the principle of military necessity equally across both realms. That meant that to hit any target whatsoever that was nonmilitary—civilian computers, university servers, anything—by hacking was opening the United States up to proceedings at the International Criminal Court in The Hague, the very place they were planning to have Slobodan Milošević and his paramilitary butchers tried. The exception might be that "the attacking force can demonstrate that a definite military advantage is expected from the attack"—such as in the case that the systems they were hacking were proven beyond any reasonable doubt to have been directing physical military attacks against NATO, locating USAF stealth planes for the surface-to-air batteries, for instance.

The report made frustrating reading for Robertson and Clinton.

The president was said to have felt somewhat flummoxed by the Pentagon general counsel's findings—especially since US forces had already approved electronic attacks on nonmilitary targets in Haiti during Operation Uphold Democracy back in 1994—an operation on which he himself had signed off.

The difficulty lay in the fact that, until now, nobody had needed to define exactly what cyber war *was*, exactly. If the field was pregnant with possibility, it was also loaded with risk.

Up to now, cyber war had been something that did not involve civilian infrastructure, for the very good reason that civilian infrastructure was not connected to the internet. Only military targets had been worth attacking—as Moonlight Maze and so on had shown.

The Pentagon's lawyers agreed. Their primary responsibility was the elimination of risk to the US military. If this were a new theater of war, then attacks on civilian infrastructure targets had to be out of bounds. Did it make any difference whether the next civilian airliner to be brought down as an act of aggression was destroyed by missiles, a bomb onboard, or somebody hacking into its autopilot and steering it into the ground? As a result, the United States and its NATO partners remained focused to a large extent on defending against what it assumed would be military-grade intrusions and on the possibilities for attacking and degrading the enemy's operational communications and weaponry. The idea that they would be fighting a dual-coded threat—in which civilian computers, university faculties, media, and even children themselves were the belligerents—was so beyond the bounds of what they considered possible as to be unthinkable.

America's ability to plan ahead was being undone by the very speed of its own success in innovation. Any report into cyber threat commissioned in early 1995, working on the basis of information available for 1994 and due for publication at the end of the year for implementation in 1996, would be obsolete before it was approved for press simply because of the global proliferation of the internet and the speed at which users, businesses, developers, and hackers were innovating for it. New browsers, new users, new domain registrations, new sites, new code, new apps, new programs, new viruses, new everything, spreading outward like wildfire. The dotcom boom was leading, and for once, US military intelligence was simply doing its best to ride the wave. It was a role to which it was ill-suited. More junior phreaks in the ranks might have helped. Then again, in 1999 they were up against a whole nation of them.

Indeed, in the current age of deepfakes and nation-state disinformation campaigns, the Pentagon lawyers' 1999 report is a fascinating window onto a more innocent age. It also preemptively quashed any hatchling plans for even a cyber-disinformation offensive. "It might be possible to use computer morphing techniques to create an image of the enemy's chief of state informing his troops that an armistice or ceasefire agreement had been signed," it warned. "If false, this also would be a war crime."

While hindsight is always 20/20, one cannot shake the nagging suspicion that these lawyers, like their generals, were less than familiar with the internet beyond its strict, top-down military purview.

The Pentagon dossier led to a period of frantic reassessment and brainstorming at NATO HQ.

Plans for a cyber-war offensive on more traditional lines had already been drawn up and presented to the president back in March, as the prospect of NATO bombardment had shifted from strong to inevitable. Strategists for air command at US European headquarters had connected with the US Joint Command and Control Warfare Center (JC2WC, pronounced "Jakewick") in San Antonio, Texas, and developed a plan to insert chaos, in the shape of fake commands, misleading messages, and false target profiles, into the systems of Serbia's centralized air-defense command networks. That plan for defensive cyber sabotage—to coincide with the very start of NATO bombing operations on March 24—had gone into the long grass, caught up in the approval process and the jumpiness of Clinton and Blair. The bombing campaign would last only a day or two before Milošević capitulated, they reasoned; why complicate it with an experimental dimension that reeked of the dangerous potential to become something they could not foresee?

The bombardment itself was irresistible. NATO had named it Operation Allied Force, while the United States, in typically florid Christian-hair-metal mode, had gone with Noble Anvil. But now while NATO was dominating the air, it was on the back foot, under sustained and somewhat humiliating attack, caught up in a new form of cyber war for which it had not planned, and in which the belligerents were civilians armed only with an internet connection, a background in sci-fi, and an infinite supply of gall.

At the start of June, the "white-hat" hacktivist group Serbian Angels, in a move they orchestrated with Russian and Chinese hacker groups, claimed that they had used a Trojan macrovirus to obtain and distribute a list containing the names and identities of dozens of members of the British intelligence agency MI6. Having done so, they sent the purported dump to more than a million addresses, starting a cat-and-mouse game in which MI6 tried to scrub the files from the internet, while refusing to acknowledge that there was any such list or, if there was, that it was genuine. Against this background, the persistent idea of saturating Russian, Chinese, and Serbian connections with a sudden flood of spam outbound from the United States and its NATO allies bubbled up yet again.

Yet the FBI's remit is primarily defensive. And while General Clark and the military continued to mull cyber scorched-earth tactics, the agencies were frantically trying to assess and limit the true damage from such operations. Swallow, Knesek, and Neal's plan got snagged up for interminable days while commanders wrestled with the almost *Catch-22* question of whether committing offensive acts could be justified as defensive if they were only offensive against one's own side's collateral.

The CIA had no such limitations. In May, it presented President Clinton with a top-secret "findings" report on ways to topple Milošević during the bombardment, even in the event that the military stayed loyal. One plan contained in the proposal involved "hitting the Milošević cadre where it hurt"—in their bank accounts. In the plan, CIA computer hackers would disrupt all private financial transactions involving Milošević and his close circle, sowing chaos at his point of leverage with his courtiers, political allies, and the mafia and paramilitary figures who freelanced for him.

It also contained a proposal that would come back to haunt it. The CIA would, through its own network of hackers, stage a series of global bank heists.

These heists would "electronically drain" the Milošević clan's overseas bank accounts of hard currency where it could find them. It believed it had identified networks of bank accounts associated with him; his wife, Mira Markovic; and his son, Marko, in a number of countries, including Switzerland, Cyprus, Greece, Lebanon, Israel, Russia, and China. Lichtenstein and Luxembourg were also suspected locations of pseudonymous Milošević-linked funds. And without its ability to confer patronage, fund hits, and reward loyalty, Milošević's mafia state would be paralyzed. Stripped of his nest eggs in "safe" third countries, Milošević might also reconsider his options.

This plan had a double upside. Using the funds from the heists of all those accounts in private banks across Switzerland and the rest of the world, the CIA itself could begin to direct funds through its own secret bank accounts to opposition groups inside Yugoslavia, as well as ordering its own hits, and recruiting potential defectors and bright stars within Milošević's regime and the Yugoslav military. They could also begin head-hunting some of the Belgrade hackers who were making their lives a misery.

This was a plan the third-way Clinton could get behind. It was almost the perfect metaphor for public-private partnership—a win-win situation in which there was a military operation that could be carried out at zero net cost.

On June 27, he ordered "government hackers" to seek out online, and block by any means necessary, funds related to Milošević or his coterie. As to whether the funds Milošević had looted from his own country would ever be repatriated, that could wait. There were leads everywhere, but such was the scale of Milošević's looting that nobody, least of all the CIA, knew how much there was, or where. Right now, and for the foreseeable future, they would be looking for buried treasure on a virtual pirate island that stretched right around the globe.

The funds were seemingly endless. A labyrinthine system for spiriting looted state cash out of the former Yugoslavia and secreting it away in accounts around the world had hubs in Cyprus, Malta, Russia, and elsewhere in the Balkans. Cyprus in particular seemed to be the international laundering and arms-smuggling hot spot. Through the 1990s, spooks, dictators, Russian oligarchs, and Yugoslav mafia men all bought large property portfolios and set up businesses and bank accounts and identities there.

The CIA identified one woman as the entire system's mastermind. Even at seventy-three, Borka Vučić was a formidable lady. A steely-haired martinet, Mrs. Vučić was fond of smart business suits offset with strings of pearl jewelry. She was also a staunch regime ally, Milošević family friend, and the Serbian president's personal banker—a position she occupied at the same time as being head of the state-owned Beogradska Banka, the country's dominant financial institution. British diplomats had dubbed her "Rosa Kleb," after the KGB villainess of Ian Fleming's Bond novel *From Russia with Love*, known for her dour ruthlessness and poison-tipped assassination shoes. Traveling everywhere flanked by two armed bodyguards, Mrs. Vučić had spent nine years heading up the giant bank's offshore subsidiary in Cyprus before returning to Belgrade to head the entire bank.

The conflicts of interest in her dual role as head of the dominant state-owned bank and Milošević's personal financier didn't seem to bother Mrs. Vučić. Indeed, it was rather the point of her elevation, as she set up and oversaw a well-organized pipeline of preferential loans to Milošević crony companies, friends, and allies. On one occasion, Beobanka, the state-owned offshoot brand of Mrs. Vučić's Beogradska Banka, was ordered to sign off on a series of "loans" to the TV and media company owned by Milošević's daughter, Marija, and to Marko's umbrella companies. These loans enabled Marko and others connected to the regime to fund bonanzas on computers and network connections throughout the country's businesses, colleges, and civic buildings, as well as the purchase of the private internet and tech business Cybernet and a utopian Serbia-themed family amusement park called Bambiland.

The Milošević regime set the young hackers at the university a discreet additional remit: helping them keep the funds dark from the CIA. At this, the hacker group received the additional directive that they should find ways to counter "hacker aggressors who were seeking the secret foreign bank accounts of Slobodan Milošević and his family."

The CIA plan was given the green light, even as US officials continued to deny its existence. General Clark told the press that the United States could have targeted regime figures, but refrained. NATO spokesperson Jamie Shea at one point declared that America, the United Kingdom, and its allies would not be deploying electronic means or hacking, as "we want to show that we are civilized." His denials raised amused eyebrows among cyber-war specialists at RAND in Washington, DC, and other American quasi-military institutions. "One should assume that financial targets were targeted," noted US naval cyber-war researcher John Arquilla in the aftermath. RAND's Martin Libicki deadpanned that this wave of

NATO pearl-clutching about being too "civilized" to target online civilian infrastructure with cyberattacks was "a little strange," given that the United States was at that point quite merrily blowing up a lot of very real physical civilian infrastructure targets, from bridges to companies, using extremely real-world missiles.

The Belgrade University hacker group quickly found themselves defending key servers against attacks coming from Germany, the Netherlands, Croatia, Bosnia and Herzegovina, the United Kingdom, the United States, Poland, and Iceland. These new NATO-backed hackers used email and logs in vast, unsynchronized waves of attack several times a day, of varying intensity and length. Some lasted just three days. One lasted almost eighty. Yugoslav sites began to vanish from the web, banking connections failing for hours at a time.

The Pentagon had indeed hacked into Serbian systems—and the denials were part of the plan to stay dark on its intentions and capabilities. The Pentagon legal report itself had raised the risk that for the United States to deploy cyber-war strategies and techniques against Serbia could trigger a global movement in the vein of anti-nuclear protests and treaties, aimed at limiting any future use of cyber weapons. "If [the techniques] are seen as a revolutionary threat to the security of nations and the welfare of their citizens, it will be much more likely that efforts will be made to restrict or prohibit information operations by legal means," the Pentagon's legal team warned.

It was a watershed moment in the development of cyber war.

Further, an attempt to hit America and its Western European allies with cyber war could be a cheap and disproportionately effective way to sow chaos. "We and our allies are the greatest targets for info-warfare," said Arquilla at the time. "Do we really want to begin this?"

It was already too late.

The last year of the twentieth century had ushered in the

twenty-first century's paradigmatic form of warfare. It was precisely the form of mass-participation, no-holds-barred cyber-enabled conflict the Yugoslav government had pioneered during the Cold War. Total War for an era of total internet penetration.

All eyes in Beijing and Moscow were on Brussels through May 1999. NATO's servers had been under sustained assault since the downing of the plane, with wave after wave of ping-of-death attacks taking down comms. In the panic, even the organization's slick PR front faltered. "We have about 100 servers, and we're afraid all the NATO sites have been attacked," NATO's webmaster Paul Magis told CNN in a rare and almost certainly unsanctioned moment of transparency. Publicly, NATO was still insisting that no serious breaches had occurred. In fact, they had little idea. NATO backroom engineers and an army of contractors brought in at high day rates worked round the clock alongside US and British military cyber commands to stem the tide of crashes and get back to operational strength. If it wasn't chaos, it closely resembled it.

The only lever they had left to pull was upgrading their systems. NATO went on a midconflict hardware spree, canning its Sun Microsystems SPARCstation 20 microprocessors, replacing them with more powerful UltraSPARCs, in the hope that the upgraded system would be able to process all the pings originating from Serbia without crashing and burning. They then upgraded from 256k connections—NATO having been operating with connections with which buffering even a short low-res video clip would take some fifteen minutes of paralysis—to shiny new T1 access lines able to process a whopping 1.544 Mbps of traffic.

Brief respite, and some clarity, came on June 1, 1999, thanks to one particularly heavy missile strike on Belgrade that saw much of the city plunged into darkness by a major power outage. Domestic internet providers were knocked out. While the Belgrade University group had alternative ways online, the attacks coming from Serbia itself lulled. This temporary and almost complete respite from attacks originating inside Serbia and Kosovo helped NATO establish for the first time something as sobering as it was crucial. The United States finally understood that if the vast majority of pings attacking NATO's servers in the United States and Europe were now originating from *outside* the Balkans, further global proliferation of anti-US acts online was a real and present danger.

For once, Russian and Chinese attackers—let alone those in the Western diasporas—could not route their attacks through Serbia. The illusion fell away, and the sheer volume of Russian and Chinese involvement became clear.

The methods of attack were also evolving. While NATO was scrambling to soak up the volume of pings involved in DDoS attacks, the Russian, Chinese, and Serbian hackers changed tack. NATO's servers now ran at higher capacity to keep ahead of ping-of-death attacks, but the floods of email it was now successfully receiving and processing were infected with fast-mutating viruses.

The organization's spokespeople continued to insist that nothing had been compromised. The simple truth was that by this time, they no longer had any idea whether that was true.

The attacks were too many, were too broadly distributed, and simply weren't coming in the form they had expected, and even when they plugged the gaps and upgraded, it mutated too fast. None of it seemed conducted at all, let alone by an opposing military command. The idea of cyber war had simply mutated, and was continuing to mutate into new strains, quicker than anyone had prepared for.

In the words of DARPA's Chris White, the man charged with bringing US military intelligence into a new digitally savvy age after 9/11: "It was *so chaotic*! I mean, it would have been *funny* that it was so chaotic, if it hadn't been so effective."

It wasn't that America and its allies had failed to prepare for cyber war at all; it was simply that they could not have anticipated the way in which conflict would speed up the process of innovation.

If there was an oversight, it was in their failure to recognize that their antagonists would turn out to be the one country on earth whose culture of fast, cheap DIY innovation had made its youthful population masters in two sectors: high tech and headfucking.

■ ■ ■ ■ ■

The increasingly global origins of the DDoS attacks made Bill Swallow's mind up for him.

Back in LA, he told case manager Neal he felt it was useless to wait any longer. Now that they had sussed that the hackers in the Balkans were connected to a worldwide network, and that some of those connections joining the attacks were in the United States itself, he wanted to move in before things got really out of hand.

As soon as Knesek's formal assignment to the job of tracking down the hackers in the United States was signed off, Swallow invited her on a work trip they would both have cause to remember. Together, they were going to pay an unannounced visit to the Serbian American hacker connection's home address.

What happened on that visit in May 1999 is—like the identity and location of the juvenile NATO hacker—still classified more than twenty years later. What we do know is that the FBI special agent and a member of the Pentagon's cyber-war team turned up at his doorstep that day. And by the time the agents' rental car left for the airport, the anonymous source had flipped. Shocked and frightened by the visit, he agreed to cooperate and immediately began supplying Neal, Swallow, and Knesek's team with information on hackers taking part in the attacks. The case was classified not only to protect the kid, but also to ensure that the information he divulged could sustain undercover investigations for a long time to come.

We also know that in the days that followed, hacker after hacker across the United States, Canada, and Western Europe started getting arrested and turned. On May 12, seventeen-year-old

Eric Burns from Shoreline, Washington, was indicted for hacking the White House site four days earlier. At his trial, federal prosecutors revealed they had Burns boasting of the White House attack online "even before it happened." Burns made a specific point of telling media he would never identify the other hackers behind his action to the Secret Service, though reportedly he was hopeful of leniency in sentencing. Then, on the evening of Friday, June 11, the security blog *Attrition* broke the news that another Western member of Team Spl0it had been arrested earlier that week. The hacker f0bic, reportedly in his late teens, was exposed to "a wide range of charges, and may bear the brunt of all Team Spl0it" work. Next, his Team Spl0it comrade nostalg1c, sixteen years old and a resident of Belgium, promptly retired from action. It's not known if that was a consequence of pressure from Swallow's team. But the information they gained from each arrest was leveraged to gain deeper, wider access to the hacker underground.

The pair now handled a growing list of erstwhile cyber warriors and thorns in NATO's side. If the rash of nondiaspora kids willing to join the hackers was disturbing, there were tonics too. To their delight, they found that the reputation of the first Serbian American kid they had visited was sky-high among the hacker teens in Belgrade. By checking in with him and syncing appearances and going through rehearsed chat routines, they could use him to get to others inside Serbia.

Swallow in particular was curious about the infowar operative inside the Serbian forces in Kosovo and used Kid X to establish contact with him too. Within days, he was a regular source of information coming straight from the front lines to the FBI in Los Angeles, and thence to the Pentagon. Establishing the veracity of this hacker's information was tougher, though. After all, they couldn't just show up at his door in American suburbia if he sold them a dummy like they could with Kid X.

Instead, they had to use a complex system of data cross-checks on his posts. If he talked about a bomb, they would check the time on the post and cross-check it against the most accurate records of NATO bombing runs they had. It wasn't an easy task, particularly on the more intense nights of NATO air action. But liaising closely with the Pentagon, Swallow and Knesek were able to delay official reports of bombings for just long enough for their source to post that he'd heard a blast close by, when nothing had gone out over the airwaves. Having verified that their second hacker was who, and where, he purported to be, they pumped him for valuable counterintelligence, not just on the other hackers, but on Serbia's entire information-war strategy. This hacker's identity is also sealed in classified files, as is all the information to which his acquisition and cultivation led the FBI.

Swallow's superiors were encouraged. They could sense that they were working toward the point where they would be able to crack people behind the attacks, at higher and higher levels. They pushed further and further, spending more time with the hackers they had flipped.

But if the research was full of small surprises, the picture that began to emerge from it was the kind of thing that sent you back checking your data. It was like nothing NATO had prepared for.

First, the hackers they were identifying were a baffling mixture. Cyberattacks were as likely to be planned and executed by American kids like Kid X, or otherwise neutral computer owners around the world, as by any member of the Serbian military. In fact, most cyberattacks on US military and government targets were now originating in countries not even involved in the conflict.

On March 31, a visibly discomfited Jamie Shea held a NATO press briefing at which he apologized for the information website's absence. "I know that you as journalists rely a lot on our website for information, and some of you may be wondering why since March 28 the service with our website is volatile," he said. But while he went on to put responsibility at the feet of "hackers from Serbia"—doubtless conscious of the poor optics of any form of anti-NATO alliance coalescing in the former Communist bloc to the East—he and the NATO technical team had seen the flood come from inside Russia. But discounting the absurd—that they were being mounted by spies, sleeper agents, or fifth columnists working for Milošević in all these countries—that raised an urgent question of motive.

It was this central question that would continue to emerge, in different forms, to define the coming twenty years, and the heart of the turmoil we see around us today. Who and what is our enemy? How and why are we under attack? How can we fight back?

What Swallow's team at the FBI had built, though they did not realize it, was a crystal ball that revealed not only the methods by which wars would be fought and politics pursued for the coming century, but the blindness and confusion of Western governments and militaries in dealing with it.

For the first time, war itself took on a meta quality now so familiar to us. Its theaters—cyberspace and physical battlegrounds—were not necessarily congruent. Nor were its beginnings or endings. The immediate result of the bombardment was never in doubt. NATO had overwhelming force on its side, as well as most of the international community.

On June 10, 1999, just seventy-eight days after it had begun, Serbian and Montenegrin forces united under the banner of a rump Yugoslav army agreed to withdraw from their positions in Kosovo. Milošević accepted the Kumanovo Agreement and the adoption of UN Security Council Resolution 1244. A massive force of thirty-six thousand international peacekeepers arrived in Kosovo to accept the withdrawal of all Yugoslav military forces.

But if the short-term objectives had been achieved, there were warnings that a longer, more overt struggle over Eastern Europe's destiny had just begun.

There had been tense moments, even at the last, including a

standoff between Russian and NATO troops at Pristina Airport on June 11, 1999, as peace was declared.

The Kremlin had been outraged by what it saw as NATO's interference on its doorstep—a fellow Orthodox Slav country, too. Its objections to the presence of US and Western European armed forces had been ignored. Now, on hearing of the peace and learning that NATO planned a joint force of peacekeepers, it looked to secure its influence once more.

Russia had hurriedly redeployed a column of some thirty Russian armored vehicles, carrying around 250 Russian soldiers, from its role in the international peacekeeping force in Bosnia, and sent it rolling into Serbia en route to Pristina Airport in Kosovo. Footage from CNN taken at 10:30 that morning showed the Russian armored column, with the letters "KFOR" hastily daubed on their vehicles, covering up their assigned "SFOR" logo. This attempt to occupy the airport ahead of NATO troops' arrival led to a tense race and a standoff between NATO and Russian troops at the airport itself. Russia put several battalions of paratroopers and Ilyushin-76 troop transport planes on standby, and General Wesley Clark ordered the airport runway blocked. For the first time since the collapse of the USSR, the specter of nuclear confrontation was back. When Clark ordered escalatory measures, British general Sir Mike Jackson refused, telling Clark, "I'm not going to start the Third World War for you," and instead had his troops (including singer James Blunt, then a British army captain, who has also said he "would have faced court-martial" rather than follow what he regarded as General Clark's foolhardy orders) isolate the airport in the knowledge that NATO already controlled the air corridors, so the Il-76s would not get through. After pressure from NATO, neighboring states Hungary, Romania, and Bulgaria also refused Russian air passage, and the Russians were left with no choice but to stand down.

The Cold War's last vestiges seemed to have been cleared away, with the Western alliance's almost casualty-free stroll to victory and Russia's acknowledgment of the new realities.

In just seventy-eight days, some five hundred civilians had died in Serbia and Montenegro, including journalists and staff in the Chinese embassy. In that same time, it is estimated that millions of cyberattacks had been mounted, targeting NATO member countries and the organization itself. The true number is unlikely ever to be known, such was the nature of the incursions on military, government, civilian, corporate, and international targets, from the United States to Western Europe.

The world had seen bombardments before, but it had seen nothing like this. In many of the ways that mattered most, it still didn't see it. The work of withstanding attacks on NATO's central structures had fallen to a tiny team of admins alone, to a tech-support team and a procurement list. The work of tracking and mapping them, to just 150 FBI agents in offices across the United States. The work of mopping up the damage, of chasing down any lingering breaches and serious cyber threats, would fall to individual countries' security agencies, like the Londoner and the Yorkshireman who showed up at my office.

There remained a nagging prospect that NATO's reassurances about the lack of serious breaches of its internal systems were as hollow as its assurances about not targeting civilian targets and finances itself.

But we were simply not trained to see what was unfolding out there. That Russia, China, and the criminal networks that facilitated rogue states had found their angle for the coming years.

The Serbian hacker laboratories' war was over. But between them, their pioneering work and the US response had created the conditions for a far bigger global war without end.

And this one was just getting started.

Part III

Metastasis

(How Total War spread from the East and took over the world)

Chapter 11

The Big Bang

As the new millennium dawned with the first rays of the rising sun over the tiny Pacific island of Tonga, the shadow of the last night of the 1990s fled across the seas and continents, and into history.

The darkness of the last long year had borne a new model of conflict: distributed, networked war for an internet age. Yet in the most positive reading by diplomats and soldiers, so much seemed to have been settled. Kosovo had seen not just the last defeat of the West's erstwhile archenemy Russia, but the last of the Balkan wars now surely fought. Moreover, peace had come through a US-led NATO intervention almost universally acknowledged in the West at least as just and well managed. Either you were on the same train as all the strategists, investors, and generals, or you were a Cassandra. By every metric that could be counted, America won. It didn't matter how many permutations or possible worlds you worked through on the available data. On the data, from here on in—commercially, militarily, technologically—America would always win. There simply was no other conclusion.

All that premillennium tension, the Wall Street jitters about the potential effects of the Y2K bug, the threat of civil unrest, madness, disaster had passed without so much as a sigh. The stock market surfed higher and higher, buoyed aloft by the weightless, magic foam of the American internet. Here it was, dissolving the world's borders, opening up economies, collapsing the time between thought and action, putting the powerful a mere tap away from the common person in the street. It was the democratizing, Blakean prophecy to the world that was America itself, made electric and manifest and irresistible.

Even the uncanny clamor of an overheating dot-com bubble now just weeks away from bursting could not shake the feeling that the world was cruising into the new century like a Corvette into the endless orange glow.

Russia and China too stood on the threshold of their own visions for the way forward. The internet explosion that had swept the West was coming, and with it would come challenges for ruling parties and authorities used to regulating information tightly. Both had already begun formulating their own approach to cyber war, inspired by the strange field maneuvers of 1999, and the way they had seemed to catch the West off balance with almost no effort or expenditure.

In Russia, gray eminence Vladimir Putin had been anointed successor to the ailing, increasingly drunken, and chaotic Boris Yeltsin. From Moscow, this brave new world in which America saw its business to intervene everywhere looked very much like a unipolar world governed by America alone. This was the year Putin would set out his own plans to use the internet's dominance against America. Yet such was America's self-regard at the height of the dot-com wave that it could see in the expansion of the global internet nothing but a reflection of itself.

In 2000 America looked at China, Russia, and Iran and saw only more America about to be born. They would become free-market economies. They would become mature democracies. They would be what the internet—like McDonald's, like American intervention—made things. The twenty-first century would see global peace through more Pets.com. The internet would bring global harmony.

In March 2000, President Clinton welcomed China's accession to the World Trade Organization. It was, he said in his address, a sign of its openness to the "development of a free society." This was the standard Western reading: the Chinese Communist Party had realized it needed to be more open, and without that openness, it could not hope to compete as a modern economy. In the same speech, the president speculated on how the growing influence of the internet itself could become one of the forces to open China. After all, he laughed ruefully, he knew only too well how trying to crack down on the internet was "like trying to nail Jell-O to the wall."

The Chinese diplomats in attendance were aware how tricky America had found trying to keep the internet in order.

In the six months since the Chinese embassy bombing, China's own internet user base of four million had jumped, doubling to eight million, urged on by the government's push for greater Chinese citizen engagement—not least on the issue of the bombing. But while it entered the new millennium with users concentrated in Hong Kong, Shanghai, and Beijing and President Clinton proposing it could become a force for openness, the Chinese Communist Party's leadership had seen over Kosovo that the internet was far too powerful a strategic weapon to waste on openness. "Eight million users out of 1.3 billion Chinese people is still insignificant," declared the Communist Party paper, *People's Daily*, in 2000. The aim was no fewer than one billion.

While Russia and other Eastern European countries had entered the 2000s with a surfeit of highly educated youths and no money, China was in the business of making lots and lots of money, quickly becoming the world's producer for export. Yet the Communist Party's control of politics, licenses, and patronage at local, regional, and national levels was still intact. The *hongke* had proved that the internet could be a force with which to advance Chinese interests in the realm of warfare and foreign policy.

Even as Clinton spoke of openness through connectivity, the Chinese government was pressuring US companies to collaborate with them in identifying and persecuting users online. By 2004, it had successfully wrestled the name of an anonymous leaker in China from Yahoo! on the basis that the leaker, a Chinese journalist, had used a pseudonymous Yahoo! Mail address to leak documents to the US press about a Chinese government directive to internet users to shut down conversations about the anniversary of the Tiananmen Square massacre. It then worked with Microsoft to fire employees critical of the Chinese government. It is easy to accuse the Clinton administration of naïveté, but it was a naïveté perpetuated by successive Bush administrations through the decade; America's tech-solutionist blind spot to the ways in which Silicon Valley's code evangelism is turned against populations, from the Rohingya to Ukraine, and QAnon to Brexit, remains as strong in the age of Facebook, Elon Musk, and the AI-industrial complex.

Bill Swallow and his team continued to comb through what they could glean from their sources. But at every step, they found themselves working against institutional blindness in the US government and military, as well as its partners in NATO. A bunch of *civilians?* In different countries? Who didn't even know each other? That wasn't even an organization, let alone an army. And that meant it wasn't army business, or even covered by any of the organized-crime definitions that would have allowed US law enforcement a unified view and a clear run.

America wanted things it could see and understand. Pressure to find simple lines of command and attribution for the attacks was great. It came together with the US KFOR peacekeeping force's efforts to identify war criminals, and the International Criminal Court's search for lines of command that pinned specific atrocities on Milošević or his commanders in the field. To identify cause and effect, chain of command, and to make it stick. The MI5 officers who questioned me wanted to establish my contacts on the assumption that the people I had gotten to know were part of a group, and that they were organized, and acting on command.

When there was no grand, unified plan, no network of spies working to secret commands, it became necessary to invent one. There seemed to be no limit to the number of times the same "suspected Serb spy within NATO" story could float. Again and again from 2000, the organization leaked stories anonymously to friendly press contacts about the discovery or confirmed existence of a human spy inside NATO's Brussels HQ working for the Serbs. Each time, a new, anonymous briefing to a friendly journo came. "NATO chiefs" suspected a spy had been leaking secret documents via obscure digital means to the Serbs. A spy inside NATO had been arrested, marched out into waiting vans. Or they were just about to arrest someone. Or indeed, "bungling NATO scientists" had leaked their own secret documents. The stories took on their own lives. Intelligence services would leak briefings to friendly reporters. The reporters would speculate in articles on the basis of the briefings. The intelligence services monitored the press, and found its own concerns uncannily mirrored, then used the articles as leverage for funding, backing, and action. Plots had been uncovered and exposure was imminent. Traitors had been identified. Watch for arrests. It kept morphing, rearing its head every couple of months. Yet nothing ever materialized. The trail of crumbs reads now like a strange, internally orchestrated QAnon, almost two decades before QAnon itself.

But successful information management meant weak self-examination. While this story kept resurfacing, there was no need for the United States and its NATO allies to admit that they had been more comprehensively penetrated by hackers than anyone could possibly have imagined. Or that the new cyber front they had been desperate to avoid opening up in the global theater of war had in fact been opened up indeed.

We can speculate as to what a more urgent, honest reckoning with the US military and intelligence services' inability to see, predict, contain, or fight networked threats might have been in those brief months between Kosovo and 9/11. What difference would a serious attempt in 2000 to address the potential for domestic civilian engagement by online information warriors of hostile opponents have made? How effective might a policy of greater engagement with civilian vectors have been? Had they been forced into a genuine reckoning with the nature of the totality of the methods and vectors they had found themselves confused, paralyzed, and ultimately outmatched by, who knows how the wider spectrum of vigilance might have changed history?

We would have had a chance to be more prepared for Russia's rise in the wake of Kosovo as a vector of information warfare along the lines of that model. Almost certainly, the way in which we understood and fought loose, distributed diaspora-based networks has changed the way we monitored and ultimately sought to combat al-Qaeda and ISIL. But might we even have been better prepared for their rise—even their attacks on America in 2001—if we had seen that the Yugoslav model of harnessing discontents in a continuous, entrepreneurial, and asymmetric push for advantage was the way forward for the West's enemies outmatched on the battlefield?

The ridicule around my questioning in April 2000 might have provided anther wake-up. But again, given the chance, the United States and its allies shrank back, with cover stories and buried reports, and put their heads in the sand.

That darkness lost valuable time. In the wake of the cease-fire, it wasn't just China and Russia calculating how to best use this amazing asymmetrical method of war. It was the Belgrade hackers themselves.

Belgrade was an angry and exhausted shell, its daily life tense and simmering in the wake of the bombardment. The coming months would see it transformed into a paranoid, decadent setting for spy-meets-spy and the settling of scores. Through 2000, it became the West Berlin of John Le Carré—a strange no-man's-land where spies, governments, criminals, and opportunists from Moscow, Beijing, Washington, and San Francisco descended and traded over the balance of power in a world to come.

If in the West the hacks had been something for NATO to cover up, in the East they were regarded as that gleaming, bright future itself. That gave each of the hackers a stark choice about what they did next.

They had been lionized, celebrated, upskilled in live combat. Now they were plugged into global networks of hackers, intelligence, and influence. And the very last thing they were about to do was put down their keyboards and fade back into school life.

Neither the Belgrade University hacking group nor the Black Hand irregulars stopped work after hostilities had ceased. But the paths each took were to have far-reaching consequences that echo down through the years to us today in the different models adopted by China, Russia, and the West.

Around the millennium itself, at a low-key evening ceremony in Belgrade's military academy, the coders, information specialists, translators, online provocateurs, monitors, and social engineers were awarded medals and given cash in US dollars "in thanks for their service to the nation." Recipients were from Serbia itself, as well as China, Russia, Ukraine, and the Serbian diaspora in the West.

The army was under no illusions, nor was the fiery young information minister Aleksandr Vučić, a former propagandist himself who'd put his backing behind the university group. Like the rocketeers and fuel scientists of Nazi Germany's late sprint for a decisive weapon that could turn the tide of war, their work had been something wholly new. The systematizing of cyber war around interdisciplinary teams activating global networks felt like the future. But it had come too late to save the regime. Now the race was on to salvage value from them, and Vučić and the military were already pivoting to talking up their success, packaging it up for global clients.

Mirjana Drakulic had warned the spooks at the Belgrade University hacker center that without the common cause of protesting bombardment, this hothoused generation of hackers, social engineers, and viral content specialists "could become hackers for some other motivation." Now that's exactly what was happening. But it was happening at a higher level than even she had thought possible. Their knowledge was not dispersing so much as it was being sold as a template. Cyber war in a box.

"If there was another attack on Serbia of the kind of the NATO air strikes, hackers could considerably contribute to the country's defence," explained government cyber-war researcher Milan Kovačević in his pitch for the viability of a scaled-up version of what they had just trialed in the live arena. "NATO operates fully on the GPS. They scanned every inch of Serbia via a large number of satellites. NATO generals supervise military operations on the ground via satellites and cameras, just like in many strategic computer games. They would be rather lost if somebody brought down their navigation and disrupted communication."

But by this time, its backers in the Serbian intelligence community were claiming the credit for every autonomous action carried out across the country and the world against the United States and its allies. Even if the Belgrade hackers hadn't changed the course of the war, their story could win everybody a piece of the action. Trade delegations in 2000 from China and a state visit to Beijing that year by Milošević's foreign minister both featured two key points of discussion. One was the issue of territorial integrity—Serbia reassuring China that its claim to Kosovo could be understood in the same way as China's to Taiwan—and the agenda item of "Defense Cooperation," covering Kovačević's pitch for a full-fledged "electronic defense" function and how Serbia might help China to found such a thing, either through its know-how or via its experiences during the conflict.

The young too were now at the center of an undignified scramble by military groups, intelligence agencies, business leaders, organized-crime syndicates, and extremist political networks to harness their talents, by fair means or foul.

At the street level, the Black Hand was busy preserving its brand by getting rid of the independent hackers. Those who stood in the way of their access to whatever servers they wanted no longer simply had their computers hacked. They were now having their bodies smashed and broken.

Zoran Rosic, the young hacker who had gone from messing with the university servers to participating in the Kosovo hacking, didn't recognize the phone number, but he answered anyway. "Hey," said the Belgrade-accented male voice on the other end. "A mutual friend gave me your number. I hope you don't mind." The mutual friend was cool, so no problem. "Look," said the voice, "I'm having problems with a proxy server, and they said you were the person to call. Is there any chance you could come over and help me fix it?"

An hour later, around noon on the spring day in 2000, the young hacker stepped from the center door of his bus. The rows of shelters in front of the tattered, gray New Belgrade bus station were the rendezvous. The guy from the phone call was there too. He stepped forward, recognizing Rosic, a little older than him, but nothing to make the twenty-year-old suspicious. The stranger greeted the young hacker. "Hey, man, thanks for making the journey here. It's not far. Shall we go?"

They were halfway across the street when the stranger said, casually, "You will be very surprised to see who my boss is." Rosic half-turned his head to ask what the man meant, when he heard footsteps close behind him and felt the impact on the back of his skull, sending him pitching into concrete and darkness. Then everything went blank.

When he arrived home, Rosic couldn't remember anything. He didn't know his own name, could not recall the start of a sentence he was trying to utter, nor what had happened to him. In the hospital, it started to come back. He recalled that while his attackers had been kicking him in the head, they had repeatedly asked him for a password. "I remember thinking that I wanted to give them the password, but I couldn't remember it. I was crying, 'Stop! I can't think!'" In the lonely hours in intensive care, he began to remember more. The password they had wanted was for one of the university servers.

The young hacker spent the next few months recovering from his injuries in an intensive treatment unit and frantically attempting to patch together his own past through the brain trauma. Rosic was working through the war and the early 2000s as an admin at the Belgrade University Center. As things gradually came back from that night, he called the center. In the wake of the Belgrade University cyber group's success, the university's rapidly expanded computing and cyber faculties were now partly staffed by intelligence officers.

The two most important members of staff were from the party, and the third was from the domestic intelligence service. Rosic got someone on the case quickly. The spooks closed off the locked section of the computer center, and they took the data away. Rosic received a personal liaison officer from the Serbian military intelligence, whose job—so Rosic thought—would be to help him reconstruct the attack.

Day by day, his memory improved, but the pieces still didn't fit. Whenever he spoke, he noticed the officer didn't need to take any names. Slowly, it dawned on Rosic that the spook in the center knew a whole lot about the hackers on the scene already.

After one meeting, as the spook was driving Rosic home in his old car, Rosic told him he would not be assisting any further with their inquiries. Something was wrong, he said. No matter how much information he gave them, they weren't moving the case along. In fact, he said, it felt like they were just probing him. To find out how much and who *he* knew. The intelligence officer pulled over. "Okay, fine," he smiled. "Thank you for what you've told us up to now." Rosic climbed out onto the street and watched the taillights fade into the night.

Rosic, as a white-hat hacker, had become a problem. As a hack-tivist who had worked with the Serbian Angels, he had sought to stem the excesses of the nationalist hacker groups during the war and after it, intervened in criminal acts, and prevented government-sponsored hacker groups from mounting attacks that could have damaged civilian infrastructure.

His network's stance had become a problem that needed address-ing. "Black Hand hackers would hack into a server and install a bot that would act inside it, to use it for takeovers and so on," he said. "Then they would lock it to try to protect their work, so that only they could get control of it. But we would not only hack the server *back*, and clean them off it completely, but once we were inside, we would fix the server so that no one could break into it again. That was my way of solving the problem. Undo their work, in anything they hacked. Hack them, and clean them up." In the chaos of war, that had been his prerogative. But locking the government goon squad out of their own handiwork had made him a marked man.

Formerly one of many, the Black Hand was now an umbrella brand, and they were now swallowing the others, or putting them out of action. Using the same holistic "Total War" team structures as the Belgrade University group, complete with memetic artists, copywriters, linguists, and cryptographers, they became not just a hacker collective but an early online open-source intelligence oper-ation liaising with Serbian intelligence.

Rosic had been identified not through code but by cryptogra-phers and language specialists in the Black Hand, whose job it was specifically to identify enemy hackers by their grammar, patterning, and syntax. Rosic's global group, with hackers in Australia, Canada, the United States, and Germany, had exchanged emails in English from anonymous webmail addresses. Black Hand cryptographers analyzed the text to get a fix on the author's writing. Then they started fishing around on the message boards, comparing tics, pat-terns, spacings, icon use. It led them back to Belgrade and to messages consistent with public postings by Zoran Rosic. Having identified the hacker who'd been spoiling their plans to install Trojans like Anti-Smyser-1 worldwide, they decided to put that person out of action.

Rosic was caught up in the military and Serbian government's rush to harness their hacker kids' anti-Western momentum, to turn one network centered on Belgrade University into a semiofficial paramilitary. When he learned that it was the Black Hand who got him, Rosic had an epiphany. Until that moment, he'd been a naive enthusiast. Now the scales had fallen from his eyes, and he realized he was fighting the wrong side. In the hospital, he told himself, "No more hacking. I'm out."

The days of low-profile hobby hackers were at an end. It had been well and good to exist as an underground scene before they came to notice. But the scene had crossed over to the mainstream, and in the new world of powerful backers and political capital, there would not be room for independents. Rosic's stewardship of the last few uncolonized servers in the university was a minor annoyance to be cleared away. By now, the Black Hand had subsumed the Serbian Internet Army's funding. They had also taken ownership of its global database. This put it in direct control of a network of overseas discontents, hackers, would-be cyber warriors, and still-active diaspora nationalists, all of whom had shown talent in, or at least volunteered for, anti-Western hacks.

The result was a secret global network of hackers for hire and usage.

It was a resource that was dark to the rest of the world. Recruited by the Serbian Internet Army's global marketing drive on email, via early bulletin boards, and through street-level networks within Serbia, its communications were virtually undetectable. The entire network—or members in certain countries, or with particular skills—could be pointed at anything. And it would be dark to the world.

Chapter 12

The Cyber Mercenaries

On the other side of the Atlantic, it seemed America was finally catching on.

The floundering of my MI5 team and NATO's response to Anti-Smyser-1 was how it had entered the new century. It was not until after the seismic shock of 9/11 that America began to understand the value—not to mention the threat—locked up in dark, distributed networks online. And when it did, it would not be Western military or intel organizations that would start probing the global hacker underworld. It would be the dot-com giants of Silicon Valley themselves. In the wake of the World Trade Center and Pentagon attacks of 9/11, America's funding for defense, homeland security, and combating terrorism rocketed, rising by between $145 billion and $160 billion in the fiscal years 2001–2003 alone. The shock had been so vast, so deep, that money was easy, if your pitch was in homeland security or the combating of terrorists on American soil or against American interests. As America convulsed, it asked itself one big chilling question.

How the hell did we miss this?

But at last Swallow, Knesek, and the rest of the cyber-intelligence community could get traction for their hobbyhorse: that *dark networks existed* and their superpower was the undetectable crowdsourcing of hostility and violence against the United States itself.

For the US cyber spooks, they were finally able to show an

upside for America's intelligence capability to all this illicit internet activity. And it came from what they were doing right at that moment in Belgrade to track down and neutralize hackers, using one of the CIA's and NSA's own new toys.

The war in Kosovo might have led to a whole bunch of cyberattacks, but it had also led to a whole lot more internet usage period. The FBI had found the additional volume helpful. Not only did it mean more clues about what was happening, but it meant more users leaving more trails to more connections. The joint CIA-NSA grant for computer scientists at Caltech, MIT, Carnegie Mellon, Harvard, and Stanford that had funded Google was known as the MDDS, short for the Massive Digital Data Systems project. "Just as geese fly together in large V shapes, or flocks of sparrows make sudden movements together in harmony, they predicted that like-minded groups of humans would move together online," Jeff Nesbit, the former director of legislative and public affairs at the National Science Foundation, would recall of the project later.

By working with emerging commercial-data companies, their intent was to track like-minded groups of people across the internet and identify them from the digital fingerprints they left behind, much like forensic scientists use fingerprint smudges to identify criminals. Just as "birds of a feather flock together," they predicted that potential terrorists would communicate with each other in this new global, connected world—and they could find them by identifying patterns in this massive amount of new information. Once these groups were identified, they could then follow their digital trails everywhere.

For a US government still struggling to incorporate the lessons of distributed cyber war, it was as if real-world movements and explosions provided an illustration they could grasp. This was the context in which the US government finally figured out a use for Google and other popular online services as surveillance tools. Suddenly, cyber intel found the wind blowing in its favor.

Google had already been working with the FBI behind the scenes since 1999. At the outset it had helped Swallow and Knesek's stakeholders to make sense of their maps of influence, attribution, and propensity that could help them match up public signals or locations with covert actions, hacks, intrusions, or information-warfare campaigns.

Google now had scale, and scale gave it reliable data. Its teams began to scour the world for look-alike behaviors. Groups who flocked together online around certain symbols, discussions, or sites were now mines of information to be investigated. During Kosovo, Google and their contacts at the bureau's cyber team of mappers, tracers, and sleuths had been sidelined by the military effort. Now, things had changed. Google would not just help the US agencies to understand where the hackers were or who they were. Now, it would join Swallow and Knesek in "flipping" potential attackers.

Many of the kids from Kosovo had been inside sensitive US government and NATO systems. It was fair to assume, especially after 9/11, that someone out there might be very interested in what they had to teach. Rumor was not only that Chinese and Russian intelligence were gaining valuable insight from the Belgrade hackers' experiences and had been given access to all the reports and data from the university network, but that the Black Hand was going around trying to kill or intimidate anyone who resisted. So Google was going to offer these same kids something instead. Beat the Black Hand to it, if they could. And this is how they began zoning in on the same individuals.

But if Serbia's spooks had used the stick, America would offer the carrot. Instead of a beating or a medal, Silicon Valley would offer them a lucrative career in the California sun.

Still swollen, Rosic sat back at his computer late in 2001 and ran his hands through his hair. It was late, and he was running out of steam, just switching between tinkering with code and the ping of arrivals from some hackers' mailing group he was on.

The group was a small, private list for a very specific project. It wasn't well known, and while participants were based around the world, there weren't many members whose names he didn't know through at least a couple of degrees of separation. He'd settled into the rhythm of a new thread in the exchanges, when an unexpected response popped up on his screen.

This new email was addressed to him only. The sender was someone Rosic didn't know and who had not been on the list.

The young hacker opened the email. The sender greeted him cordially, by name, and introduced themselves as someone who had been made aware of his work. The sender was, they said, from the fast-growing military/intel-backed search company in California: Google. They had been following him for some time. Now they wanted to hire him.

The approaches from Google received by four other Balkan hackers I have spoken to were consistently well researched and personal in nature, and all had the impression that their subsequent conversations were at least partly informed by information gained from penetrating hacker groups they had been part of. They were right. Far from simply spamming lists with approaches in the hope of funneling out high-quality candidates, recruiters acting for Google in Mountain View, California, were working along a list of names, profiles, and contact details supplied to them by someone with more detailed, private knowledge of their work. While the FBI worked to protect their sources, they also liaised with US tech companies to capture the best talent.

Not that it mattered to some of their marks. Zoran Rosic thought for a while, then sent the HR exec at Google a one-line response that read simply, "No, I'm really not interested. But thanks."

"You have to understand that at that time, I really had the brightest people around me in Belgrade, not California," he points out. "Belgrade University computer rooms were *where it had all happened*. It was famous! It was the place where this new kind of internet activity started. Everything was coming from here." It's a sentiment echoed everywhere in Eastern Europe, from the Balkans to Moscow, today. The hackers, for that brief moment, were the epicenter of the online world—the place where innovation was happening. And it was happening not in scheduled meetings or brainstorms with PowerPoint presentations, but in real time, with missiles and microwaves, revolution and resistance.

"We were so arrogant and so sure that we were better than this Google," laughs Rosic, emphasizing the name with an ironic tonal quotation mark. "We were laughing, 'Wow, they are so *desperate.*' That they were going deep into our work, even our mailing lists, to select people they want."

He shakes his head ruefully, tracing the arc of how subsequent events would pan out for the intelligence community–funded Stanford project and the teenage hacker army. "That's what young guys are like, isn't it?" He shrugs. "Of course, now I'm like, 'Jesus. If I had the opportunity again? At that age? Absolutely.'"

One, who wishes only to be referred to as D, clicked to open an email on his home PC in March 2000. He didn't recognize the sender's name, but it was familiar and Serbian, and the subject line was a bit of current slang approximating, "You snooze, you lose." It proved to be a BCC round-robin email claiming to be from a coding competition in the United States, looking for entrants. D responded, completed some tests, and took part in some online chats. He then began receiving more tests, for which he would be paid. This segued into contracting for an American company—one of Google's search competitors—remotely at first, from Belgrade. He took the option to move to the United States on a work visa as soon as one was offered. As far as he could ascertain, there never was any coding competition. "It was like an early Cicada," he says, referring to Cicada 3301, the cryptic series of internet puzzles that appeared between 2012 and 2014, leading to harder and harder cryptographic challenges and commonly supposed to be the work of intelligence agencies, law enforcement, or software companies. Today, D lives in Northern

California. He left the search giant some time ago and now works in e-commerce. It feels like a lifetime in Silicon Valley, he laughs. So much has changed. But he was so young then, he's still only in his late thirties: "The first half of my career."

Silicon Valley's recruitment drive in Belgrade saw this brain drain of skilled technology-sector workers became so prominent through the 2000s that the Serbian government could no longer pretend it wasn't happening. Instead, they spun it as a stroke of genius-level statecraft on their part. Its mouthpiece Politika trumpeted the country's brain drain as "the best investment" Serbia had ever made. It rationalized that the diaspora's average transfer to family back home of 8 percent of their hard-currency wages in the United States, United Kingdom, Germany, or Canada and higher wages in places like Silicon Valley meant higher Western Union transfers home.

When the US embassy in Serbia reopened, the teams were briefed to try to identify some of the kids behind the hacks. Canadian and US diplomatic officials were working toward a directive described to me as "creaming off the brightest talent" and fast-tracking it for green cards and work in the American tech or government sectors where applicable. Google and its competitors were happily benefiting from an apparent foreign policy fast lane aimed at securing the American status of the very people who had inflicted such public humiliation on the United States. This policy earned the humorous nickname "Operation Paperclip," after the US grab for Germany's nuclear and rocket scientists in the wake of World War II. If the junior hackers and behind-the-scenes technologists could be bought and imported, then this strange Eastern evolutionary offshoot of internet culture could be redirected, bred back into the central American model. "Ultimately, you figure the economics will work where force doesn't," said one US official. It was a new twist on an old adage: "If you can't beat them, make them join you."

But it was too little, too late. America's adversaries were already way ahead.

Chapter 13

A Troll Is Born

So it was that, by 2001, Russia was in the mood to experiment with its own loosely affiliated hacker underground, one incentivized to grow by getting rich.

Russia was smarting. Its military had been humiliated by NATO. Its erstwhile Warsaw Pact allies had supported America and the West. The Russian military was widely regarded, even among its enlisted men and women, as finished. Its forces were outspent, outmanned, and outgunned by NATO, and morale and capability had both been in freefall since their Soviet army collapsed. Soldiers and air force personnel—many were veterans of the long, drawn-out disaster that was the Soviet occupation of Afghanistan—went unpaid for months, even years, resulting in a burgeoning criminal network of military-trained muscle for hire across the country. Burned by their embarrassment and impotence over Kosovo, the Russians were also impoverished by the vanishment of much of their defense capability into newly independent countries, from Kazakhstan to Ukraine.

At a closed-door meeting in 2000, Putin met with his generals. The West has gone too far, they argued. They needed more money, more troops. Russia had to flex its muscles in the world again. A boost in spending for military might had to be in the cards. But Putin was a former intel and signals spook, not a general. He was also a realist. He spelled out to the generals his sense of the failure of direct confrontation. Russia would not win through direct contest.

The Belgrade hackers, on the other hand, had proved an extremely interesting anomaly for Putin and his advisers. The only time outside of the Chinese embassy fiasco that they had seen NATO's organization completely thrown, up and down the chain of command, was by this group of anonymous, mysterious teenage hackers. As the incursions had drawn blood, hackers from Russia watched what was successful, and then joined in, copying the methods and upping the scale. As early as March 28, they had been initiating their own copycat attacks. At one point, an attack took down NATO's own website for several days.

For Russia's new president, the observation was decisive. As head of the FSB (Federal Security Service) in 1998, Putin had developed a simmering suspicion of America's internet. The former USSR was being plundered by former apparatchiks and new *biznesmeny*—the plural of the English word whose transition into Russian saw it become shorthand for the Russian mafia's arrivistes as slick-suited institutional looters. Shares, weapons, expertise, natural resources, jewels, and gold were evaporating from Russia.

Through the 1990s, Russian authorities had largely cooperated with the FBI in case of fraud and early cybercrime. The FBI had stepped in to assist in the mid-1990s, solving the high-profile theft of $180 million in jewels, looted from Russia to the United States. By 1998, the FBI and FSB had worked together on 660 different cases and were exchanging around 800 requests for assistance and information each year. FBI officers even began having weekly meetings with their counterparts, at the feared Lubyanka building in Moscow from which it had ruled the USSR. Then, in spring of that year, Putin was appointed head of the FSB. He immediately asked about the cooperation and began to sit in. He would simply walk into the meeting room unannounced each week, take a seat, and remain silent, watching and taking notes. FBI agent William Kinane's impression from Moscow meetings was that the stony disbelief with which the soon-to-be Russian premier sat through the briefings came down to the FBI's investigation into Moonlight Maze—the Russian government's own attempt at nation-state hacking. Perhaps, reasoned Kinane, Putin was suspicious that the US agents were using the meetings to try to amass evidence against his own agency. "I think he was just incredulous," reported the FBI officer, "that there was an FBI agent sitting in Lubyanka."

"That feeling is foundational," agrees Dr. Jovan Byford. "It informs everything Putin has pursued since. If he has a manifesto from the 2000s to today, it is one formed by these humiliations and sealed by Kosovo. That soft power he witnessed, that mix of disinformation and cyberwar, was so effective and cheap that it could be his means to an end. And that end could be summed up as Make Russia Great Again."

In Kosovo, he saw that the generals' method of direct confrontation had failed. The methods used by the kids playing havoc with NATO were what he called "the way forward." He outlined the need to consider "asymmetric war." At the same time, there was no money. The state was broken. The future would belong not just to those waging hacking and cyber war instead of confrontations of military might, but to those who could crowdsource the dirty work for free.

One can imagine the shock inside the room at the Kremlin as he briefed his generals. Yet it's the aftershocks *outside* the room—in elections, war zones, cabinets, criminal networks, chat rooms, headlines, streets, economies, global conflicts—that are still being felt.

He had expanded on the theme in Russia's strategic plan for 2000, and then again in that spring's speech to Russia's largest military-industrial complex trade fair in the arms-making city of Nizhny Novgorod. Russia's capability was still "behind that of the other countries in terms of some technological areas," he told the press. It was a signal of how Russia was going to go about meeting its strategic objectives in the years to come.

On July 8, 2000, he spelled out his thinking even more clearly to the Federal Assembly. "We do not have the right to 'sleep through' the information revolution that is under way in the world."

What followed that day now reads like a blueprint for Russia's covert operations in Ukraine, Syria, and elsewhere. Like a Bond villain, he really was spelling out what he planned to do.

"The Cold War is a thing of the past, but to this day there are attempts to infringe on the sovereign rights of nations in the guise of humanitarian operations," he said of NATO's intervention. Then he turned to information operations. "An important area of foreign policy activity should be ensuring objective perception of Russia. Reliable information on the events in our country is a question of its reputation and national security." At one point, he referred to journalism as "a convenient tool."

The message was clear. Only the United States and its allies, fresh from victory in Kosovo, were too wedded to the image of a Russian military in the last stages of morbid decay that they simply did not attend to the warning.

Russia had been a laggard in the information revolution, as Putin admitted. But this pragmatic, wait-and-see approach could be made to bear fruit. After all, internet measures would be asymmetrically powerful against a country like the United States precisely because its internet penetration and dependency for everything from news to critical infrastructure were higher than Russia's.

Just how far Russia had lagged behind is illustrated by a snapshot of Russia's information-warfare capabilities at the outset. The army's cyber capabilities were just fine, as Moonlight Maze had shown. But like Soviet-era operations, they were limited by the pool of officers who were senior enough to be authorized, and skilled enough, to be useful.

For the same reason, the attempt to wage information war against America up to that point was tiny, its team ludicrously overqualified (or underqualified, depending on how you look at it). Its key proponent was a Russian agent named Sergei Tretyakov, stationed in New York City through the 1990s. Initially, Tretyakov's daily espionage work against the United States in New York settled into a routine. The spy would report for work in his mission office at 9:00, to find a night's worth of cables from Moscow, all asking questions for him to answer. What was New York University working on in the area of genetically engineered food? What did he know about the US hunt for Osama bin Laden, or rumors of al-Qaeda assisting Chechen forces? Eventually, to beef up his answers to respectable length, he began searching things they asked about on sites such as Yahoo! and AOL before copy-pasting the answers and sending them as cables back to Russia.

Then, just like your elderly parents, the grandees of Moscow began to send him cables containing information that they wanted someone to put on the internet for them. The *Washington Post's* Pete Earley recounted in his interviews with Tretyakov: "Sergei would send an officer to a branch of the New York Public Library, where he could get access to the internet without anyone knowing his identity. The officer would post the propaganda on various websites and send it in emails to US publications and broadcasters. Some propaganda would be disguised as educational or scientific reports."

The lone Russian agent going undercover on the top-secret mission of sitting at a public computer terminal at the West Fifty-Third Street Public Library with his thermos flask and sandwiches and shitposting to newspaper comment threads on behalf of elderly technophobe generals in Moscow day after day is a character crying out for a Bill Murray vehicle. Tretyakov's man made a familiar but lonesome figure to the librarians, typing snarky rebuttals about Chechnya (a favorite early theme) and then Kosovo into chat rooms and firing off salty emails to CNN and NBC whenever they talked about NATO.

For all the expertise inside the Russian military's black bunkers—the ones who had unleashed Moonlight Maze on

Texas—it is this scene, not online troll armies or nihilistic hackers, that forms the defining image of the state of Russian cyber war before the Kosovo conflict's young cybernauts showed them how. Tretyakov was, per the CIA and FBI, Russia's most senior spy in America after the end of the Cold War. Yet he was personally ordering his man in New York to sit at a computer in a public library for hours sowing minor confusion online. Russia had failed to grasp the opportunities created by the internet. This was not cyber war. It was barely an information campaign. In the summer of 2000, when Vladimir Putin told the Russian state to wake up to the internet, he was speaking to a country still hopelessly adrift, with an almost entirely digitally illiterate population. While the former Yugoslavia had been teaching its kids to code through the 1980s, the USSR had focused from its position of numerical superiority on might and missiles. And while the rest of the world had been negotiating the hands-off 1990s, for good and bad, Russia's security forces still could not imagine, let alone countenance, anything like a loose, distributed communications network that wasn't somehow under their top-down direction.

Something had to change.

Russia drew two key epiphanies from the Balkans.

The first was that they had gotten cyber warfare all wrong. What Russia had been most intrigued by was the Serbian hackers' focus not just on hampering NATO, but on using civilian hacks, takeovers, and information hijacks to highlight the uncanny valley between NATO's image (briefings on supposedly victimless "surgical strikes," bombardments named Noble Anvil, claims that aircraft were invisible) and the dirty reality of cluster bombs and casualties. Cyber war, as the Russian and US military still conceived it, was a strategic function of technology. It was specialized, expensive, and limited in scope. It demanded access to tools and knowledge that were tightly controlled and a highly specific skill set. But this new way was a function of crowds of individual intelligences. The Total

War approach—in which everybody is a target and everything a vector—was not a surgical strike, but a spanner in the works, the gremlin in the engine. It was the embrace of chaos as a weapon. Of deliberate *un*strategy.

If America was going to try to dominate cyberspace as it was dominating physical war, then its units would find themselves out-flanked by hostile platoons of code and quotation marks. As Russia's information-war channel Russia Today would put it when it launched in 2006, "Question more."

It now began to systematize its interventions in America's great invention. Russian security services had become focused on *infor-matsionnoye protivoborstvo* (information countermeasures) online, and the intelligence services had started to become involved in edit-ing the Russian Wikipedia. In this scaling up of Tretyakov's activity was the seed of today's troll farms—government-sponsored agen-cies in Russia and elsewhere whose focus is on disrupting online discourse with disinformation, distraction, and trolling. Where the Belgrade method of cyber war had been bottom-up—kids leading the way—this sea change in Russia was managed on an industrial-ized scale, taking the lessons from the kids, and giving it a steroidal, government-funded, at-scale boost.

It is impossible to understand Russia's pivot to the Eastern inter-net's decentralizing, destabilizing method of cyber war in 2000 without knowing that this was the already flourishing ecosystem of influence and manipulation.

Pravda, the Communist Party's newspaper since the revolu-tion, had shut down in 1996 after an entirely predictable standoff between its new Greek billionaire investor owners and its veteran Soviet Communist editors. Then in 1999, the editors formed a breakaway Pravda.ru brand online. After the Kosovo cyber war, they had launched an English-language Pravda site pointed at the West and promoted by emails and downloadable apps for desktop computers. It would become the template for everything Russia would go on to do with RT.com and its information campaigns in the West.

This English-language site swiftly dedicated itself to crowd-sourcing anti-Western disinformation campaigns through its forums, which became hotbeds of spitballed ideas for everything from terrorist attacks against targets in the United States to cyber-attack plans and inflammatory viral memes promoting early versions of fake news in the anglosphere. This was the great age in the West of the email meme—the chain letter featuring jokes, anecdotes, or personality quizzes about everything from the Nieman-Marcus cookie recipe to the Taliban. Pravda.ru fitted right in. Posts on its forums crowdsourced rumor and built to disinformation and were then picked up by the main website, generating everything from fake reports of further attacks on London and Paris amid the confusion of 9/11, which Pravda.ru then published and amplified via email lists, to lines of code that could be used and adapted to plant viruses inside Windows machines.

It was backed by a fresh-faced thirty-year-old whiz kid called Konstantin Kostin, a young Moscow journalist turned information warrior and magnate. Kostin had risen meteorically through Russia's cocaine-and-Kalashnikov-fueled adland in which a campaign briefed to a PR agency was as likely to be "dark publicity" and advertising presentation decks to clients might include proposals for blackmail, smear campaigns, or having the opposition's CEO arrested. Kostin became Mr. Fix-It to Moscow's political class, selling what he termed "preelection technology strategies" as a way of trialing the Belgrade hackers' methods in the domestic arena, as an electioneering tool. It proved a sweeping success. By 2000, he had masterminded Putin's first election victory.

It was to Kostin that Putin turned for advice on how harnessing bored, talented, impoverished young internet users could turn Russia's fortunes around.

Their model was to identify and amplify all the things that had worked well against NATO in Kosovo, through the same distrib-uted mechanisms.

These semidetached, plausibly deniable units of hackers, informa-tion specialists, and social engineers followed the Belgrade formula in their commitment to the opposite of strategy. Theirs was a heady cock-tail of cyber war and disinformation, in a continual, uncommanded, but entrepreneurial push for advantage that is funded both directly (by their governments) and indirectly (by the tacit agreement that they can keep the spoils of anything they do when they are on their own time and will be protected).

The Eastern internet became a map of "bulletproof" destina-tions for servers dealing in illicit material. Even if their security forces had not been complicit, their legal systems weren't harmo-nized with the rest of the world. You could begin a case against someone in Russia, but it would be so costly and long-winded, and was so likely to fall victim to corruption and red tape, that nobody tried anymore. It was with this feeling of bulletproof invincibility that some Russian and Ukrainian hackers were about to open a business that would go global.

A Ukrainian hacker called Roman Vega, a.k.a. Roman Ste-panenko or his screen name BOA, had launched boafactory.com around the turn of the millennium as a clearinghouse for trading anything that could be hacked, plundered, and used to commit financial crimes, from fake passports to dumps of bank numbers, blank credit cards, and stolen checks. With protection from senior figures in the Russian and Ukrainian security services, the Factory became a blueprint for what would follow.

In 2001, a face-to-face meeting at a restaurant in Odessa, Ukraine, brought the cream of credit-card data thieves operating in Russia and Ukraine together to discuss a plan for global expan-sion. Boa was there. So were Dmitry Golubov, a.k.a. Script, another Ukrainian hacker inspired by the kids of Belgrade, and a twenty-year-old hacker from Moscow, Vladislav Anatolievich Horohorin, a.k.a. BadB. All three connected to groups that were part of the action in 1999. As the organization's hype man and PR magnet, BadB harbored such animus against the United States that Carder-Planet, a hub for cybercriminals whose specialty was in hacking, obtaining, and selling third parties' credit-card data, almost immediately began to stray from simple cybercrime into actions of a darker nature. He was a cartoonist and promoted the service with *South Park*–style short ads that depicted every bank account users emptied as an act of war against America, with Americans shown dying in various ways as a result of the bleeding of finance. In the final one, their actions cause President George W. Bush to shoot himself through the head. The call to action invited internet users to "Join the Army" of hackers working against the Stars and Stripes of America.

It had no lack of official support in this, with backers including Russian military intelligence and security services.

The role state-sponsored criminal networks play for the Russian military and government is similar to that of the British government's secret World War II organization the Special Operations Executive (SOE), suggests Dr. Mark Galeotti. The organization was founded in 1940, its mission to carry out sabotage, espionage, and reconnaissance in Nazi-occupied Europe. "The model of the SOE is more helpful in understanding these shifting, semi-autonomous hacker collectives in Russia and the former Communist world," says Galeotti. "So yes, they had set missions and goals. But in the meantime, they were told, 'Look, honestly *anything* you can do to cause inconvenience or the reallocation of resources, just go for it. Set light to some newspaper in a train station if the smoke causes alarm. Commit continuous low-level crimes that drain your opponents' people, money, resources and focus."

For Russia, that felt like a winning strategy, especially if it could pay for itself in the proceeds of crime. The more FBI agents they had running around trying to stop a bunch of scammers, the less attention the agency had to pay to the other work they were doing, intrusions into government systems and information countermeasures. It degraded America's sense of strategic decision making, introducing the sensation of being out of control. The result is that defensive organizations—the FBI and MI5, say—overallocate to it and miss the bigger picture.

In the weeks following the Odessa meeting, the Russian sponsors of the International Carders Alliance got a perfect illustration of the terrifyingly asymmetric effects of surprise attack. September 11 saw almost three thousand people die on the day. Yet the American reaction was to attack a third country, then another. Eventually, all the Americans who died and were wounded in Iraq and Afghanistan—service people, civilians, contractors—dwarfed the initial toll. Then consider the civilian death tolls in those countries—millions. Then look at the economic, material, reputational, and political cost to America.

For all the US scare talk of a "cyber Pearl Harbor" at which point war breaks out, this continuing sense of insecurity, sabotage, draining of resources, and the creation of miscalculation *is already* the war. And it is a tactical, opportunistic war that the West, with its strategic view, is not terribly good at defending.

Indeed, when Script was finally arrested and imprisoned under pressure from the United States, following months of painstaking investigative signals intelligence work by Postal Inspector Greg Crabb liaising with the Secret Service and FBI, it was despite years of being blocked by Ukrainian authorities working closely with Russia. Only after the Orange Revolution swept the country in 2004 was the Ministry of the Interior willing to listen. Still, he knew too much to stay in jail for long. Six months after the guilty verdict, two members of parliament influenced a judge to release him, whereupon he was installed as a member of the Ukrainian parliament running as "the Internet Party" in order to grant him immunity from any future investigations. (A stock tactic in the former USSR. In 2007, former KGB man Andrei Lugovoi, wanted by

British authorities for assassinating Russian whistle-blower Aleksandr Litvinenko with radioactive polonium in a London sushi bar,
was summarily appointed to the Russian parliament as evidence
against him was announced.)

The hackers present at the global gathering of carders in Odessa
that summer had made it through the lawless 1990s by knowing
how to work with the powers that be. Now, Kosovo had shown the
authorities too that a well-fed hacker underground could benefit
their national defense, while contributing cash to the coffers from
the proceeds in the form of informal "taxes." It had formed the crux
of Putin's briefing to Russia's generals in the spring of 2000. Now
the hackers had every reason to feel confident in the backing of
their governments.

The project they were gathered to launch seemed revolutionary at the time. Its name was CarderPlanet. The organization's core
activity was to release dumps of credit-card data to paid membership lists. Those members would then use the data to convert into
money or goods. It was the perfect black market: there were no
logistics risks or transport costs. Risk was low. Credit-card companies, like banks, have always been notoriously reluctant to admit
to having been hacked and often prefer to settle up with their customers on the quiet. In fact, it was just a prototype for what was
to come.

The International Carders Alliance's operations quickly became
a source of more than just the information the carders needed. The
carders and their affiliates quickly became invaluable to its sponsors in the Russian state and security services, not for the money
they stole, but for the access the ops gave them to identities and
networks. Their incredibly prolific, industrial-scale pipeline for
passports, credit-card details, and raids on bank accounts quickly
became a source of manufactured identities for Russian intelligence's own doppelgänger armies.

By 2003, these crime-funded hacker auxiliaries counted some

seven thousand active members across the world, all regularly hacking and trading bulk drops of card data, passports, IDs, and financial and other information obtained from the US government, businesses, and individuals. As it extended beyond the Russo-sphere, it had mutated from a Russian-language-only hacker setup into something stranger. It added an English-language dating-style component, matching American, Canadian, Australian, and Western European hackers—so-called hacker mules—with Russian handlers, hacking on demand in exchange for an early trace-hard form of digital money called eGold from the Russian cadre. For its backers in the former ex-Soviet security services, this free-for-all was not simply a Yugoslav-style revenue-generation opportunity; it was nothing less than a supercharged incubator for the cultivation of a skilled hacker underground.

Again, the West was unable to think in the new ways this blurry new behavior demanded of it. Western intelligence and law enforcement communities, still working in neat categories two years after the lessons of Kosovo, saw the problem as one of cyber-crime, not of defense against cyber war.

It formed part of a failure on the West's part not just to address this new form of warfare, but to even conceive of it. From London to Washington, DC, the connection between statecraft and the cyber-war capabilities of America's strategic foes hovered, yet even as Russia incentivized the growth of a new ecosystem of a state-backed hackerati, the penny would not drop.

Into this void stepped two things. One was a post-9/11 fear of terrorism. The other was a chiropractor from Sewickley, Pennsylvania.

Chapter 14

Life on the Wire

Robert Boback was relaxing after a day with patients at his home practice in the town of Sewickley, just north of Pittsburgh, in 2003. He worked hard, not just as a chiropractor, but in his real-estate sales side hustle. Relaxation brought a little TV channel flipping, and as he pushed the button again and again, he happened on a *60 Minutes* report by Lesley Stahl about the new breed of peer-to-peer file sharers setting their sights on pirated movies. At this, he stopped pressing the button and watched.

Like a great many small-town patriots, the ambitious thirty-two-year-old was taken with the idea of this new threat to the American way of life. He figured someone, somehow, should find a way to stop the travelers on these murky and opaque digital highways from undermining the United States. He gnawed on it, and the more he dug, the bigger the threat became. Everyone was concerned about piracy, but Boback was among the few who saw the real threat. Truly malignant actors were out there among the kids wanting something for nothing. The Russian Business Network (RBN) was releasing malware to hackers everywhere through peer-to-peer. Terrorists were using hard-to-monitor file-sharing platforms like LimeWire to share plans and secure messages. If you were running the software, they could be inside your hard drive too. Who knew how many soldiers or government researchers, aerospace engineers, or politicians' families that included?

Finally, he hit upon the idea of tracking the dark web of connections between file sharers. This was no easy matter. Peer-to-peer platforms didn't "hold" any appropriated files anywhere at all. They just connected the software running on the machines of millions of civilian users across the world.

Where there was a will, there was a way. Alongside a chiropractic patient of his, a wispy but intense thirtysomething programming whiz called Sam Hopkins, he developed a program that scattered virtual users, or "nodes," throughout the LimeWire network. These artificial nodes in the network acted just as contrast-medium dye injected into a network of arteries illuminates critical pathways for medical researchers. Once enough of these nodes were connected to each other, in theory, the whole network would become visible for the first time. The extent of the threat would be known, as would the locations of its flows. It would also mean they could trace the location of the files they found. They called the program Tiversa, an anagram of "veritas." It was perfect. Like the code itself, it revealed hidden truth, seen only obscurely. Once you knew, you knew.

At a meeting in Washington, DC, with Orrin Hatch, chairman of the Senate Judiciary Committee and a strong antipiracy campaigner, Boback and Hopkins showed him a presentation from their laptop—which they referred to as the "football," in reference to the US Secret Service presidential detail's case containing the nuclear launch codes. As they clicked through the slides, Boback spelled out the potential for their product, pitching for some government investment. Hatch seemed interested, if a little lukewarm, when they talked about its potential for stopping file sharers of movies and music. It was only in the final few slides that he sat bolt upright. The men mentioned that it wasn't just music and movies that the Tiversa program could locate, but anything and everything else that was being shared, deliberately or inadvertently—from documents to code, presentations, Excels. Hopkins then explained that since that meant national security was a concern, he had created a second interface for the Tiversa platform. Boback showed Hatch some of the things it had picked up. Here was Russian and Chinese malware. Here was a Balkan hub for the plunder of email viruses from Western systems. One showed a file sharer in Australia to be in possession of jihadi literature and bomb-making instructionals, stored on a hard drive that they were unsuspectingly revealing through Hopkins's code. To Hatch, they called the program not Tiversa, but the far more compelling Patriot Spy.

It was great marketing. If the Bush administration was hawkish on piracy, post-9/11 it pursued the War on Terror almost to the point of mania. Hatch's instinct for traction kicked in. He told the men to stop what they were doing, and within moments he had CIA director George Tenet dialed in on speaker for a précis. By the following morning, they were face-to-face with the CIA's Directorate of Science and Technology in Langley, making the same pitch.

The men settled into a rhythm. Boback undertook meeting after meeting, while Hopkins worked on upgrades and advances to the program. One advance worked on the same principle as Rudy Giuliani's "broken windows" policing methods in 1990s New York City: if the program sniffed out anything interesting on a user's hard drive, it would drag down and reveal everything else on that hard drive. They called the new version EagleVision X1—the "X1" was for the stamp on classified files, the "EagleVision" for its ability to see granular detail at an unimaginable remove. That changed everything. The number of leads for investigation exploded.

Sure, there were false positives. Absolutely, these methods created alarm where there may be no cause. But for an America now deeply embroiled in the War on Terror, entrenched in Iraq and Afghanistan, and full of inflationary patriotism and zeal for vengeance on whomever, these bugs were given the status of features. And slowly, the US intelligence community went from sleep to a permanent state of hypervigilance not seen since the Cold War days of McCarthy and mutually assured destruction.

Through the 2000s, the more America knew, the more it seemed there was to know. Chatter online, once regarded as just that, was now always a harbinger.

As Russia's cyber war on NATO took the headlines again, America was all ears. On Tuesday, July 24, 2007, the final seconds ticked toward ten on an already-searing morning, the bright morning sun pouring through the windows of the US House of Representatives' Rayburn Building in Washington, DC. The sign beside the double oak doors read simply, "Room 2154. United States House of Representatives Committee on Oversight and Government Reform."

The excitement was high. Already that spring, the newswires had been thrumming with reports of a massive Russian cyberattack on NATO member Estonia that had brought the tiny Baltic country across the sound from Finland to a standstill. If the United States had slept through the birth of the new realities of cyber war, and still had trouble understanding it, talking about it in terms that any Cold Warrior or terror hawk could grasp was the role Boback was born to.

Representatives from some thirty US states and their secretaries waited, attended by assistants. There were business delegations, from the music and software industries, academics from the world of security, tech, business, and media. A deputation from LimeWire, the file-sharing network that had risen as one of the many peer-to-peer file-sharing successors to Napster, was closest to the large, polished doors to the chamber. Mark Gorton, the founder and CEO of LimeWire's holding corporation, the Lime Group, sipped his coffee and looked around for his opposite number today. The closed corridor space thrummed with sotto voce chatter, which lowered briefly to a reverent whisper as he arrived—a silver-haired, dapper man in his midsixties, tallish and tanned. He was Wesley Clark. The former supreme allied commander of NATO was here in his new capacity. In November 2006, he had joined the Tiversa Advisory Board.

The pair had made for a compelling proposition in their pitches. Boback was slick, almost hypnotic in the way he delivered his pitch, a winning blend of energy, expertise, and eloquence. Hopkins was the backroom boffin—quietly spoken and fascinated by the possibilities they might open up with their work. A compelling proposition, sure—but not an irresistible one. For that, they needed influence, credibility, and contacts. Clark, still basking in the glow of his successful bombardment of Serbia and its forces in Kosovo, came with all three. In Room 2154, beside the group was an easel board, on which a large printed sheet of paper displayed the event about to start: "Special Hearing. Inadvertent File Sharing on Peer-to-Peer Networks." The goal of the hearing was to tackle a problem that had become acute for America—its businesses and corporations, government, security services, and military.

It was a problem that sounded unnervingly familiar to Wesley Clark from his time as NATO's supreme commander. While America's enemies—from foreign powers to terror networks and organized-crime syndicates—were inside their computer systems, gaining access to classified, sensitive, and potentially dangerous documents, not only did those American government, military, and business bodies have no way to stop them, but they were, for the most part, completely unaware that they were compromised.

NATO, the Pentagon, and MI5 had all been fatally behind the curve in 2000; now, more than seven years later, they were behind the very same curve. Even as they sat here, America's secrets were being put to use by hackers, criminals, terrorists, and strategic enemies belonging to no elite cadre. The world was a mass of discontents, cyber mercenaries, and criminals. The continuing attacks on Estonia—clearly the work of Russia, but tantalizingly hard to pin down—were proof of that.

This was a hearing to uncover the extent of the problem file-sharing platforms posed to America's national security. Boback had every reason to feel confident. EagleVision X1 was proving day after day that the threat to the United States was real, and it went beyond business. Its hourly successes each read like front-page headlines. The program had located a document belonging to the US Air Force F-35 Joint Strike Fighter program on a hard drive in China. It had found a user only an hour away from President George Bush's Texas ranch whose hard drive contained files about sniper rifles and photos of the president's daughter. He had passed information on its searches for "jihad" and "Chechnya" to the CIA. With EagleVision X1, Tiversa had turned into a valuable source of information for the Secret Service. Suddenly, there were enemies *everywhere*. The threat of a "cyber Pearl Harbor" was making government memos, TV news, military briefings.

Boback's testimony spelled out to the representative committee how EagleVision X1 was revealing that some of the most sensitive material in the United States was out on the open market.

It included patent work in markup, thousands upon thousands of administrative passwords and user IDs for private corporate networks, ongoing clinical drug-trial data, countless legal documents, financial data that opened the door to hackers and cyber heists, including "an outsourced telecom provider which shared the entire wide area network of one of the largest, most recognized investment banks in the world." Then he turned to terror.

There was a large government outsource provider that did security threats to transit authorities for various US cities. In that report they were given carte blanche access to the security measures of these various cities. Then they released the report inadvertently on the peer-to-peer. This information gives very precise information on where the bombs should be placed to have the maximum damage—where are the vulnerabilities in this city that could impact our national security. A city hired this company in an effort to *decrease* the risk facing that city, and unfortunately it *increased it severalfold*, as individuals are able to access that information.

Clark and Boback zoned in on who these national security threats were, incorporating the data trails the Black Hand and Russian Business Network themselves were leaving everywhere. "People are accessing this information from outside the United States....[T]his information does head to Pakistan. It does head to Africa. It does head to Eastern Europe."

The hearing caused a sensation. The US defense establishment finally sat up and listened.

Tiversa was backed by the CIA as America's first line of cyber defense. It quickly picked up one blue-chip client after another, inside government and beyond—Capital One, Lehman Brothers, Goldman Sachs, and AmEx all signed on, paying a whopping $75,000 each month for its tracking of the information trail. General Wesley Clark had fronted what seemed like a significant blow against the growing communities of hackers targeting America economically and militarily at last.

And indeed, the EagleVision X1 proposition was heady, powerful stuff. While there would later be concerns that Tiversa was overstating the danger and picking up false positives, there is no doubt that on the evidence presented, it felt like a no-brainer for the hearing that day. The history of America's engagement with cyber war and the threats hackers pose to national security is studded with such champagne moments. Great leaps, huge pitches, huge investments, successful products.

Yet just like the decision to cover up the long plundering of NATO's files in 1999, EagleVision X1 in 2007 was another *Sliding Doors* moment. The investment in automated intelligence measures flattered the leaders in the field of high-tech and AI, while ignoring the root cause of the problem. It was a technical Band-Aid for an issue that lay far deeper. Time and again, the West's adversaries were attacking in ways that are all too human, in an unceasing, entrepreneurial push for advantage, weak spots, leakage, intelligence, and errors. Yet America's solution has always been more investment in technology. Where its foes were networked, insurgent, and unpredictable, America's response was to turn to technological silver bullets. There's a saying, "To a man with a hammer, the whole world looks like a bag of nails." In the same way that Hollywood movies and the National Rifle Association cleave to the idée fixe that more guns in more hands is the solution to society's ills, so America's near hegemony in the field of high-tech made the answer to every problem more money for high technology.

But the questions being posed weren't technological in nature. They were human. Despite these leaps, innovations, and technological mastery, America's engagement with cyber war is ultimately a story of slow, drawn-out failure. Like its drawn-out and dispiriting wars in Vietnam and Afghanistan, it is a chronicle of winning every decisive battle, yet somehow contriving to lose the war.

Even as Tiversa's trackers were rolling out across America, that hothoused, financially motivated scene with its Russian and Ukrainian intelligence *krishas*—literally "roof" in Russian, a *krisha* is a sponsor or guarantor, usually in the higher echelons of government or the FSB—was growing and diversifying into something far less easy to describe or combat, a series of fully fledged state-backed hacker armies disguised as private enterprises.

One of the most notorious was the successor to CarderPlanet. The St. Petersburg–based organization the Russian Business Network was the Russian government's vision for a dark, self-funding cyber-war economy turned on the West with a vengeance.

Appearing as a registered domain in 2006, RBN was a curious emergence, with a flickering, semisubmerged presence. Yet it quickly became an industrialized, at-scale version of the Total War studio that Markovic and the Belgrade network had pioneered on the fly amid the fire and darkness of the bombardment. Russia's adoption of the model for its own cyber capability was wholly strategic.

The Russian Business Network contained the DNA of so much that we have seen since, from the Kremlin's bot networks to China's cyber nationalists. But though it called itself a business network, it was never incorporated, or even registered as a company. Nor was there any way of tracing a legal paper trail to ownership of the domains it used. It took a different path, opening itself up as a dark-web marketplace for everything from state-on-state cyberattacks, to pirate music and malware, to cash transactions, espionage, sabotage, disinformation, organized campaigns of geopolitical cyber war, illegal pornography, and stolen credit-card numbers. It was, in the succinct summation of one Russian member, an "online marketplace for the apocalypse."

Its founders and leadership structure were unknown, except for its prime figure, a twenty-four-year-old hacker known as Flyman. Flyman was the nephew of a well-connected Moscow lawmaker and politician and had been one of the Russians to copy and multiply the Serbian hackers' work against NATO at the turn of the century. Even he did everything he could to stay off the radar. The RBN owners' contact details were a series of anonymous webmail addresses. They were, legally and for all practical purposes of detection or identification, entirely nonexistent. It did not promote itself; if you wanted to contact the RBN, you could try one of the anonymous webmail addresses, or an internet message service. It took bounties, state work, and commissions in eGold.

Its very existence made a mockery of continued Western attempts to class online malfeasance as either "cyber war" or "cybercrime," "hacking" or "information war." Like the Belgrade hackers, the outsiders of RBN and its sponsors in the Russian government had discovered the great truth of an internetworked world with more clarity than the West. Whether your primary goal online was profit, espionage, or adventurism, you could double your protection, your patronage, your resources with one easy formulation. *Everything was war.* Diverting US policing and intelligence resources toward hacks into its energy infrastructure? *War.* Draining the accounts of everyday Americans? Cause panic on the stock market? *War.* Stealing and sealing off classified government secrets and intellectual property? *War.* Erode faith in the American internet, from the security of online payments to the veracity of messages from your government? *War.*

That dual branding of criminal enterprise was what got them protection, leverage, and patronage. War in the twenty-first century was not always in the roar of planes and explosives, but the constant, low-level background hum of the internet itself. While its hackers and middlemen, information architects and admins certainly became wealthy, the upside for the Kremlin went well beyond the informal taxes they collected. RBN became a new form of cyber regiment turned intelligence agency. Outsourced, entrepreneurial, and ruthlessly unaccountable.

"RBN is a for-hire service catering to large-scale criminal operations," read one US infrastructure report in response to its rise. "It hosts cybercriminals, ranging from spammers to phishers, botherders and all manner of other fraudsters and wrongdoers from the venal to the vicious." One Trojan operation alone unleashed on America and the West made RBN $150 million in less than twelve months. Their ambitions for stealing secrets, IP, cash, and the contents of servers and hard drives were outlined in malware with names like Corpse's Nuclear Grabber. "Every major trojan in the last year links to RBN," reported US cyber detectives. After one Trojan campaign, they successfully hacked into RBN's own computers. There, they found a treasure trove of data that showed at least thirty thousand incursions' worth of highly sensitive stolen material.

Yet behind the mask, even RBN could not keep its members completely secret. US company VeriSign determined the physical locations of RBN's servers, but US and European law enforcement simply could not get their Russian counterparts to pursue an investigation. "RBN feel they are strongly politically protected," said the report. "They pay a huge amount of people. They know they are being watched. They cover their tracks."

The uncomfortable truth was one that US intelligence agencies had trouble recognizing, even as first Estonia, then Georgia, then Ukraine, and finally America and Western Europe themselves fell victim. Our opposite numbers in Russia, the Balkans, and China were not interested in creating hacker armies. They had been busy creating nothing less than a cyber-war economy.

And they were about to get their taste of hot war.

Chapter 15

The New Russian Way of War

In the Baltic, the days are long and the light—from sky, from water, from churches and office buildings and cars—always shot through with silvery blue.

Like the former Yugoslavia, the Baltic states—Estonia, Latvia, and Lithuania—were at the very hem of the Iron Curtain. Unlike the former Yugoslavia, they were on the inside. All three became Soviet Socialist Republics of the USSR at the end of the Second World War. They had achieved independence, often at great cost, as the Soviet Union crumbled, though the last small detachments of Russian troops did not depart until 1995. Yet by 2004, all three were members of NATO.

By the USSR's collapse, Estonians—the closest Soviet people to a Western transmitter, across the water in Finland—had lived in a dual reality for decades. They didn't need fantasy for their futurology. For years, they had watched the future beamed to them through airwaves and come to them through cables. The newly free republic of Estonia knew exactly what to do. It liberalized early and set up support for innovation in homegrown businesses. By 1995, every school in the country was wired to the internet, with all computer terminals in the school building remaining open before and after school hours to encourage free public use. In 1997, Estonia transitioned to e-governance. By 2000, the Estonian government made it the first country in the world to declare internet access a human right, and e-tax became standard. By 2001, a mandatory digital ID card was introduced for all citizens, saving Estonia the equivalent of 2 percent of gross domestic product every year. Estonia introduced blockchain technology way back in 2008—a whole year before it was first tested as a distributed ledger for Bitcoin. Today, Estonia is the most advanced digital society in the world. It has more unicorns—private companies valued at more than $1 billion—than any other small country in the world. It is the birthplace of Skype, Taxify, and TransferWise.

It's easy to see mania for high technology, telecoms, and cyber as Estonia's own posttraumatic response to conquest and mass slaughter at the hands of the bears on its doorstep. "There are all sorts of advantages to being an early mover in technology, and having that small-country transparency," says Baltic geopolitics researcher Aliide Naylor. "But the downside is that it makes Estonia a perfect little test tube. It's a laboratory in which Russia likes to carry out experiments in things like covert influence and cyber war."

So as the RBN's network surged beyond its growth phase and became a force online, Estonia was the perfect place for Russia to send a message to NATO. It would do so in a way so clear that its misreading by NATO itself is almost miraculous. And it would do so by adopting the Black Hand's playbook, and some of its code. Moscow was in the mood to offer a view as to who had a say in the countries in its vicinity and who did not.

All through the early part of the decade, Russia and NATO had been in an increasingly fraught deadlock over the ultimate status of Kosovo. All early spring, a controversy had built up steam. NATO put pressure on for independence. Russia pushed back. How, it asked, could one guarantee that if Kosovo were allowed its independence, that would not give Chechnya, or anywhere else that felt like seceding from Russia, the same right, on pain of NATO interference? In a refrain that has become familiar in Ukraine since, Russia asked where its sphere of influence would stop being eroded, if not here. Finally, when a UN resolution backed by France, the United Kingdom, and the United States proposed granting Kosovo independence and sovereignty under international control in 2007, the hammer came down. Russia threatened to use its UN veto. The last thing anyone on NATO's side wanted was a confrontation between armed forces. But a confrontation of armed forces was the last thing on Vladimir Putin's mind.

That spring, another curious controversy with the potential to become an emotive, anti-NATO culture war had been rumbling in the former Soviet northwestern borderlands. It had the potential to become emotive in just the same way that Serbia's claims for Kosovo were. It was also a story of fallen heroes, sacrifices, and spilled blood, in a place that, for one side at least, would forever be defined by it. And it all revolved around a bronze statue in Tallinn, Estonia, scheduled to be moved to a new home.

Erected by the Soviets in 1947, the statue, known locally as the Bronze Soldier, had been dedicated to "The Liberators of Tallinn" in the Red Army. A third of Estonia's population are ethnic Russians, just as, one might say, a minority in Kosovo are Serbs. For at least some Russian Estonians, the soldier symbolized their sacrifices fighting the Wehrmacht. But for the Baltic states, history is never quite that simple. In 2007, memories of the Soviets in Estonia were of occupiers themselves. And in its attempt to forge its own path, the small, independent, and Westward-facing Baltic state made plans to move the statue, quietly, from its central square to a more discreet cemetery on the outskirts.

But quiet was one thing it was not to be. First came a few blog and social media posts. Then aggrieved editorials in Russian-language media, then something like an early attempt at fanning the flames of a culture war. Online reports, all false, all in Russian, all on forums with large Russian domestic audiences, began to circulate, claiming variously that the statue had been desecrated, that the Estonian authorities were planning to destroy it completely, and that Russian war graves were being defaced, destroyed, and disinterred.

The night of April 26 was mild and brought crowds into town, intent on protesting the removal. As the crowd swelled, the mood turned ugly. Police attempted to keep the protesters back, causing an inflamed crowd to surge. The center of Tallinn erupted into violence and looting. The rioting lasted for two days and nights, resulting in 156 casualties needing hospital treatment, 1 death, and more than 1,000 arrests.

On the second night, the vector of attack switched. From pumping false reports into grassroots forums, someone began pumping huge gluts of internet traffic into Estonia, clogging servers. They were using the same mechanisms the Black Hand, Belgrade hackers, and Serbian Internet Army had used—not just industrializing the takeover of zombie computer networks through malware, but urging people in chat rooms and on email lists and peer-to-peer file-sharing platforms to download and install "patriotic" files.

Wave upon gigantic wave of automated spam jammed servers across the world's most heavily digitized society, as traffic jams a road. Nothing else could get through—certainly not the tiny day-to-day volumes of traffic generated by Estonian banks, media, government, or private individuals. This wave of DDoS attacks was typically primitive, massive, and highly effective. It could have been pulled off by almost anyone with a botnet or two at their command to synchronize the spam and autogenerate requests.

To Estonians, that meant more than email problems. Estonia was already fully digital in the way it ran its government and public services. Government servers failed immediately. Newspapers and broadcaster organizations found that they could not upload or publish content. ATMs went down and stayed down. Some banks themselves went offline, unable to access account details for customers, let alone log or transfer funds. Amid a second day of looting and rioting in the capital, computerized government services and police records were disrupted.

America and its NATO allies again sent in its cyber detectives, intent on tracking down the culprits. The first arrived in Tallinn just two days after the attacks had begun. But the closer the cyber-security team got, the deeper it dug, the further the attacks seemed to swim out of focus.

Almost immediately, the Estonian government pointed the finger at the Kremlin. Then, in the days following, it walked the claim back. "I cannot state for certain that the cyber-attacks were managed by the Kremlin, or other Russian government agencies," admitted defense minister Jaak Aaviksoo. "It is not possible to say without doubt that orders came from the Kremlin; or that, indeed, a wish was expressed for such a thing there."

Russia denied all involvement, and in May, it offered assistance in tracking down the attackers. Then, in June, Russia's supreme procurator rescinded the offer, citing its interpretation of technicalities of the two countries' cooperation treaty. On May 2, activists from the Kremlin-backed Youth for Putin organization Nashi invaded and disrupted a press conference in Moscow by Estonian ambassador to Russia Marina Kaljurand, afterward attacking the car of a Swedish diplomat in which they guessed Kaljurand was hiding. Speaking to Russia's regional Rosbalt news agency in the aftermath, Nashi activist Konstantin Goloskov boasted that he had "personally" taken part in the cyberattacks. The message was clear. The physical and digital attacks were combined toward the same end, and by the same people. They were a continuum, no more, no less.

Goloskov was careful to deny that any Moscow state offices had been used as bases for the attack. Instead, he pointed to an obscure breakaway region of Moldova called Transnistria. And this is where the puzzle became a riddle. Because Transnistria is a place that is no place. It is also a key. Part of the past that has become the blueprint for the future—of cyber war, crime, and international statecraft—for all of us. But to understand how it is a key, you first have to understand the joke hidden inside it.

In the aftermath of the Soviet collapse, Moldova, like neighboring Ukraine, became an independent post-Soviet republic. Within its borders there is a narrow slip of land, just 1,607 square miles in total, between the river Dniester and the Ukrainian border. That land is known as Transnistria. It soon launched a breakaway bid itself, this time from the independent Moldova of which it was part. From March to July, a small but vicious war of secession raged, in which the breakaway forces were backed first by "volunteers" from Russia, then by the former Soviet Fourteenth Guards army division. The cease-fire came with a tripartite agreement between Transnistria, Moldova, and Russia. Transnistria declared its own capital (Tiraspol) and its own laws, currency, parliament, and vehicle registration.

Transnistria became an oddity—a flickering, traveling presence in time and place. Today, it is not recognized as a country internationally—except, that is, by three other breakaway zones, post-Soviet "frozen conflict" countries propped up by Russia despite lacking global recognition: Abkhazia, Artsakh, and South Ossetia. Its national industries are somewhat mysterious, too. It is thought that its national gas and oil distribution company Transtiraspolgas is owned by Russian giant Gazprom, controlled as an arm of foreign policy by Vladimir Putin. However, Gazprom will neither confirm nor deny this.

Its web domains are unusual, too. Entities there register as .md for Moldova, .ru for Russia, or .su for the Soviet Union that ceased to exist three decades ago. This was the land where Russian-backed former president Igor Smirnov somehow netted 103.6 percent of the votes in a regional election. Where international ballot monitors are discouraged, but Russia acts as guarantor of fairness.

Through the 2000s, while I was tracking illicit shipments of arms, drugs, and other contraband across the globe from the former Soviet republics, Transnistria was infamous as an organized-crime and trafficking hub with links to Russia. It was suspected

by UN and nongovernmental organization monitors alike of playing a major role in small-arms trafficking and the production of
unmonitored weapons for illicit trade. Reports repeatedly cited it
as a drug transshipment point. But most of all, it was notorious for
its lack of transparency. Consignments enter and vanish, only to
reappear transformed into money and contraband, often trafficked
by vehicles operated by the Russian military.

To this day, plausible deniability and uncertainty remain its
global brands and chief exports. It is an in-joke among international
monitors, governments, law enforcement, and traffickers alike. To
do something "via Transnistria" is to do it in a way that the labels
are changed, the reporting does not exist, and only those in the
know—often high up in Russia—will ever get. To say that something you are being asked about happened "in Transnistria" is to
tap the side of your nose, and to wink theatrically, to those in on
the joke. "It is like telling a pal who asks where the HD TV that you
are carrying down the street from the scene of a riot came from,
that it 'fell off the back of a truck,'" muttered one UN monitor of
the traffic in arms and destabilizing commodities. "In this case, a
Russian truck."

Only this time, the joke was not intended for any audience in
Russia. It was played out for NATO, delivered with a bow and a
canned laugh via the official Russian Baltic news agency. For Nashi
to claim a part in the cyberattacks on a NATO member, and to say
it all happened because of Transnistria, was to ask NATO's reeling and frustrated investigators whether they recalled a similar
incident—a team of spontaneously operating schoolkid and student
hackers humiliating them in connection with a breakaway republic that lacked international recognition, like Kosovo, perhaps. The
punch line was that in Russia, NATO was picking on someone its
own size. And that Eastern Europe was still very much Russia's
patch. Cyber war, it turned out, was diplomacy by other means.

And still, the attacks continued. On April 30, 2007, users of the popular Russian blogging platform LiveJournal posted a long list, containing the email addresses of every one of Estonia's parliamentary deputies, along with step-by-step encouragement for everyone who saw the post to share the list and send multiple emails to the entire list containing the Russian phrase "Congratulations on Victory Day." Cue a two-day outage of Estonia's parliamentary mail mainframe.

Next to appear were sets of more complex instructions. Anonymous and pseudonymous users began to post lists of commands for Internet Control Message Protocol attacks—taking down the means by which routers communicate success or failure to send along the line—to message boards, blogs, and chat spaces across the Russian-language internet. The commands were sometimes laid out, sometimes held in batch files for Windows. Links and instructions popped up as comments under online newspaper articles, posts to military community boards, blogs on youth political sites, and early social media. The commands were received in a frenzy of execution.

A third wave peaked between May 3 and 9, 2007. It saw a further escalation of complexity. This time, the dominant method was SQL injection—a method whereby information input by a connection user is intercepted by a third party, then manipulated and sent on in its new form. Again, the recruitment of humans in sending out emails as part of an otherwise machine-led DDoS attack was an unusual step seen only once before, from the Serbian hackers during Kosovo. "We've also seen non-botnet tools (human-net, so to speak) that turned people's computers into packet sources," said Jose Nazario, a researcher at Arbor Security in the United States. The script uploaded as http://fipip.ru/raznoe/pingi.bat, which was being used to send ping floods to eighteen different Estonian sites, was a typical example. "This has been shared around on Russian language boards by various people," he reported.

As in the case of the Serbian hackers, the Russian diaspora got involved, as did those who suddenly felt drawn to intervene, with some signs that an "anti-NATO" alliance of interests was coalescing. "None of the sources we have analyzed from around the world show a clear line from Moscow to Tallinn," said Nazario. "Instead, it's from *everywhere around the world* to Estonia. There's no 'smoking gun' of a Russian government connection." Pressed to nail the attack to a government, he stopped short, conceding that in the hard evidence he could capture, "We see signs of Russian nationalism at work here, but no Russian government connection."

Russian news sites picked up this lack of a direct-command trail and turned it into exoneration. "Russia is not involved in DDoS attacks on Estonia," piped *PC News Russia* on May 6. "Nazario notes that the Russian government was not involved in the attacks," its anonymous journalist fibbed. "I won't point fingers," said one NATO official. "But these were not things done by a few individuals. This clearly bore the hallmarks of something concerted."

Everybody *knew* what Russia was doing. Everybody *knew* that its attacks were quotation marks from recent history, only turbocharged—a warning to NATO not to tread on Russia's backyard.

The West seemed as paralyzed as Estonia's internet was jammed. Almost a month later, as the attacks subsided, America and its NATO allies were still locked in negotiations about how to respond. America was still behind the curve. Its own Pentagon lawyers' indecision over Kosovo had seen the question of cyber aggression shelved.

Now the question rose again. Unlike NATO in Kosovo, someone was attacking civilian infrastructure wholesale. Was an attack like this an act of war? A war crime, even? And if not, what was it? Did it merit escalation and response? Nobody seemed to know. Nobody could agree.

"NATO does not define cyberattacks as a clear military action," shrugged Estonia's defense minister, Jaak Aaviksoo. "This means that the provisions of Article Five of the North Atlantic Treaty—in other words, collective self-defence—will not automatically be extended to the attacked country. Not a single NATO defence minister would define a cyberattack as a clear military action.... This question needs to be resolved in the near future."

Finally, a single suspect was arrested. A twenty-year-old ethnic Russian Estonian, a student in Tallinn called Dmitri Galushkevich, had used his home PC to join the attack, specifically to swamp the website of the ruling Estonian party. In January 2008, he was found guilty and fined $1,642. The frustration was palpable, not at the light sentence, but at the very idea that this one student had been—as was reported in the international media desperate for facts—"behind" the attack. He had, news websites reported, "launched" it.

"He wanted to show that he was against the removal of this bronze statue," sighed the Tallinn prosecutor's spokesperson Gerrit Maesalu. A pause, then he added, "At the moment, we don't have any other suspects."

On June 4, Vladimir Putin faced questions from a group of journalists at the conclusion of the G8 summit in Heiligendamm, East Germany. He was in simmering attack mode, in which he felt the need to draw the connection for everyone present between Russia's greatness during Soviet times and the need to tell NATO to back off.

Asked about NATO's membership by a German reporter, he compared its relationships to Russia's one-way control over the Communist world in the Cold War. "There was a joke in East Germany: How can you tell which of the telephones on Honecker's desk is the direct line to Moscow? Do you know this joke? The answer is: it's the one with only a receiver and no mouthpiece. It's the same with NATO. Only instead of the telephone going to Moscow, it's Washington." The room laughed with him. Then the journalist from Italy's *Corriere della Sera* asked about Russia's position on Serbia and Kosovo. For anybody who'd been tracking Moscow's cyberattacks on Estonia, the answer would have raised eyebrows sky-high.

"If we want to place the principle of a people's right to self-determination—the principle behind the Soviet Union's policy during the time when peoples were struggling to free themselves from colonialism—above the principle of territorial integrity," he replied, "this policy and this decision should be universal and should apply to all parts of the world, and at least to all parts of Europe. We are not convinced by our partners' statements to the effect that Kosovo is a unique case. There is nothing to suggest that the case of Kosovo is any different to that of South Ossetia, Abkhazia," he smiled, "or Transnistria."

Russian government officials were elated. They began to joke about the lack of suspects for NATO that this plausibly deniable form of networked cyber war and information war, coming together, had left. Sergei Markov, a state Duma deputy from Vladimir Putin's United Russia party, quipped: "About the cyberattack on Estonia... Don't worry, that attack was carried out by my assistant. I won't tell you his name though, because then he might not be able to get visas."

As the threat of retaliation and war receded, Konstantin Goloskov popped up again, in a role that has since become familiar as that of media surrogate or sideshow. He was, he said, taking credit for the attacks. In March 2009, he claimed the whole incident was, after all, initiated by him as part of a Nashi youth-group initiative. When he was asked about the odd claim that it had originated in Transnistria, he would only say that it was "a private joke."

Of the three places listed by Putin at the G8 presser that day in June 2007 as analogues to Kosovo, one punch line, "Transnistria," had already been delivered. The other two, South Ossetia and Abkhazia, were slow burners. It would take until the following summer for the Kremlin to unleash cyber war on Georgia under the spurious auspices of "providing military assistance to separatists" in South Ossetia and Abkhazia.

Their attacks were just the first wave of a wider action, preparing the ground for military intervention by sowing confusion and communications paralysis. Early on, they crashed and kept offline the official website of the Georgian government and all of its online communications. Under direction from the US government, Atlanta-based US service provider Tulip Systems intervened to try to keep official Georgian websites functioning, only to find its own servers in America attacked.

Tulip Systems' Tom Burling blamed a flood of bogus traffic that had been dispatched from Russia to crash the sites deliberately. The attacks were coming from mysterious servers in Russia and Turkey, with malicious visits outnumbering legitimate ones five thousand to one. Tulip brought in the FBI. Once again American admins and law enforcement found themselves working around the clock to defend against attacks that were diffuse in their origins, almost free to stage, and, ultimately, undefendable. The government site of the Republic of Georgia, and the site of Georgian president Mikheil Saakashvili, and a number of other online strategic targets for those who wanted to put the upstart, Western-leaning former Soviet republic back in its place remained down.

Visitors to the Georgian sites were rerouted through servers in Russia itself and in Turkey. The servers were controlled by the Russian Business Network. Almost immediately, it became clear that the attacks on Georgian sites were being conducted not by cyberwar divisions within any army or government facility, but through the RBN.

These servers had long been vectors for activity that matched the Russian government's goals for distributed cyber war, its positions, and its statements. Now, for the first time since Kosovo, the networks who controlled them were attacking the United States itself.

Again, America found itself frustrated. The FBI worked diligently, but encountered obfuscation, denial, and red herrings in its attempts to establish even something as basic as ownership of the servers. Meanwhile, the Russian government denied responsibility. The Russian Business Network sounded like it was private individuals, so why didn't the American authorities name them?

In fact, the network was well named. It is almost an emblem for the new form of cyber war and for Putinism as a whole. Russia analyst Dr. Mark Galeotti compares Russia's approach to cyber war and foreign policy after Kosovo to the TV show *Shark Tank*.

Putin's innovation was simply to embrace the bottom-up policy he'd witnessed in Kosovo. But rather than leave it to chance and circumstance, he simply let it be known that he was open to ideas. "It's really rather like an ongoing beauty contest of ideas that people will bring to him," says Galeotti.

If someone's doing something, and it makes its way to him through his network and sounds good, he'll say, okay I like that. Here's some cash, or here are some contacts, or just get on with it, you'll be allowed to do what you do to fund it. Don't keep in touch, just, you know, have my people let me know how it goes. And if that goes well, you have a policy. And eventually, you have something that resembles a strategy. It's going to be one that's not only cheap, and agile, and completely plausibly deniable. The thing is, it's also going to be extraordinarily effective. That's what Russia did. It trained them on CarderPlanet and with Russian Business Network, then deployed in Estonia, then Georgia. It's a strategic approach that is in fact an *antistrategy*.

For a Russia playing catch-up on the global internet revolution in the 2000s and without the necessary skill inside the army or intelligence services in anything like the numbers that would be required for a standing force of cyber warriors, this newly minted, hybrid criminal-security complex was the only game in town. Russia's young people were often highly educated and technically trained, but were also often living in conditions of extreme poverty in a Russia reeling from economic shock after economic shock under Gorbachev and Yeltsin. This perfect storm made the idea of siphoning money from the West through piracy, carding, cybercrime, and other digital means an incredibly popular option for those with access to an internet connection. In fact, Russia was replicating the conditions in 1990s Serbia.

In Georgia, the cyberattacks brought down the government systems, jammed military communications, killed telephone lines, and blocked broadcasts. The confusion and paralysis of government, military, and civil society absent mass online communication made the ground invasion that followed easy. Georgian soldiers and government functionaries found themselves waiting for clarity, for orders, for permission to act that never came.

This was a step on from Estonia. Russia was pointing its legions of self-financing auxiliary hackers as strategic forces, deployed in the name of defense of Russian interests. Again, its opponents had found themselves flat-footed. What the new form of cyberattacks did, by making themselves unattributable and blurring the line between what was civilian hacking or protest and what was a military operation, was to remove the clarity.

NATO had lost the initiative and found itself unable to react in any meaningful way. Investigations, expressions of diplomatic ire, and dark hints about Russian responsibility were fine things. But they were also admissions of impotence. The Western failure after 2000 to address these loose and plausibly deniable networks— instead covering up the extent to which it had been outmaneuvered, shutting down inquiries, and focusing on technological updates— had lost its momentum.

Even now, there was failure to grasp quite how fruitless it was to express displeasure to Russia's diplomatic corps, or even its leaders. Foreign minister Sergey Lavrov had been appointed by Putin in 2004, with, it was said, the brief to "be a stone in [the West's] shoe." He was the perfect tool for the job of directing and denying online activity—a winking, nudging prototype for the proxy figures that would coalesce around Trump, Johnson, and the online Right in the years to come, largely in response to the way in which Lavrov had succeeded in his dog whistles to online troll armies. The figure that emerges from diplomatic reports is of a pragmatist and someone who has no moral compass but is tactical and entrepreneurial in the ways big and small in which America could be trolled, inconvenienced, shown up, and outmaneuvered.

Under Lavrov, the Kremlin's and the Russian state's responses to accusations of sponsoring attacks were frustratingly bland, and they might have been disingenuous, but they also contained at least a kernel of truth. These cyberattacks were not the work of state actors. They were not following any orders given by the government. It was entirely plausible that the foreign minister believed they were nothing to do with Russia, strictly speaking. It made a mockery of the very concept of the United States applying diplomatic as well as military pressure. These were enemies who simply appeared, caused chaos, spread fear, and then melted back into the shadows. Their self-financing activities meant there was no paper, financial, or data trail tying them to Russian state structures.

The sense of having stumbled upon something game-changing swept through Russian networks, from embassies to the Kremlin. In their internet-choked circumstances, lagging light-years behind the American digital and military juggernaut, the Serbian model had enabled them to punch above their weight, and to do so deniably, and in a way that was almost entirely self-financing. "That was most pleasing on the inside of the Russian government and military, no doubt about it," says Dr. Mark Galeotti. "If Russians have a specific genius, it is to fuck and do over anyone and everyone who has tried to impose or lord it over them, and that was a prime example. This, though it was the industrialisation at scale of something they had seen in Kosovo, was hailed as another example. And frankly, why stop there? It had worked in Estonia and Georgia. They thought perhaps it would work in Ukraine, as Russia re-established its presence on the old Soviet doorstep. But even the West itself, had we but known."

Cyber war was the new game for remaking the world's strategic blocs of influence. It could succeed where open confrontation failed. Trolling was the new patrolling.

But if Russia was using the cyber war to stage its own comeback from the dead, it had company.

Chapter 16

Storms and Deserts

The world was growing heavy with illicit cyber networks, spinning out like galaxies from the big bang of millennium Belgrade. Behind closed doors, Western militaries and governments were increasingly anxious, not just about their potential affiliations—the prospect of another Estonia or Georgia—but about the very free-floating quality that sustained them.

Indeed, membership of different hacker networks was no longer clear-cut. Rather than the "family" model of organized crime, the new breed of hackers saw their actions in terms of alignment, in the same way one might "join" a subreddit or chat room. They friended and unfriended, joined and left, collected memberships of hacker networks ad hoc, curating portfolio identities—the individual was the brand, and hacking activity was the proto–social network through which they moved. If it was a new way of forming criminal associations—ephemeral and floating, rather than earned and trusted—it also made patterns and motivations frustratingly difficult to pin down. Former members of the Black Hand and other Belgrade teens moved into new groups as the 2000s drew to a close, splitting and coalescing in ways that seemed driven as much by excitement and image as mission, in the same way that music fans might move to a new scene.

One such hot scene was Anonymous, formed in 2003 on the 4chan boards and taking its name from the default posting of new content to the /b/ board as from "Anonymous," posters quickly coalescing around the idea that all the "Anons" on the internet made a faceless yet powerful collective. Its standard ops were pranks and online flash mobs—one such against Finnish game site Habbo Hotel saw its Anonymous profiles blocking and reporting regular users—which became popular and began attracting more and more participants. By 2008, it was styling itself both as a source of fun and as a vigilante organization. Flash mobs and ping attacks began aiming to even up the score on oppressive regimes, too powerful businesses, and criminal organizations such as websites trading in child pornography. The name of its offshoot Lulzsec seemed to poke fun at the very idea of the West's idea of cybersecurity.

Meanwhile, Wikileaks, its early web presence established in Iceland in 2006, had added to American discomfort in the aftermath of the Estonian cyberattacks. That summer, it had released documents showing the gravy train of expenses and contracts that formed around the coalition's invasion of Afghanistan, and in November it published the operating-procedures manual for Guantánamo Bay prison, containing instructions on how to psychologically break prisoners, intimidate them with military dogs, and deal with hunger strikes. While journalists and activists cheered its first releases, for the US and UK military and intelligence communities, it was doing exactly what Anti-Smyser-1 had done with the Kosovo rules of engagement. By Trojans or leakers, its business was illicitly obtaining and publishing documents that were proof of what it saw as Western governments' mendacity, hypocrisy, and instinctive drive toward secrecy and obscurity. In April 2010, it published *Collateral Murder*, a release of footage from a July 12, 2007, US airstrike on Baghdad in which US aircrews gunned down Iraqi Reuters journalists and other civilians. *Collateral Murder* was just the tip of the iceberg.

It's impossible to see the reaction to *Collateral Murder*—from a thirty-five-year prison sentence for leaker Private Chelsea Manning, through years of embargo and prosecution of Wikileaks—as anything but a belated reaction to Kosovo. The penny had finally dropped with the US military and its allies.

In tech solutionism and siloed thinking, they had backed the wrong horse. Now they saw it. Cyber war was not about the protection of military infrastructure or the ability to degrade the enemy's weapons. It was about degrading the enemy's ability to function at all—through information war, direct assaults, draining resources through the sowing of chaos, terror, mistrust in institutions, and economic damage.

Year after year, the United States and its allies were being plundered. In 2007 alone, the year Estonia was hacked, the US Department of Defense "lost" between 25 and 27 terabytes of data from its systems—about five thousand DVDs of information, a huge amount at that time, greater than some European nations' total of digitally held data. That data was not being lost to formal acts of war, but to slow attrition through incursions.

Yet still they needed structure, just as they continued to chase people through Afghanistan and Iraq they called "commanders," "lieutenants," and "high-ranking figures" in al-Qaeda. Military chiefs briefed and sounded alarms almost continually about the threat of a "digital Pearl Harbor," or "digital 9/11," all the while failing to spot that the threat had already materialized and was slowly compromising American cyber supremacy, not to mention eroding its strategic and military advantages.

Even NATO insiders were tearing their hair out. In the wake of the Tbilisi attacks, staff at its Joint Advanced Distributed Learning Center were exasperated by the alliance's failure to expand its definition of war for the cyber arena. "Even though it might not be NATO's mission to classify and define everything in cyberspace," read one report, "it *is* the alliance's role to prevent crises, manage conflicts, and defend one another against attacks, including against new threats."

"Cybercrime is different from cyberwar," concluded another. "But the difference is only in the motivations of those behind them." In his own online operations to unmask members of Anonymous and its offshoot Lulzsec in the United States and United Kingdom, pro-America hacker J35t3r drew the distinction between what individual members of hacker collectives may think they are doing and what those who point them toward targets are doing. How, he asked, did they know who their fellow Anons were? Could they be sure they weren't being used?

FBI and MI5 unease about groups such as Anonymous morphing into a freebooting, grievance-fueled online vigilante hacking network that could be groomed, diverted, and ultimately directed by Russia, Iran, and other strategic opponents of the United States blossomed into open briefings. The West was finally cottoning on to the thing that had spooked Mirjana Drakulic in the flickering blue of the Belgrade hacking room more than a decade previously. The aftermath of any mission is simply a cadre of skilled-up hackers who are open to new motivations. And motivations, in the age of the hashtag, were everywhere.

This point was borne out in March 2011, when the Black Hand reemerged—not as a nationalist hacker group at all, nor as the criminal collective they had morphed into, but as a free-floating cyber army for hire in the midst of one of the worst conflicts of the Arab Spring.

On December 29, 2010, a Tunisian market-stall trader named Mohamed Bouazizi had doused his clothes in gasoline and set himself on fire to protest his harassment by state officials. It sparked a wave of protests, first through North Africa with Egypt and Morocco. By January the wave had spread to the Middle East, with Oman, Jordan, and Syria, in February Bahrain, Kuwait, Iraq, and Libya. Social media and email groups became central to the worsening civil conflicts, groups not just organizing in ways that governments found difficult to control, but using it as the Serbian Angels had against NATO, quickly debunking government claims about police actions with from-the-ground photographs and video that spread quickly around the world.

As one of the last to tip, Colonel Muammar Gaddafi's Libya had some time to prepare. Gaddafi's advisers knew what was coming and saw the crucial role played by online communications networks among the rebels and protesters. The problem was, even though they saw it coming, they had no way to counter that movement.

But they knew where they could borrow one. And so began the strange second life of the Black Hand as a global franchise bringing cyber war to bear on the Muslim world.

Libya-Yugoslavia relations went back to the Non-Aligned Movement under Tito. After Gaddafi's 1969 coup brought him to power, the two countries became thriving partners in both the licit and the illicit trades in arms and technology. Gaddafi had personally led UN and diplomatic pressure against the NATO bombardment of Serbia during Kosovo; alongside Vladimir Putin, he had been one of a small band of leaders—a vanishingly small fourteen worldwide—who filed letters of opposition to Kosovar independence at the International Court of Justice. Going into the Arab Spring, the links of dark finance and arms deals between the two pirate states remained strong, and it was both a thank-you and a marketing exercise that had seen Serbia send units from its armed forces to perform at a grand display in Tripoli in 2009 for Gaddafi's fortieth anniversary in power. The Black Hand's journey from autonomous group at the outset of the 2000s to fully fledged Serbian military proxy had kept it unusually close to power in Belgrade. Gaddafi knew who to call to get access to its ready-made, highly exportable package of connections and know-how. Illicit Ilyushin-76 flights to Libyan desert airstrips outside Benghazi and Tripoli itself were already operating a thriving trade in bullion, cash, narcotics, technology, arms, and expertise between the two outlier states and old allies. Libyan high command was well aware of the importance of irregular support in the global court of public opinion, and nobody had harnessed that force better than the Black Hand.

While prep time was short, it made it simpler that the enemy was a familiar one. On March 17, 2011, the United Nations Security Council had passed Resolution 1973. It established Libyan airspace as a no-fly zone and authorized the "robust" enforcement by member states of Resolution 1970's arms embargo against Gaddafi's Libyan regime. It also gave UN states the authorization "to take all necessary measures...to protect civilians and civilian populated areas under threat of attack in the Libyan Arab Jamahiriya, including Benghazi, while excluding a foreign occupation force of any form on any part of Libyan territory."

The United States wasted no time. President Obama initiated Operation Odyssey Dawn on March 19, the flight orders flying from the final minutes of a UN Security Council meeting in Paris. Odyssey Dawn's initial goal was to enforce a no-fly zone and to degrade President Muammar Gaddafi's Libyan army forces, preventing them from attacking the rebel opposition Libyan Youth Movement and massacring civilians (as Gaddafi had threatened to do, in a speech that was swiftly sampled over a dance beat by an internet user, turned into a viral meme, and shared around the world by an opposition that knew how to get traction). French fighter jets screamed over the scorched African desert toward Benghazi; US and UK forces followed up with missile strikes on Tripoli from warships, while submarines launched Cruise Tomahawks. Then came a second wave of aircraft, streaking down to obliterate Gaddafi's ground forces outside Benghazi. But what had started as a UN mission quickly got morphed. By March 30, it was a NATO operation, renamed Operation Unified Protector.

The Black Hand was not just seen as a potential savior by Gaddafi. It also got his allies out of a sticky patch. In doing so, it ushered in a new age of proxy wars, fought by hackers on behalf of allies and third parties whose support had to remain deniable.

The Serbian government, a great beneficiary of the continued sanctions-busting arms trade with Libya, was in something of a pickle. It could neither openly join nor oppose the attacks. Over the initial days of the crisis, Serbia's foreign minister insisted to the Western media that he fully supported Libya's territorial integrity and sovereignty and deplored any intervention. Often within the same breath, he had to point out that he also supported the UN Security Council's decision to intervene. It was no time for the rogue Balkan state gradually coming back in from the international cold to be forming any kind of axis with a global outlaw and dictator who was attacking his own people, whose days were clearly numbered, and who seemed determined to fight NATO.

In the Black Hand, Gaddafi's Serbian allies had a war-hardened generation of youthful idealists who had become a global brand as an army of cyber mercenaries.

First came the wave of information war. Suddenly, in February, in what seemed to be a coordinated fashion, hundreds of pages and profiles appeared online. In addition to the emails and blogger sites were now Facebook, Twitter, MySpace, YouTube, LiveJournal, and other social platforms—all enlisting support for Gaddafi and making his case as an icon of solidarity with those who "resist aggression" globally. Their posts read:

- "Gaddafi is fighting against the people who ruined our childhood."
- "Gaddafi sent oil to us while we were under sanctions."
- "Gaddafi did not recognize the independence of Kosovo and was the first to rebel."
- "After the bombing in '99, Gaddafi sent money to help our country recover."
- "Gaddafi gave our people jobs when we had nothing to eat here."

Others were marketed at a different, more diffuse, audiences. Some targeted the world's discontented online young in the wake of the credit crunch and global financial crisis with depictions of Gaddafi's head in the style of the Che Guevara stencil and the legend "Colonel, win for all of us!" The creatives amplified memes of American force allied with old enemies, conspiracy theories, and anti-Semitic tropes. George Soros had been one of Slobodan Milošević's bogeymen in the 1990s wars because his Open Democracy foundation had given grants to dissidents. Now here he was again, cast as a puppet master trying to keep Muslim leaders down. Twitter was subjected to wave after wave of huge bot activity, in which identical posts slammed the West's double standards on words the American NATO briefings had kept returning to, such as "freedom." These campaigns—seemingly spontaneous, but coordinated in timing and design—often drew on the same templates they had a decade before when posting about Slobodan Milošević, whom they recast as a freedom fighter who'd stood against NATO for the benefit of the downtrodden of the world. The difference was in the level of coordination. The Kosovo bombardment had seen an entire new ecosystem kick into life. Now, more than a decade later, that ecosystem was established, had spread, and was dense with life and directable purpose. The activity now sprang up readily in a variety of languages and platforms, using the latest social marketing techniques—from live monitoring and hijacking popular hashtags to bot networks and spending on amplified posts—to cut through to audiences out there, among the world's online disengaged and disaffected. It was a warning of what was coming our way.

Then came denial-of-service attacks and Trojan malware. Libyan rebels and areas under their control found their transport, military capability, telecommunications, and broadcasting crippled. "Lights on the runways of the airport and aircraft carriers have been turned off," enthused the Serbian daily newspaper *Novosti*. "Data is either unavailable or inaccurate. Navigation, internet and telephones are not working." It named the two Serbian nationalist hacker brands Black Hand and C1337ORG as being behind the attacks.

"Thousands of internet users from Serbia attack and take down our sites every day," said Mohamed al-Sabah, director of communications for rebel army the Libyan Youth Movement. "Or they are so congested with anti-NATO and EU slogans that they are completely unusable."

Serbian cyber-defense specialist Milan Kovačević watched the attacks—information war, denial of service, and pinpoint strikes against Libyan Youth Movement infrastructure—with the mounting feeling that the support went further than simply reassembling the Belgrade Hackers or giving the Black Hand targets and resources. Kovačević, who had authored Serb government books on hackers, cryptography, and digital banking, knew that the greatest weakness in any system is its human component. He had been warning Serbia's burgeoning citizen cyber army for years that brute force and numbers were fine for attacks focused on spectacle and inconvenience, but military systems were tougher nuts to crack without someone working on the inside to leak authorizations, passwords, and vulnerabilities. He concluded that the more specifically targeted cyberattacks against the Libyan resistance had to have been carried out with the support of an insider among the rebels. They clearly had someone there, among them, who was telling the Serbian hackers where, and how, to attack.

It all sounded rather familiar from my own questioning at the hands of British military intelligence and the Woozles briefed by NATO in 2000. If there was an insider, that would explain the continual leaks—the way the attackers always seemed to have information that helped them negotiate access. The hunt for this mysterious insider was on among the rebel forces, just as it had been for General Wesley Clark, NATO, and the Pentagon a decade earlier.

One giveaway in this case was Kovačević himself. He was the

same Serbian government figure who after the Belgrade hackers' strikes under the Kosovo bombardment had floated the idea of a Serbian "national electronic defense force" made of irregular hackers who could be called on to intercept and knock out NATO's GPS positioning and communications infrastructure. Someone was inside the Libyan rebels' systems all right, but it wasn't one of the rebels giving away their secrets. The Black Hand's hackers in the Balkans and worldwide had been breaking into their communications on a nightly basis and using their knowledge to sow confusion among the rebel forces, as well as mistrust in their own genuine communications.

The problem for the West was that the Black Hand's infiltration was now obscure in terms not just of its patronage, but of its objectives too. These were not Libyans protesting a bombardment, but easily operationalized online antagonists who could be pointed at anything at all.

This was an overseas third-party force, effectively set upon NATO and whatever course it was tacking—a loose international cadre of cyber mercenaries. Because their conflict activities were carried out online—even if they did target physical infrastructure and expose military positions—they escaped the scrutiny due to soldiers of fortune, from Libya to later engagements working on behalf of Russia and President Assad's forces in Syria. This group represented a fundamental mutation from the idea of national hacker armies. It was now a free-floating group of hackers and information warriors, and it could be pointed through the antagonistic energies of its core members toward almost any cause. In this, it was akin to mercenary forces that crop up in conflict zones in which their sponsors must appear to have no business—to send no official troops or to interfere—but require plausibly deniable actors on the ground to secure their interests.

Founded in 1984, amid the Cold War's Hollywood-induced *WarGames* panic and Yugoslav computer fever, Belgrade's Institute for Strategic Research holds the brief to apply the latest science and technology to the fields of defense and security. In effect, it is today the country's combination of RAND and DARPA. The institute— formerly the Institute of War Skills—specializes in planning for contemporary conflict, with the emphasis on information and technological warfare. It lists as its key stakeholders three faculties at the Belgrade University: the Faculty of Political Sciences, the Faculty of Security, and the Drakulices' faculty, Organizational Sciences. And that spring, its rooms and terminals had been unusually busy. One man especially was watching events with interest.

A lively young officer with smiling eyes and a flick of dark brown hair, Colonel Dejan Vuletić is the army's liaison point for hacker groups. He gained his PhD in cybercrime at the Belgrade University, studying under the tutelage of Dr. Mirjana Drakulic and Ratimir Drakulic from 2000 to 2004, and, by 2011, he was one of the few government employees who remained connected to the Belgrade hacker group and the Black Hand. He was also considered his military's chief authority in cyber and information warfare. Since 2004 when he joined as a captain earmarked for great things, he had been a researcher and program manager for cyber war at the institute. He was fascinated by the way in which the Black Hand's networked force was at that moment impacting global history and frustrating a NATO force and its in-country allies in Libya, using the same unsophisticated methods it had a decade earlier.

It was almost comical. They were costing the government hardly any money, and incurring zero risk, but were inflicting damage, confusion, and cost on the combined NATO and rebel war effort in Libya. For all its mastery of the high-tech world, America seemed stuck in its posture, holding up its dukes and demanding its militarily weaker opponents come out, show themselves, and fight fair.

More than a decade on from the CIA's finding for President Clinton, the US State Department was continuing to mull whether cyber activities fell within the scope of any UN charter or international law governing "use of force." It would not be until 2012 that it would issue its verdict that cyber activities counted as force only if they resulted in death, injury, or significant destruction, such as opening a dam and causing floods or downing aircraft by interfering with air-traffic control. Even a full decade into the War on Terror, as Wikileaks turned the leveraging of information flows into an art and Anonymous and Lulzsec coalesced around targets, the State Department could not quite plan for a theater of conflict that was in fact a gray area, where chains of command ceded to loose, flat networks operating on patronage and mutual benefit, one in which attribution—finding out who was behind an attack—was not just difficult, but often simply fruitless.

Instead—in a pattern that has shown itself time and again—a broad goal is defined; a group primed, incentivized, and enabled; and a host of potential desirable outcomes generated and promoted among groups whose participation can come in exchange for any number of currencies, from grievance to favor, from money to freedom.

Estimates from network admins inside Libya during the bombardment had more than fifty thousand cyber warriors from inside Serbia itself joining the attacks on the rebel army's digital infrastructure and communications. It is a number so huge as to be fantastical; even Serbian intelligence chiefs were quick to point out how absurd fifty thousand hackers was, given the population of just over seven million and access to the internet of around 42 percent. It would have made one in sixty internet users a pro-Gaddafi hacker taking on NATO.

"Some of our hackers are really behind the attacks on the sites through which the Libyan rebels communicate," corrected Milan Kovačević. "These are two hacker groups involved—C1337ORG and Black Hand. But there is no way the number is 50,000 *Serbian* attackers. Ours are part of the international team. A good proportion of the attackers are actually foreigners hiding behind the internet addresses of ordinary users from Serbia."

The Black Hand was never just a brand for the people who were original members. It had become a global franchise. The pioneers of the untouchable, impromptu citizen cyber army had turned themselves into a highly prestigious global marque of rebellion against NATO; now the country itself was serving America's enemies as something like one gigantic physical VPN. It was cloaking attacks against Western allies by enemies of America on a massive scale.

It was the first global warning that America's strategic opponents were packaging and producing their own cyber-war brands for the global public. In the years to come, China would take this design, like so much else, and scale it up to irresistible proportions before letting it flood the world.

Yet in America's reliance on the things in which it was master— the resolutions, the declarations, the military might—it remained seemingly all but oblivious to the strange, invisible beings who traveled the wires and currents of the American internet.

And all the while, hidden out there in plain sight, America's strategic opponents were experimenting with new ways to hothouse and cultivate armies of these beings. On the streets, in specially equipped jail colonies, in universities and schools, the next great generation of citizen cyber mercenaries was rising to challenge the West. And the story of their sponsors' ongoing tense relationship of deniable influence over them is told by the trajectory of one of the best, brightest, and most dangerous.

Chapter 17

The Google Archipelago

Miloš Čujović was a skinny sixteen-year-old with dark hair from Belgrade when the bombs fell.

As Zoran Rosic watched the burning factories across the river reflect in the windows of the tower blocks, "Cujka," as his friends called him, was a few streets away. As the noises subsided, he sat at his desk and booted up the computer his army father had given him. He felt calm, because his overactive mind now had a focus. In that moment of chaos and noise, he had direction. It was a feeling he would find himself chasing again and again over the coming decades.

Teenage Miloš had a face that was equal parts young David Duchovny and adult David Schwimmer. Born in 1984 into a country whose great and only hope had been computing, his father, Braco, had worked for the Yugoslav military in Slovenia. Braco Čujović was a man of high-up connections, in the military and the intelligence services. And if by the time Miloš was eight years old the country was embroiled in the murderous Balkan wars, their effects on his life were refracted through the economy and his father's colleagues and friends.

The family spent Miloš's early years on intelligence work abroad that saw the young computer whiz kid living in Switzerland and the Middle East, mastering English and an uncanny variety of its accents before returning to Belgrade. They were well off by

Yugoslav standards, and by those standards they also enjoyed stability and a global outlook, with friends and connections overseas, a whitewashed family house with shutters for the summer, a car, and well-tended hedges out front. It was a lifestyle one would recognize from any well-heeled American suburb.

Čujović was not one of the jocks, but he was spectacularly bright. He got consistently high grades and spoke six languages. His gift for detail-perfect impressions of teachers and other kids alike kept him from getting beaten up, and his way with words earned him the reputation of being a charmer. If he was a little too eager to court approval from the wrong peers, he was still young. The teachers felt he had a bright future in technology or military intelligence.

Like so many young people, Kosovo was a disruption to his early years. Čujović became part of a hacking circle that—though possibly unknown to him at first—included some of the hackers who hung around Belgrade University. The government network had raised the young hackers as Robin Hoods, with America as the sheriff of Nottingham. Their political, military, and law-enforcement patronage had given them a sense of absolute invulnerability. Their work had encouraged daring and inventiveness. Miloš himself brought a natural flair for taking on roles and for uncanny mimicry.

Friends had seen him haunting the strange twenty-four-hour computer sessions. The stuff they had done, making memes, getting inside websites, thinking and talking like admins, had been exciting. But for him, being hailed as a hero was *addictive*. He'd discovered that his primary skill was not necessarily to do with software or technology, at about the same time as the intelligence officers monitoring the hackers had noticed too.

"His method," says Serbia's chief cybercrime prosecutor, Branko Stamenković, "was to play with people's minds. He is not a hacker in the way that most people—particularly in the West—understand the term. He is not passionate about code, or some nerd guy. It is his tool, of course, and he is probably one of the leading exponents we have in terms of exploiting vulnerabilities. His hardware is computers, but his software is your psychology." Marko Vešović, a crime reporter who's been following his trail through governments and missions for more than a decade, puts it more succinctly: "Miloš Čujović doesn't just hack computer systems. Miloš Čujović hacks *people*."

The army and the police, the Ministry of Information, and the intelligence services all began coming to him with special jobs. He always took them. He had felt most alive in the heat of the hacking and cyber-war ops, working off the others, thinking on his feet. It calmed his apparent ADHD, liberated him from the hunger for excitement, gave him the stillness he craved. But the bombardment had ended, and it seemed to be Miloš who suffered from lack of direction after the cease-fire. Like a gambler elated by the first high, when the war finished he found he couldn't. "Something in him stopped like a broken watch at 17," says one former hacker.

It was the blessing and the curse of Čujović and his generation of Eastern European hackers that they had cyberspace to retreat into. The authorities hothoused his talents, so that he became infamous and cash rich. But like a Soviet Olympian discovering life after steroids, it was never going to go smoothly.

According to his associates, he was headhunted by American companies and approached by Western intelligence amid the broken embers of Belgrade. But if he was, the now seventeen-year-old Miloš did not leave the country for any of the possible futures on offer. He was already an in-demand figure within the circles of the Black Hand and the Serbian intelligence services increasingly aligned with Russia and China.

He is said to have pinged between work for the authorities, himself, collabs with members of overseas networks like RBN, and domestic organized crime. The security services saw him and his generation as geese that laid golden eggs. They were the perfect army. Best of all, they were gratis to employ.

Čujović quickly developed a specialty. He became a doppelgänger, accessing state secrets and Swiss bullion vaults using social engineering—his gift for languages, details, and mimicry—and his gift for accessing hard drives through the dark-web networks of peer-to-peer sites like LimeWire. The incidental, invisible detritus of our online existences—soldiers, intelligence officers, laboratory heads, lawyers, private citizens—became his passport into the lives of others. He would assemble full identities, access codes, passports, bank statements, classified intelligence files, weapons systems. It was the internet's own dark matter, the limitless mass of telltale data. And the more he combed through the ether of the internet through the 2000s, the more Čujović began to realize that global law enforcement was entirely oblivious to what he was doing. This strange floating ephemera of the internet fell outside of the realm of things laws were made for. America was denying his existence, and Serbia itself had studiously avoided bringing in any laws whatsoever governing cyber war or online crime.

The hacker prodigy's favorite pastime in his apartment was long nocturnal hours of probing, casting around, testing and checking for the next victim. He could do it high just as well as—maybe even better than—straight. His favorite hunting ground was LimeWire and other file-sharing platforms—Bearshare, Kazaa, and the rest of the Napster successors.

By 2003, file sharing and enterprise-wide systems had opened up hard drives and servers on a global network. Now their leakage, their unwitting shares, winked at him from accidental results and mistyped queries, leaks from hard drives, automatically generated logs, autosaves, and oversights. It was the very CO_2 of our digital existence. And it was everywhere. Almost all of it, even when you looked directly at it, was meaningless. But among the waste data was the stuff that opened up the most closely guarded secrets of individual lives, corporations, and nation-states around the world.

As the likes of Napster and LimeWire became globally notorious around the turn of the millennium, new branches of internet law enforcement sprang up dedicated to policing and monitoring them. US lawyers for rock bands and Hollywood movie studios were crawling all over these same file-sharing platforms, seeking and taking down copyright material. Metallica and Madonna both fought Napster and LimeWire in- and outside of the courts, putting the spotlight on file sharing and dark networks.

Yet incredibly, until Robert Boback's visit to Washington, the security threat inherent in these file-sharing platforms remained below US defense and intelligence radar. Čujović and his cohorts were stunned that the Americans could see no further than taking down copyrighted IP, while all along the strange, incoherent mass of incidental leakage of individuals', corporations', military, and government private files went completely unobserved.

It didn't show up in most searches of the platforms, and it if did show up, it just looked like useless gobbledygook. Yet here were html documents, notes, word processor files, spreadsheets pages long, stuffed with stolen credit-card numbers and bank-account data. Then there were large caches of files leaked and radiated by employees of governments and security services. It was easy to use it if you wanted. You just had to know what you were looking for and have the smarts to work out which locks out there the keys you might be able to assemble would fit.

Čujović began spending his days online. He was freelance, like a journalist, being given briefs for fact-finding jobs. Only those jobs involved breaking into government systems in the United States. They might come from criminal networks, or from the Serbian government, intelligence, and law enforcement. In any case, the groups overlapped and were often the same people. He lived high off the plunder, too—the security agencies allowed him to do what he wanted, so long as he didn't get any big ideas.

That was the tricky part. One day in 2003, in the grimy Čukarica suburb of Belgrade, police cars converged around Čujović's home, machine guns drawn. The cops forced their way in, to find the nineteen-year-old still sitting at his computer, executing commands. The hallways into the apartment were so crammed with priceless specialist objects that American citizens had been reporting missing to the FBI and others that the raiding party had to slow down and pick their way through. Here were four electric guitars—a couple of $2,000 types, all the way up to a vintage 1950s Gibson Les Paul valued at $25,000, Kawasaki Ninja motorbikes, a BMW, musical equipment, video cameras, tech, and everywhere cash. And among it all, stacks upon stacks of ownership certificates, cargo bills, and customs declaration documents. The goods were arriving so thick and fast that even while the raid officers bagged goods, they realized more were descending to land out at the airport. During the search of his apartment, police found paperwork for a consignment arriving later that same day. A Lufthansa cargo flight was landing at Belgrade airport, the hold containing a motorbike— a Kawasaki ZX9R from Oregon, racing specification. A unit was scrambled and quickly dispatched by squad car to the Belgrade airport, and there it was. A racing motorbike worth tens of thousands, in its transport cage. There was no sign of the BMW beyond some transportation documents, and a host of other treasures were missing whose presence in the apartment prior to the raid they inferred from the papers they'd seized.

While Miloš Čujović had been assembling a couple of false identities in American online communities, he noticed that there was a community in the United States trading in vintage electric guitars, Fender Stratocasters, Gibson Les Pauls, all being traded with payment through an escrow service. These services offered for a fee to guarantee that Person A paid a certain amount of the money through their account to Person B. Then Person B would release the item to Person A. The escrow was the bank of high-value remote. purchases, from condos to Lamborghinis. Čujović would arrange to buy goods, recommending a real provider called EscrowEurope. It was a reputable company, so they were happy. They registered with EscrowEurope, and in due course, they received notification from them that the money had been remitted and was waiting for them, so they knew payment had been made, and at that point they sent the goods.

Even when Čujović went quiet, dropping off from messaging on the guitar forum and not responding to emails, they figured he had gotten his stuff, so there was no issue there, and they corresponded with EscrowEurope, which had their funds safely held, and diligently followed its policies for inquiring about funds, dealing with different departments when necessary, or admins in the case of delayed comms. "The thing was," sighs prosecutor Branko Stamenković, who organized the police raid, "he *was* Escrow-Europe. He was the admin. He was the bank guarantor. He was *everything*. He had set it up as an online sting."

His false site was EscrowEurope.net, not EscrowEurope.com. The website was an exact copy—complete with Visa, American Express, and Mastercard logos. The domain was registered by Čujović, listing the same apartment as the air-freight documents, to which it is estimated that several hundred thousands of dollars' worth of luxury cars and racing motorcycles, classic guitars, hi-fi equipment, home theater, recording equipment, and antiques made their way.

The police identified five accomplices from records of transactions, emails, and phone records. They included a member of a known organized-crime syndicate and a government employee. But there were some odd anomalies to the bust. Čujović's computer was seized, but when the forensics team came to examine his hard drive, its contents had been erased. Someone had reformatted it while the hacker was in custody. Then there was an odd exchange at the pretrial hearing. Speaking to the judge, Čujović had claimed, "The whole thing was arranged by the police themselves." At one point, the hacker himself simply said, "I don't understand. We didn't do anything that we weren't asked to."

His time in prison was made pleasant, and it was brief. Within a matter of hours of leaving custody in 2004, he was back in business. He looked like a skinny kid, but he talked like a movie star, and this was a country in need of Robin Hoods and folk heroes who could fuck the West back.

Čujović became a star—part Artful Dodger, part Scarlet Pimpernel, and a hot character for the gossip-hungry Balkan tabloids. By 2005, he was talked of as the hacker with links to the Balkan security services. Everybody knew him, and everyone knew he drained American secrets for the government. He swigged Courvoisier in glamorous starlets' hit pop videos; he robbed Swiss banks. The paparazzi loved him. Like the sports cars he blasted through the cocaine-blizzard nights on the highways of Eastern Europe, anti-US cyber mercenary Miloš Čujović was a dandy Information Superhighwayman.

He was like a one-man RBN, a phenomenon. He was also drawing too much attention, making a lot of people uncomfortable. And then, in the spring of 2006, he just vanished. The next time he was seen, in the summer, three fingers on his left hand were missing.

The young Serb hacker never talked about how he was mutilated, but others did. It was reported that he'd been ignoring warnings from the security services, and it was they, his sponsors in the army and government, who had made the decision to make an example of him. There were other rumors. He'd played with fire unwisely, wrote the newspaper *Kurir*. "Miloš tried to light a large Russian-made firecracker, which exploded in his hand." The anonymous report was unusual in its description of the firework's provenance and was widely seen as a coded message not to fuck the Serbian intelligence services over by playing them off with the Russians. Newspaper *Vijesti* implied that the Black Hand was involved. "Although he is known to us as a top hacker, we have information that a certain Belgrade team had been let down in dealings with him, and that they tortured him and cut off three fingers on his hand." No investigation was ever launched by the authorities. Čujović fled from the hospital and vanished. His apartment was empty. His network went dark. The tabloid-star veteran of the anti-NATO hacks, just into his twenties and the intelligence services' dark horse in the race to penetrate American security services through the back door of its human capital, had simply disappeared.

As it turned out, he had been spirited away to Podgorica, the capital of the wild coastal neighbor state Montenegro, taking his girlfriend at the time, the mother of his child, with him. "I needed to get away from Belgrade" was all he would say when asked what happened. He had reportedly been placed in something like a witness-protection program by the Serbian authorities. Only instead of a star witness, Čujović was a secret weapon. The plan was that he would take it easy, go back underground, lay off the tabloid life, and stop messing with rival intelligence services. He rented a large apartment inside the secure perimeter of the old Podgorica military airbase, where he was installed with computers, phones, and high-quality connections. He was supposed to get back to work, as his country's virtual mole inside computer systems from Washington, DC, to Brussels, and Beijing to Moscow. In this secure apartment, the goose would lay on demand—a battery fowl farmed for state secrets.

It was a cunning plan. It was also a terrible mistake. Čujović's handlers hadn't considered the casinos, the sun-kissed beach girls, and the long, cool drinks of the Montenegrin Riviera.

By the time Čujović had collapsed onto his bed in the airport apartment for the first time, the airfield was already a notorious transshipment hub for illicit cargo. Arms, heroin, cocaine, cash, and people made their way in and out, and the apartments around the airfield were widely regarded as transshipment safe houses. They were places where you were as likely to find an empty suite full of suitcases of cash or fugitives as fugitives under the protection of the secret police.

Podgorica is proud of its somewhat sketchy, sly reputation. Today, busy Bokeska Street is home to a reconstructed English-style pub called the Nag's Head. It is named in tribute to the fictitious pub in South London's then-down-at-heel Peckham from a long-running BBC sitcom called *Only Fools and Horses*. In the show, the Nag's Head pub is where its small-time South London criminal protagonists, brothers Delboy and Rodney Trotter, fence stolen goods and cook up new schemes with other Artful Dodger types each episode. Another popular bar in second city Niksic is simply called the Delboy. Čujović had found his tribe, quickly connecting with the underground there.

Through the late 2000s and early 2010s, the airport itself had become known as a major transshipment hub for dirty cargo— illicit Russian and Ukrainian arms flights and shipments of munitions and cash to Turkey, North Africa, and the Middle East. In this time period, big-money clients began drifting in their yachts into the picturesque Montenegrin harbors close by, among them a Russian oligarch named Oleg Deripaska who sat at Putin's right hand as his most trusted confidant. Another was an American hustler for the Republican Party by the name of Paul Manafort whose aide Konstantin Kilimnik had ties to Russian intelligence. The Russians held parties along the Riviera in which they were introduced to a parade of "operators" who could help them.

Miloš Čujović's work was overseen by a cold-eyed former Yugoslav intelligence officer turned security chief in his midforties known as "the Wolf." The Wolf, alias Vuk Boskovic, was discreetly armed, and his own guards were watchful. He was known as the man who could make things happen for foreign visitors with the right amount of money—oligarchs and cocaine kingpins a specialty. He flanked Čujović like a pimp with his hooker.

Čujović was a big hit. He explained his methods like they were close-up magic tricks. At the hacker's new base, the Wolf began to arrange visits from more intermediaries from Russia and else-where, eager to understand how he could be of use. Čujović received them, a cyber mercenary for hire. He would later explain in detail to a judge how he accessed secrets that would give him the key to people's lives and whole organizations' data banks. He accessed classified US government material time and again, and past associ-ates say he sold material he found there. The Balkan intelligence services, in turn, had found someone they felt they could control.

What he did—one party guest hailed it as "mindreading America"—made its way into a number of conversations around Kremlin circles. While US political pundits obsessed about the potential security implications of American companies or politi-cal parties holding "Big Data" on Americans in the political main-stream in 2012, the cadre forming around Čujović had already been giving overseas intelligence services access to Americans' hard drives, private lives, affiliations, bank accounts, peccadilloes, and propensities by scraping the dark web for years. He was soon styl-ing himself not as a hacker, but as a superpredictor, and a brand. He would boast that he was working for intelligence services.

It was hardly the "fresh start" the mother of his children had been sold. "She left me," he told a judge later, after she'd packed her things in the car and gone back home. With her moderating influ-ence gone, Čujović threw himself into the life of a playboy, getting high and using his charm and skill with languages—not to men-tion the bulletproof confidence the powders and pills gave him—to cut a swath along the bars down in the resorts, networking with clients and buying whatever he wanted between stints back at his screen. He had bank accounts in China, Russia, Switzerland, Ser-bia, Montenegro. He was a subversive superstar, snorting lines of coke behind the roped-off areas, photographed leaving with starlets and supermodels. Sunglasses at night, three fingers missing, work-ing the screens and the phones, working the political operators.

His patrons were often at odds. The intelligence services'

indulgence of his criminal behavior was the least of the problems with supporting him. The kid was an absolute nightmare, they argued. A liability. He might be amazing—the very best at cracking Swiss banks' bullion-backed accounts and top-secret CIA files—but every day was a new exposure. How were they even supposed to be a "secret" intelligence service at all when their oh-so-secret weapon spent evenings rolling slowly along the Montenegrin seafront in local mobsters' gold Humvees, blasting Eminem while he high-fived drug dealers through the open windows? His top-secret state-sponsored hacker status was his stock chat-up line at the beach bars, for God's sake. He was a trouble magnet. Yet he was more than worth the trouble.

"While less than a minute is enough to break into a computer with a standard level of protection," wrote Serbian cryptography and cybersecurity specialist Milan Kovačević at the time, "military networks represent a higher level. It is more difficult to penetrate them, as the access path is constantly monitored. However, there is a solution here as well, and that is identity theft. Hackers break into someone's computer, decrypt the password and then carry out an attack from the computer of a man, who thus becomes a scapegoat. With well-protected systems, it is still best to have an insider, who would facilitate access to the enemy system by disclosing certain information."

And that meant he was valuable from a strategic, even military, standpoint.

LimeWire was one of the new generation of peer-to-peer filesharing platforms that by March 2005 had 1.7 million users, the vast majority of them in the United States. And the reason hackers could gain access to US corporate, government, infrastructure, and military networks through LimeWire was as dumb as it was ingenious. LimeWire and the wave of peer-to-peer file-sharing networks that arrived in the wake of Napster's rise and fall were designed and built with one oddly persistent UX, or user-experience, flaw in the interface. Users who downloaded the client and then logged on were asked if they were willing to share their libraries too. This was a file-sharing service, after all. But in electing to do so, a great many of the service's users selected not just their downloads library under "Share," but their entire hard drives. That meant that every single item on their computer was now not only being shared, but fully searchable by anyone out there who realized what was going on. "In pursuit of a free MP3, jihadis and federal contractors, soldiers and diplomats, executives and celebrities were doxxing themselves," explained the *New Yorker* almost a decade and a half later. "Because the people who used LimeWire were looking almost exclusively for music, this mass exposure had gone largely unnoticed."

First, Čujović chose the obvious targets—the names of private banks he remembered from Switzerland or others from Lichtenstein and Luxembourg. Billionaires. Passport details. US military bases. Access codes for government networks that would allow him to join the admins in monitoring all of the department's payroll, or emails, or plans. Large US corporations with priceless IP or plenty of sensitivity.

Then he really went to town. He infiltrated US arms and infrastructure giant Halliburton and its subsidiary Kellogg, Brown & Root, during their involvement in Iraq as contractors for military and oil-field infrastructure, and in the United States as the constructors of Guantánamo Bay–style internment camps run by the army and intended for Iraqi and Afghan prisoners. The US government was next. Then he infiltrated Microsoft, Apple, United Airlines, Berkshire Hathaway, Bank of America, MasterCard, the FBI.

His personal collection of English-speaking doppelgängers expanded. He became real people, with real security clearances and Swiss bank accounts: Simon de Villar, a wealthy doctor from Chicago; a wealthy US citizen named Romijn V; Englishman Simon Taylor, who spoke in such a singsong British accent while he waited on the phone for the clerk at Kaiser Ritter bank in Lichtenstein to connect him to his personal manager. All real people, whose online doubles he had carefully assembled, using hacked, leaked, and human-engineered data to become them online. He was a real-life "Talented Mr. Ripley." If the hacker couldn't get into your systems one way, then the digital double of your most valued client or your commanding officer would.

Yet while most of his lesser compatriots remained below the radar, he was unable to. The former government-sponsored child hacker of the bombardment became exactly what Mirjana Drakulic had feared when she'd told the hacker collective that they had created a monster. That meant the intelligence services had to accommodate him again.

By 2012, he knew too much, and spoke too freely. That meant drastic measures.

The guards, guns, and blast barriers surrounding Podgorica High Court were doubled the day they tried the Zagorje crime syndicate: brothers Nikola (twenty-four) and Nebojša Marković (twenty-six), Bojan Pejović (twenty-five), Dragan Kovačević (thirty-two), Radonja Vulević (thirty), Slađana Medenica (twenty-seven), and Vidoje Stanišić. And at their side, also cuffed, the hacker Miloš Čujović.

Together, they stood accused of running a cybercrime and mercenary enterprise spanning continents, offering services from Chicago to China. Čujović was alleged to be the master hacker in the group, while the others were muscle; honey traps; military, political, and far-right connections; and marksmen for the Zagorje gang, one of the Balkans' most notorious paramilitary and mafia outfits and Eastern European military and intelligence services' go-to outfits for dirty work. Like the Russian Business Network, the gang hacks security protocols worldwide, raids banks, and turns cash into arms and cocaine, and in return, the authorities get to use Čujović and his colleagues as their own private army. This makes the military and intelligence services themselves tantalizingly hard to attribute actions to, let alone motives.

Now Čujović had become too valuable, was privy to too much to be risked out there, where he was a danger to himself and others. A safe house inside a military airport wouldn't keep him safe. In such cases, their intelligence services have a fallback option.

Leave Podgorica through its northwest suburbs, and the city fades fast, countryside opening up on the motorway toward Danilovgrad. You feel ZIKS—the locals' name for Spuz prison complex—before you see it. The earth is brown, the country-side cleared; then there it is, the guards' towers silhouetted over mountains of encircling wire. The guards themselves are armed with machine guns and rifles. The prison is secure, its reputation daunting. The gray concrete and modern red bricks suck the life from the skyline, lacking even the energy to aspire to brutality. Its seven units—from punishment and solitary to extreme secu-rity and semiopen—are overcrowded by 30 percent. Officially, this is because ZIKS has become a key facility in the fight against organized crime. In reality, it has become a government-funded residential center of excellence for hackers, a cyber-age take on the Victorian workhouses, in which the talented delinquents are sepa-rated out and put to use under supervision.

As the online iteration of Total War has taken off, the authori-ties' relationships with these semideniable bands of hackers has danced a pattern of wanting more control, yet greater deniability and mystery. The prison-workhouse model has suggested itself as a win-win solution for authorities keen to control their hacker cad-res and be seen to stand for law and order at the same time. These compounds are opaque to the outside world. Any suggestion that hackers are working from the prison can be put down to a corrup-tion issue, rather than a deliberate feature of the places. Yet peniten-tiaries like Spuz have become Tin Pan Alleys for cyber mercenaries to ply their trade under battery-farm conditions.

The Serbian and Montenegrin governments had been early pioneers in Total War. But the story of Miloš Čujović shows that even having harnessed the power of these Lost Boys of the bombardment, the authorities struggled to scale up. They saw the talent, and instead of growing it, they had exploited it for personal gain. The chaotic and competing interests from criminal gangs, military intelligence, and law enforcement in two different countries had squeezed it until it bled.

They were rookie errors.

But one of the countries that had been watching since the original Lost Boys had earned their stripes under the NATO bombs of '99 was far more methodical in its approach. And its giant scale was the one thing it already knew how to flex.

When China began hothousing cyber warriors, it would do so in a way nowhere else on earth could even begin to imagine.

Chapter 18

Dark Guest, Red Guest

If the rise of the celebrity hacker had presented Eastern European intelligence services with a problem they needed to work around, there were no such qualms in China.

From Russia to Serbia, former Communist authorities had taken to working from the shadows. With the United States in their backyards, NATO and UN forces combing through their militaries, the FBI chasing anyone who got too high profile, their hacks needed to remain inscrutable, their motivations obscure. When their cyber warriors like Boa, Script, or Čujović became too high profile, they became liabilities. They had to be exited, prevented from having to answer questions and revealing the chain of command that flowed from state to apparently criminal acts online.

The years since had played out like a *Sliding Doors* experiment in which Eastern European governments would explore the different ways to license, protect, and jettison their cyber irregulars.

By 2005, Čujović had been busted and jailed after becoming the focus of American attention in the Stratocaster case; he was now out, missing three fingers, and lying low in a Serbian intelligence safe house in Montenegro. CarderPlanet's Dmitry "Script" Golubov was nabbed in a US-backed raid by Ukrainian special forces at his home in Odessa, after an investigation by the FBI, US Treasury Department, and the postal inspection service put pressure on Ukraine and Russia to clamp down. He would be out within months and would soon become an MP immune from prosecution, but had learned never to court the headlines as a hacker again. Roman "Boa" Vega (a.k.a. Roman Stepanenko, Randy Riolta, and RioRita) was sweating out booze in jail in Cyprus awaiting extradition to the United States. He'd been on his way from a trip to the Russian arms-running and money-laundering hub of Malta to Ukraine when he'd received an invitation to stop and see an old contact in Nikosia. After a night's vodka-fueled reminiscence about operations in Myanmar, he'd returned to his hotel room to find police officers waiting. Cypriot cops had imaged his computer and found a half-million US credit cards on it, alongside proof that some fourteen million had been captured by him. He'd spend the next few years attempting to resist extradition—miraculously managing to carry on hacking activities from jail, despite being officially denied access to the internet—but would eventually be sentenced by the Federal Courthouse of Brooklyn to eighteen years in a US jail. BadB graduated from urging cybercrime as a political act that could kill Americans to hacking into the systems of NASDAQ and Dow Jones themselves, attempting to cause stock-market chaos in the United States with the aim of civil unrest. The Ukraine-born Russian-Israeli citizen, real name Vladislav Horohorin, had been pursued by the US Secret Service for years when he was finally arrested on the French Riviera in 2010, boarding a flight from Nice to Warsaw.

Their mistakes had been becoming the focus. Give unceasing, low-level, nation-on-nation sabotage a face, and it becomes easier to fight. Like Osama bin Laden, Saddam Hussein, Russian arms-dealing "Merchant of Death" Viktor Bout, and countless others, they allowed the American delusion to turn a threat that was complex and diffuse into a series of faces that could be put behind bars.

In their place, supercharged state-assembled cyber networks like the Russian Business Network rose and prevailed. They made an explicit feature of their anonymity to launch cyberattacks on

NATO members in Estonia and Western-facing Georgia. Everything from the branding to the methods—disguising their origins in Turkey or Transnistria—was intended to distance them from their sponsors in the Kremlin.

This model of cyber war has become the globe-spanning antithesis to America's strategic method. It has even taken root in real-world conflict. The infiltration of eastern Ukraine in 2014 by Russian soldiers and irregulars posing as local rebels and separatists against the Ukrainian government in Kyiv—they became known as "little green men" in reference not only to their Russian-issue fatigues, but to their seemingly inexplicable presence in places Moscow denied ever sending them—was nothing if not a rollout of the methods first trialed in its decade-long, Belgrade-inspired cyber war against the West.

Yet it was not the only paradigm the West now faces.

From that same big bang in Kosovo, we can trace a second evolutionary line. This one is the descendant not of the Russian Business Network's illicit hacker economy, but of the proud, nationalist cyber-warrior networks of the Black Hand.

China and Russia both took lessons from the way the United States had been left flat-footed in the war for cyberspace at the turn of the millennium. But the lesson each saw in it was very different.

Russia's was that unceasing, unattributable acts of sabotage could turn the hegemonic strength of America back on itself, distracting, confusing, draining, and dismaying a more powerful opponent, and exploiting any inconsistencies or weaknesses in its narrative of events. It saw the future of cyber war against the West as one that it would play out in the shadows.

China's was different. They saw the Serbian army awarding medals to the Belgrade hackers. They saw how the Serbian Internet Army's branding—its appeal to the global diaspora, students, allies, and discontents—to defend the country and its principles against aggressors—had become a force multiplier. China saw in the wake of the embassy bombing that the activities of China's internet users could steer global opinion.

It also saw that the nationalist projects of the Serbian Internet Army and the Black Hand had made the defense of the country cool among kids. No matter that those kids also chafed against their own government; defending their country online was badass. The Yugoslav national project of arming and equipping a generation of cyber warriors—not just through greater access to computers and unlimited internet connections but through cyber-cool magazines, radio shows, TV shout-outs, official recognition and rewards, and high status—was all the proof of concept the Chinese government and military required.

The templates were followed so closely, they resembled the cheekily renamed products of China's industry in bootleg Western goods at knockoff prices, the equivalent of the uncannily accurate fake Apple Stores in Beijing, so like the real thing that even employees thought they worked for Apple, or the "Michaelsoft Binbows" software company of Shenzhen that circulated in viral photos online in 2012. The Chinese homegrown version of the Black Hand and Serbian Internet Army became the Green Army and Whampoa Military Academy.

As President Clinton had floated the idea that the internet would bring China closer to the American philosophy that had spawned its own model for the world wide web, the Chinese authorities saw the opportunity in very different terms.

It had similar qualms about flat and unaccountable networks of hackers sharing comments online. But unlike Russia and Serbia, it did not feel itself to be in a position of geopolitical or economic weakness in relation to NATO. Even back in 1999, its hackers and information warriors had not been silent and shadowy like the early Russian and global diaspora hordes to swarm in support of the Belgrade team. They did not hide behind the rerouting of traffic through Serbian lines to carry out their ping attacks. They proudly announced themselves as Red Visitors, not the Dark Guests of hacker custom. Just as the Black Hand had defaced sites with messages of national purpose, "Rocky" and his fellow Chinese hackers left manifestos.

The Green Army and Whampoa Military Academy had stuck up for China's interests publicly—defacing American sites, calling for NATO to back down, and functioning as a powerful voice of a mighty and overwhelmingly large people, in a country that had hitherto been careful not to let its people have anything like unfiltered access to any international conversation. In doing so, they had not just proved that cyberattacks and information war were cheap but effective forms of soft power at a point where China had no other levers it could pull without risking full escalation into war. They had shown that given the right stimulus, online conversation could become an engine for national revival. The country's economic engine was running hot. This would make that muscle felt. Universities expanded, online businesses grew, and through it all was the tacit understanding that if the party required services, those services would be given. The standing resource was huge. Whereas at its height the Serbian hackers had numbered perhaps a couple of thousand, China had numbers that made the head spin. University intakes were measured in millions. Through the 2010s, internet-based companies quickly became more numerous than in the United States and Western Europe combined.

This was a project that went deeper than hacking; it was about the refashioning of China's economy, its relationship with the government and with public services, and its social relationships, all as one continuum. By 2012, China had 389 million internet users— more than any other country on earth. By the end of 2020, its online population numbered one billion daily users.

If there was a sense in the Balkans that online citizens were dual-coded guerrillas, and in Russia the line between cybercriminal and cybersoldier was dissolved, in China the business of cyber war was business itself. Even as the Green Army collective split in 2000, it signaled a fundamentally different approach to the idea of how public a collective of hackers could be. The Green Army dissolved into the Shanghai Green Alliance and the Beijing Green Alliance amid acrimony over whether cyber war was to be a profit-making venture (the Beijing faction's position) or something carried out for idealistic purposes (Shanghai). In contrast to the way groups elsewhere were informal and shady, sorting their differences out in public beefs, the two factions dissolved their collaboration in a lengthy court case that owed as much to corporate demergers and contract disputes and reads like the stuff of a comedy sketch. As the hackers traded suit and countersuit in court, both sides accompanied the courtroom action in real time with massive hacks and counterhacks of each other's servers. At the climax of the case, the judge awarded some 300,000 yuan in damages to the Beijing hacker collective. They got custody of the URL.

That this early fault line was even possible illustrated a particularly China-specific approach to its distributed networks of free-lance cyber warriors.

Even as China embarked on its program of national economic rebirth, harnessing internet users' fervor and pride to mount attacks on government, corporate, and military targets overseas, China as monolithic, directed state cyber aggressor was, and has largely remained, a myth. It was a myth so powerful that it even became known in hacker circles as the "King Kong Delusion."

In fact, through the 2000s, China's exploding internet made it home to a vast subculture of young hacker-influencer-marketeers who saw no difference between promoting snacks, raiding overseas servers, or mounting information campaigns on behalf of their sponsors. This was far more difficult to control, or to predict, than any strategic state directives. Yet again, the West seemed to find that almost impossible to conceive.

The links between the countries were deep and strategic, with

China relying on the Communist computer-crazed country for the technology that would power its economic resurgence (Iskra Delta, the company that had teamed up with IBM and the CIA to supply sabotaged computers to the Soviets through its KGB deals back in the 1980s, had been the largest supplier of computer systems to the Chinese government) and at least some of the hacker reinforcements and military signals assistance China had offered Serbia through the bombardment coming in recognition of that relationship. Now, in the way it sought to position itself for the future, China took a leaf from its former Communist fellows' playbook.

The result was a breathtakingly entrepreneurial, bullish approach to cyberspace from a government with a keen eye on what got published and what didn't and a transformation of society that was as swift as it was complete. And at the center of a massive wave of education, supply, and public messaging were teenagers.

Suddenly, stores, news, and TV shows popped with hacker-themed spots. The glossy, sexy youth lifestyle associated with computers and the internet was everywhere—a permanent twenty-four-hour fiesta of cyber chic. A policy of "forceful positivity" from the authorities suddenly saw hacker magazines covering the shelves of city-center stores and suburban kiosks; cyber war–themed fashion flooded into the market, with printed T-shirts and jackets and code-themed accessories flooding malls. The burgeoning Chinese celebrity machine soon started throwing up hacker TV talent stars—it was as if Miloš Čujović had been winning *American Idol* each week, or, perhaps more to the point, as if his equivalents were part of the same churning machine that throws up China pop acts and fandoms daily.

SharpWinner was one such. A skinny, mildly photogenic eighteen-year-old, he rose in 2008 from the ranks of young hackers referred to dismissively by more experienced hands as "script kiddies" for the way they simply lift and use ready-made code to try out defacements and incursions. He'd been part of cyberattacks on White House and military web structures, declaring to reporters with a grin, "Those [American] .gov and .mil sites are always our targets!"

SharpWinner was as much media creation as he had ever been cyber warrior—and that was entirely the point. He was dramatized by interviewers, shot by photographers, pictured just as heroically as any iconic peasant of the Mao-era posters of the 1960s.

By 2010, SharpWinner's glossy, ghostwritten hardback autobiography was decking bookstores across China. In *The Turbulent Times of the Red Hackers* he referred to himself—always in the third person—as "the handsome, bright youth" who spent quite a lot of time batting off text messages from squads of female groupies after each hack on a foreign site.

This was the high life of Yugoslav computer kids taken to its anabolic, high-volume, cash-rich limit—a parade of aspirational, if ephemeral, figures, thoroughly modern equivalents of Communist-era stories of virtue and hard work for the improvement and modeling of the young. In 2006 the Shanghai Academy of Social Sciences surveyed five thousand Chinese primary schoolchildren about their ambitions and dreams. An astonishing 43 percent of those interviewed said they "adored" China's hackers, while 33 percent told the researchers that they "dreamed of becoming a hacker someday." One student said, "Hackers are very cool. Hackers leave people an impression of high intelligence, and are able to do whatever they like and get whatever secrets they want. That is what I lack, but dream of."

"Hacking in China is more than surface appeal," concluded Scott Henderson on the survey in his Chinese cyber-war treatise *Dark Visitor*. "It is a way of life, a sub-culture, and a dream. It offers an independent path to a future of one's own choosing and not a life dictated or controlled by the state."

But even if the way of the Dark Visitor was distinctly rock and roll, these hackers were being packaged for public consumption and aspiration.

Groups launched, focusing on identities and personalities as if they were boy and girl bands on teen TV. The first of the female-only groups to rise in the mid-2000s was Six Golden Flowers; when they split, a new group was pushed: the China Girl Security Team. Like most of the hacker groups, it had its own domain on the web (registered on March 12, 2007) and immediately began recruiting female hackers, quickly hitting the thousands. Its slim and camera-happy nineteen-year-old "leader," Xiao Tian, lives no less like an Instagram style icon than SharpWinner, snapping V-sign selfies in the latest street fashion, posing at home, and chatting live to fans as well as fellow hackers.

Both these wholesome, oddly public figures represented a par-ticularly Chinese progression on the tacit collaboration between state and hacker armies in Eastern Europe. They were part of a project to create an army that would be far more effective than the ad hoc, somewhat paltry resources available to the Russians through RBN. They had created a generation of hackers only too ready—in the words of the Black Hand a decade earlier—to "mount an electronic defense of the interests" of China, and they would do it *because they wanted to.*

In doing so, the Chinese authorities had created—or, rather, incentivized, enabled, and nourished—a cyber-warrior subculture for the age of the influencer.

Like a dark cousin of China's massive social media influencer schools in Shanghai and Beijing, so for the past decade a massive sector of universities, seminaries, and online webinar courses and schools have promised to teach kids how to become Dark Visitors and Red Visitors.

Sites such as chinahacker.com and cnhacker.com didn't just have the usual Western pasteboards of code to copy, or tutorials on skills, but ran massive live courses and advertised in-person evening classes in cyber-warrior life, skills, and security.

One of the least-reported legacies of the Belgrade University cyber-defense group was the way its structure was imported as a template for the way China would upskill its own "electronic defense" cadre. Postbombardment intelligence briefings and a rash of knowledge-sharing presentations between Serbia's military and China's through the early 2000s had persuaded China on the cross-disciplinary university model. It spent the next decade building strength in depth at its most bustling universities.

By 2010, many of the most famous Chinese universities, including Hainan University, Southeast University, Shanghai Jiao Tong University, Xidian University, Zhejiang University, and the Harbin Institute of Technology (HIT), had begun offering courses as military-civilian fusions, designed to train hundreds of thousands of hackers to move seamlessly between lab work, the world of business and media, and cyber combat.

The course activities often bordered on the surreal. At Southeastern University in Nanjing in 2014, students in the courses took part in a live cyber-war competition in which points toward a winning total could be acquired by hacking real, live targets in the United States.

Such was their confidence in America's inability to accurately attribute the attacks, not to mention its impotence even if they did, that the university set about not war games as an exercise, but live attacks on real American targets. The competition was sponsored and designed by a Chinese security firm contracting to the country's Ministry of State Security.

The competition, which was hosted by professors at Southeastern, caused a sudden peak in cyberattacks in the United States originating from China. Yet this peak itself was just a small taste of what was to come. The competition's attacks by the students were used to refine and perfect the malware that on February 4, 2015, would be used in the infamous Anthem raid on 78.8 million Americans' medical records by a crew calling themselves Deep Panda—a Chinese crew also calling themselves APT 19—or the influencer brand-savvy Kung Fu Kittens.

At Xidian University, meanwhile, where the courses are over-seen by two members of China's state security services, the students have been put to work on a gigantic AI/machine-learning project that's been hailed as "doing for cyber war what Google did for search." Its job is simply to crawl the net endlessly and at huge scale, looking for and identifying software vulnerabilities that can be fed back to the government's database. It will then use what it knows about each one to search more efficiently for more. Network and Information Security School students are each paired with Ministry of State Security officers for the duration of the course.

The gigantic Chinese-brutalist edifice of the Harbin Institute of Technology in China's Far East, meanwhile, functions chiefly as a large-scale recruitment center for Chinese cyber-intelligence officers and warriors. The equivalent of Harvard, it is one of a very few Chinese universities authorized to work on top-secret government projects. In common with Chinese universities and illicit hacking groups, it parades the trophies of its activities quite openly. While the hacker groups usually upload screenshots of successful defacements they have carried out or code they have changed, HIT's cybersecurity school's web archive proudly announces that many of its staff and alumni now work for the Chinese army's Electronic Intelligence Department. This group is charged with the massive 2017 Equifax hack in the United States, for which the US Department of Justice took the highly unusual step of indicting four serving members of China's military on February 10, 2020, on a total of nine charges.

Yet again, the West lacks the tools to deal with the diffuse nature of this threat. "The phenomenon of Chinese hacking is made up of four-parts," wrote Henderson. "One part nationalism; one part tech interest; one part financial; and one part fame. When political strife and interest begin to wane, it is money and fame that holds the organizations together. Many Chinese hackers are capitalistic entrepreneurs who not only finance their activities through illegal methods; they also generate income by marketing pop culture."

Chinese military doctrine sees civilians as the fundamental building blocks of the nation's power. Former USAF intelligence officer turned Washington, DC, cybersecurity maven Richard Bejtlich warns that this means the Chinese government simply sees no disjunction between working with independent hacker groups to achieve national security goals and working with them as businesses toward achieving global economic goals. In China, hackers are the ultimate portfolio workers.

The Western media calling hacks the work of "China" not only is unhelpful, but betrays a blindness to the nuances that characterize the way cyber war is waged today. In the space behind that large target, many literal millions of hackers coalesce, for just as many reasons, around targets. Like the Serbian hackers, they may be no fans of the government, instead driven by a subtle mixture of things— economic need, national pride, social momentum, professional prestige, peer pressure, the trade of favor for favor, criminal motives, playfulness, badassery, boredom, money, loyalty, and a thousand others. Depending on the day, and on the job, they might be swamping and attacking targets in Japan, the United States, or the houses of Parliament in London. They might be backing or protesting a new policy by a large company inside China—hacking its servers or counterattacking those of its hackers themselves. They might be for or against the government, or one of its policies. They might be taking part in criminal acts, or in the world's largest black hole for piracy and intellectual property theft. They might be fighting global hacker wars, or attacking servers from Russia or Canada or Europe, or mounting an information offensive in Australia. Sometimes they are paid for. Sometimes they are working on government business. Sometimes they are just kids.

Yet again, the West risks viewing the phenomenon through its own deceptive distinctions of state or private sponsorship. "That the government would condone or even encourage industrial spying and data theft for fiscal gain is a very remote idea for us," writes

Henderson. "However, the Chinese government does not divorce itself from domestic industry and all assets located inside of China are viewed as assets of the state. Financial institutions are deemed a vital component for the health and stability of the nation and are at least on par with, if not on a higher priority than the development of its military capabilities."

Unlike Russia's cyber war underground, China's is an open, publicly funded cyber-war ecosystem. Whereas Russia built a dual-coded, self-funding hacker economy based on the cyber warriors of the streets, China branded and empowered theirs after the Black Hand.

Where Russia's attempt to remain obscure, China's are hidden in plain sight, industrialized and fully incorporated into the state's, economy's, and military's schematic of their resources. Where the Russian Business Network was a legitimate business organization in name only, China's cyber-war actors include well-known branded companies, civilian media agencies, and individuals of all levels of skill, fame, and professionalism.

For that reason, it remains almost impossible to tell the motivation of almost any act of cyber hostility from China against US or other Western targets. "The hacking scene in China probably looks more like a few intelligence officers overseeing a jumble of talented—and sometimes unruly—patriotic hackers," reported investigator Mara Hvistendahl.

"It's chaos," says one Chinese hacker who's willing to talk. "That's what you must understand. Or, not chaos, but fuzzy. The chaos, it's uncertainty, like being in a crowd. It means that nobody tells you individually what to do, more that the dynamic is important. The group helps, it means you know the targets, you know how much you can do safely.

"It's like auditioning for a lot of us. Just, like academic work. Like, how good was your last assignment? Oh wow, that good? Okay, you can come and do another one. Here's someone you should work with."

I ask if he knows many of the people within these groups, so that he can be sure of motives. "The motives are really that we want to support each other, and of course at some point win respect," he replies. I ask if there are no briefs or checks or balances to what happens, but it's a route he doesn't follow me down.

That's when I realize we're talking about two different things. My vision of this gigantic crowd of loosely defined actors, fizzing with the effervescence of youth, national pride or grievance, entrepreneurialism, posturing, badassery, and often barely contained anger is a recipe for disaster. It is the mob, uncontrollable and unpredictable. A Dionysiac nightmare made manifest, plundering and defacing, hacking and trolling whatever gets in the way of its perceived mission of that moment.

For Chinese hackers, as well as its business, political, and military interests, it is the future. The internet transformed China indeed, just as President Clinton had predicted. But instead of Westernizing it, it turned the country into the flat-structured, nonhierarchical dynamo of people power that Communism had always promised it could become.

The energy of that first big bang captured, like lightning in a bottle, had turned into a *perpetuum mobile* of war and industry. Leaderless, and irresistible.

Chapter 19

Ignorant Armies

The wild child-hacker days of the internet are a fond memory for people like me who were there and just old enough at the time to be questioned by MI5. For two generations since, that internet has only ever existed in millennial movies and digital folklore. The giants have moved in, hoovering up pests and closing loopholes. Yet in 2010, one ingenious operation showed that in a networked age, it wasn't the force behind an attack that mattered, but how many unseen vectors you could open up for it, how many parts of the network you could recruit. And though nobody knew it at the time, it would define everything from political shifts to marketing, and cybersecurity to terrorism, in the mobile-first decade to come.

Natanz is a small town in Isfahan state, Iran. It is home to some 12,500 people and is known for its winds that rake through the desert and mountains, parching the skin and stinging the eyes with dust and sand, and for the sweetness of its locally grown pears and other fruit.

On the flat vermillion of the desert is a small hill and what looks like a large industrial park. Covering two and a half acres, its buildings are silver and white, the gates barbed and locked, approach tracks patrolled by slow jeeps and security cameras that whir and pivot and take in the approach road. But its true secrets are two dozen feet below the desert floor, covered by two concrete shells eight feet thick. The hill is in fact the seventy-two feet of earth piled on top of the hall containing up to seven thousand centrifuges. This is one of Iran's uranium enrichment plants and the key plank in the country's fledgling nuclear weapons program.

Since the early millennium, the United States had been expressing alarm at the development of the site, while Iran continued to insist it was simply a power plant for domestic use. Now it was 2010, and still nobody was getting anywhere.

That same year, a cybersecurity researcher in Minsk, Belarus, noticed a strange traveler on the global currents of the internet, one that seemed harmless enough as it was, but suggested so much more than met the eye. On June 17, Sergey Ulasen of Minsk-based Virus-BlokAda received a report from a Windows PC stuck in a reboot loop. He investigated and found some unusual code—a wholly new virus. He reported it as a Zero-Day—a new vulnerability that was already live, giving developers zero days to patch it before they were exposed.

That got the world's attention. Researchers called it the Stuxnet worm. It was, they agreed, "the most sophisticated piece of malware known to humankind." Yet even among those who found and analyzed it, nobody could get a clear idea of its purpose. It simply did not act like any malware that anyone had ever seen in the wild. It gained access to systems, but it seemed to leave them alone entirely. It did not delete data. Nor did it raid any of the systems it gained access to in order to leak information, damage files, or cause any harm to the systems themselves. What was this?

First came speculation. Stuxnet must exist for one very specific purpose. One very specific set of circumstances. That meant that unlike, say, most Trojans, this was not a numbers game. It didn't want to be just anywhere. It wanted to do one job, in one location. But what?

Stuxnet was fiendishly clever, the ultimate sleeper agent. A multipart worm, it spread through USB sticks inserted into computers running Microsoft Windows. In some ways, it was as straightforward as Anti-Smyser-1. Once inside a PC, the virus would search it for Siemens Step 7 software, popular with businesses using their PCs to regulate automated machinery in factories, assembly lines, or power plants. If it found any trace of Step 7, the worm's mysterious second stage would deploy.

This was all its early discoverers knew. As biological viruses do, Stuxnet passed completely asymptomatically through anything that did not suit that purpose, circulating through the global digital ecosystem without incident, or even being detected.

Ten years on, the same veteran Helsinki team that had tracked Anti-Smyser-1's strange metamorphoses across the web in 2000 worked with others around the world to determine the nature of the virus. Mikko Hyppönen and Katrin Tocheva began peeling back the layers and matches for its second stage. They found it contained a set of riddles and nudging references that appeared to play no part in the code. Artifact references left inside the code referred to "myrtus." The Latin name for the myrtle plant, it struck some of the teams as a potential biblical reference and sent them scouring through its potential significance as clues, from ancient myths to cooking and botanical chemistry. This curious, gnomic reference had a Holmesian quality to it. Why was it even there? It ignited a frantic period of puzzling in parallel to the analysis of the code. Hyppönen's team too puzzled on it. It was hard to figure out what myrtus could mean. He broke down the words—were they code? They could just as easily mean "my RTUs"—the remote terminal units used in large factory systems and automated plants.

"Under the right set of circumstances?" warned Hyppönen. "It could adjust motors, conveyor belts, pumps. It could stop a factory. With right modifications, it could cause things to explode." But if that was the case, which RTUs did the writers of the virus want to take ownership of? What did this clever little virus want to make explode?

The code was giving up its secrets. It was as stealthy as it was deadly. Once it was inside a machine, Stuxnet's root would deploy, updating its code without its user knowing, over any open internet connection. Still undetected, it would then start sending destructive commands to any automated machinery the PC controlled; it would command machines to overheat, programs to ignore safety parameters, safety gauges to suppress alerts as the damage mounted. Yet even as it sent the machinery into a spiral of self-destruct modes, causing extensive and irrecoverable damage across the operation, the virus sent falsely reassuring feedback to the control center. Even supervisors monitoring the equipment closely would have no clue that the equipment was being destroyed until the destruction, breakdown, and malfunctions had reached visibly catastrophic levels.

It was primed to destroy a very specific set of Siemens systems in a specific formulation. But the puzzle only deepened there. Siemens itself was able to verify in 2010 that as far as it knew, despite the code, none of its customers' machines had been harmed at all. The mystery deepened.

Another odd piece of extraneous data seemed to wink at the sleuths. A strange number in the code, used as an infection marker: 19790509. In date form, it had little significance in global security. Frantic Wikipedia efforts revealed only one serious international incident. It was the date in 1979 of the execution in Tehran of an Iranian Jewish businessman named Habib Elghanian on a charge of spying for Israel.

The Iran connection sent a flurry of inquiries through the intelligence chain. What came back sent a chill down everybody's spine. Over the past couple of years, investigators working with the International Atomic Energy Agency had become perplexed by the findings in their periodic inspections at Natanz. The IAEA team had found anomalies in the cascade rooms housing eighty-seven hundred uranium-enriching centrifuges. They noticed that the usual rate of attrition—of new centrifuges the plant could expect to replace per year—was about 10 percent, or around eight to nine hundred centrifuges. Yet the latest figure was many times that. Natanz was burning through between one and two thousand centrifuges in just half a year.

At the same time, trackers at Symantec determined that at least 60 percent of the infected computers worldwide were in Iran. Yet officially at least, Iran had no systems that fitted the profile. Now intelligence learned that the Natanz plant alone was running the vulnerable configuration of Siemens equipment and Windows. Siemens had not sold the equipment to the regime, sanctioned as it was. "Everything about it just made your hair stand up," recalled one Symantec detective. Iran had gotten the equipment illicitly, probably through a network stretching from Pakistan to Europe. The long web of false end-user agreements and resales disguised the machines' role in Iran's nuclear program even from Siemens itself.

The Siemens-powered P-1 centrifuges in Iran's nuclear enrichment plant had been fizzing, crashing, burning out, developing cracks, and malfunctioning at phenomenal rates, putting Iran's path toward nuclear capability back a decade or more. "Enemies of the state" were at work, seethed Iranian president Mahmoud Ahmadinejad as Iran searched in vain for flesh-and-blood saboteurs just as NATO had a decade earlier. But they were not. The truth was far more far-reaching.

In the months that followed, that Habib Elghanian reference winked from the code. Then a series of further nudges began to hint at the origin of Stuxnet. American officials maintained their official line that they had not created the virus, yet President Barack Obama's adviser Gary Samore broke into his own barely controlled grin when an interviewer asked about US involvement. Israeli intelligence officers too broke into broad smiles even as they denied all knowledge or involvement. Then in 2011, Israel Defense Force chief of staff Gabi Ashkenazi threw a retirement party. Onstage at the bash, a video montage of his "greatest hits" rolled behind him. Among them was a single coy reference to Stuxnet.

But even as its success was celebrated, the double life of Stuxnet swam only slowly into focus.

The problem with advanced, hyperengineered cyber weapons is that they are only yours for the first-use advantage. The moment they are deployed—or perhaps discovered—they become defendable, and obsolete. But the bigger problem is that they also enter public domain, their code pored over, learned from, pulled apart, adapted, redeployed. One of the reasons researchers find Western cyber-war capability so hard to quantify is the West's reluctance to use its most advanced code, the equivalent of saving the expensive wine for a truly special occasion. It is the same disjunction again, between strategic deployment and bottom-up, crowdsourced guerrilla cyber war. In the East, cyber war is carried out as if it was a series of Silicon Valley start-ups. Spot the opening. Launch beta. Fail fast. Fail better next time. Bingo.

Meanwhile, Western governments work with Silicon Valley. They develop big, effective cyber weapons they can deploy in the most serious circumstances. But they're like nuclear bombs; you need to think very carefully before you push the button, and once you do, you hand that advantage over. And so it was now. The bottle was open. And very quickly, everyone, the Iranians included, simply started reverse-engineering Stuxnet.

In the aftermath, governments weighed publicly the possibility that their own nuclear facilities, or even launch bases and early-warning systems, could be compromised by the descendants of this now public-domain code. Under President Obama, the United States itself adopted a "left-of-launch" policy on North Korea, in which it would use covert means, from cyberattacks to supply-chain interference, to hobble North Korea's rocket tests and slow its development of offensive nuclear capability.

But the Stuxnet code was diabolically clever. It was elegant. It was specific. It was hard to detect. It was even quite witty. But it was also distracting. Because perhaps its greatest innovation was a lesson from Kosovo. What Stuxnet had been, before it was even a weapon, was an invisible recruiting tool through which noncombatants, previously unknown to any security service, would all become vectors. It crowdsourced inevitability.

Hundreds of thousands, perhaps millions, of computers around the world had become infected with Stuxnet over the course of just over a year. But in contrast to most virus attacks, almost none of them had experienced any problems whatsoever. Machines had been turned into zombies and botnet components before, and they would be again. But this was about the turning of huge numbers of small, tactical realities into one overwhelming strategic one, in a way that owed as much to quantum physics and the movement of crowds as it did to military strategy. Like the application the Serbian hacker HQ in Belgrade had encouraged citizens and sympathizers around the world to install on their machines, turning them into zombies so that the critical mass could be reached to swamp NATO's powerful systems, Stuxnet had enlisted computers worldwide for the sake of a mathematically overwhelming focus on one target alone. Their role was simply to become unwitting civilian vectors for further infection, each time moving the virus one degree of separation closer to activation, which would take place just once, in one very specific place. Every new machine was simply a quantum push to get the probability of that single event closer to 1. Like the calculus behind turning cyber war into a public mass-participation event in 1999, Stuxnet's method was breathtakingly, beautifully simple. This was not merely a virus for a networked world in which civilians were combatants; everybody was online, and the internet was ubiquitous. It was an exercise in nothing less than the crowdsourcing of inevitability.

And it was in that approach, not in its code, that it became the final step toward the world we inhabit.

In its aftermath, Stuxnet's slow creep to 1 became a Rorschach test; what it meant was very different depending on the baggage of the beholder. To cybersecurity analysts working with militaries, governments, and software consultancies in the West, it showed that long, strategic plays with expensively developed code were still the devastating last word in victimless surgical strikes. Technology reigned supreme, putting into their hands knockout blows they could land against physical collateral through cyberspace. The world's best coders could cause real-world damage where airstrikes were impossible.

But to the architects and denizens of the Eastern internet, it was the lesson of Kosovo manifest. The future lay in the crowd-sourcing of specific outcomes by flipping millions upon millions of noncombatants into damage generators that could then be pointed at specific targets or events.

Hackers I spoke to in Russia and Serbia saw Stuxnet as America and the rest of the world belatedly and expensively cottoning onto the methods they had pioneered with the PC-flipping programs and global crowdsourcing of critical-attack mass a decade earlier. Repeatedly, Eastern hackers referred to Stuxnet in terms of fabled Serbian inventor Nikola Tesla's groundbreaking ideas being stolen by the media-savvy American Thomas Edison. It was specifically to reclaim this pioneer brand for the new age of physical targets that the Serbian nationalist hacking crew Tesla Team formed in 2010.

As it had been in the Cold War, in Kosovo, and in Iran, America's advantage was in big, strategic cyber weapons. The East's was about the quantum world, Tesla's empire of the invisible. It achieved its effect by slow accretion. By enrolling more distributed particles of the internet and sending them pushing not toward anything as basic as a denial of service, but toward a single tipping point in the big world of physical machines and human choices.

As the always-on, mobile internet slowly took the world—76 percent of Americans used home broadband in 2010, with 59 percent using mobile internet—so did their potential as quantum particles of a new kind of weapon. And this is where the legacy of the Belgrade war room's teens is still being felt most directly. Because

Stuxnet had proven that what you could do to a physical machine through the spread in viral load at this quantum level, you could do to a political machine too.

The mobile internet's rise brought a new front in the global cyber war. But the front wasn't just in hacking phoneware instead of Windows. Phones brought about a new relationship with the internet. It was no longer a task-oriented activity. Through the 1990s and 2000s, internet companies and media had talked about their websites being "destinations." These destinations—these bookmarks—were being swept away in the unceasing flow of timelines. The internet was not something we visited to get something done; it had become a constant companion—a hotline direct into the consciousness, location, and engagement of the individual. This critical mass—by 2010, three-quarters of Americans had their phones on them all the time, refreshing Twitter, Facebook, YouTube, news, email, and other apps an average of ninety-six times a day—meant that links sent to their phones via social media, email, or RSS feeds had become their primary source of information.

That meant higher online consumption, as online shopping exploded and lining up outside a nightclub or waiting in a bar now became shopping time. It also meant soaring valuations for Silicon Valley companies that could show that they were able to capture and deliver the lion's share of that attention. They were primed to deliver whatever made its way into their ecosystems, packaged and wrapped up as viral load. The consequence—and the second big change that swept the world in the early 2010s—was the switch of cyber war from big targets to small ones. Like the internet itself, cyberattacks were about to enter their always-on, direct-to-consumer phase. Victory in cyber war was not simply defined by what the technologically equipped *attackers wanted to achieve*, but by what kind of leverage over civil society the technologically equipped *target represented*. For a West now rapidly approaching always-on saturation through mobile devices, that meant the hacking of networked democracies themselves.

America's two giant opponents both operated hacker econo-mies at different levels, but both had to some extent globalized. Russia's cyber-mercenary economy birthed FSB-aligned crews like EvilCorp (so named to mock the hypocrisy of Google's founding "Don't Be Evil" credo). EvilCorp swiftly cornered the market in ransomware directed against the West, co-opting networks of money mules just as CarderPlanet and RBN had before them, and conducting hacks for Russian intelligence and security agencies when required, as the price for letting them get on with amassing millions of dollars' worth of stolen US cash, secrets, and IP.

Both Russia and China, concerned about the influence of the American internet, had begun carving out their own internet architecture and blocking and limiting the growth of the Western giants. Their goal was to make cyber war a one-way street. Lever-age those global diasporas in the West, while knowing that no such diasporas exist in China or Russia. It also meant securing the flow of news. In 2009, China had banned Facebook, Twitter, and You-Tube. In 2010, it blocked Google. In 2012, Russia's parliament passed bill 89417-6, publishing a black list of "undesirable" internet sites. It included swaths of English-language websites and much of Wikipe-dia. By the decade's turn, both had their own bootleg Silicon Valley giants. Russia's Vkontakte was designed as a Facebook spoiler for the Russophone world, even down to the logo; Yandex was Rus-sia's parallel Google, its traffic-based algorithm manipulated by the government so that news unfavorable to the Putin administration was suppressed.

As the internet developed its own virtual Berlin Walls, cyber-space began once more to resemble the tripolar world of the Cold War. Once again, nonaligned countries and border states were stra-tegically important. And as the Russians turned to the offensive possibilities of the information war and memetic capabilities that had flourished with the rise of Google and Facebook, they looked to the nonaligned Eastern European borderlands.

Chapter 20

Darkness Visible

On his release in 2011, dope sick and paranoid, Čujović succumbed to a full-blown breakdown. Holing up with friends, seeing raids and enemies everywhere, convinced he was being followed, and moving under cover of darkness, he fled Montenegro in secret.

Now on an Interpol warrant, bug-eyed, sweating, and reflexively hiding his distinctive mutilated hand inside his jeans pocket, he fled over the Alps to Switzerland. But everywhere he went, his talents followed, and so did the people who needed them. Days after his arrival, he was arrested with a duffel bag of cash at Zurich's airport. At this point, during his remand in the Lugano jail, the Swiss authorities realized that he was the Eastern European hacker who'd been raiding their banks' gold bullion–backed funds on the regular. Tense at the thought of losing control over what he knew, but with his pop-star girlfriend and his child still in Serbia and Montenegro as leverage, his Balkan handlers negotiated his extradition—no easy thing, as Switzerland was the injured party. They were tense days. The Serbian and Montenegrin intelligence services cooperated, each pushing the case that they both needed to investigate crimes against the other so that they could assure Switzerland he was a sensitive individual from the standpoint of national security, without letting the Swiss authorities see that what they had in prison was not just a cybercriminal, but a secret weapon that had allowed them to develop full digital likenesses of US and European government personnel at the highest level.

Montenegro worked hard to negotiate his repatriation as a special case, with the guarantee that he would stand trial at home. Quite why that was so important became clear at the trial, when Čujović told the judge in Podgorica that the whole thing had been a big misunderstanding between the countries' security services, adding, "Everything we ever did, we did with full permission" of the Montenegrin authorities. It was a strange thing to say. Stranger still was that it seemed to pass everybody in the courtroom by entirely. Still, if he was asking for help, or making a veiled threat to tell more about his backers in the security services, it worked.

He would spend the next couple of years in and out of the ZIKS center, in the way that other people do military-service tours. The leash is played out and then shortened by the security services who manage him. Good work earns him time outside. Notoriety, crossing lines, politics earn him time back at the archipelago. It hit something like a rhythm. It could not last.

At his most recent trial in 2018, Cujka was convicted of a number of heists of Swiss banks. He couldn't take another tour of coked-up cyber-espionage duty. Something in him broke, and on the stand, he repeated that he was working for the security services. Only this time he volunteered to spill the beans on everything. He started talking about additional incursions he had managed that weren't in his indictment. He pointed out to Judge Vesna Moštrokol that he was going into far more detail than anything he was charged with and suggested everyone take note. And that's just what his handlers did. Čujović was given bail and placed under house arrest. He was not to leave Podgorica. His passport and ID were canceled. He could not get through customs. His world seemed to be getting smaller and smaller, and now he was trapped. And then, like that, he vanished.

I was woken by a ping from the bedside phone that morning. It was Marko Vešović, a crime journalist in Podgorica. The message said simply, "Čujović escaped."

A scheduled check-in had him missing. Now all hell broke loose. He'd not been checked on at the last scheduled appointment. His papers appeared to have been returned to him by mistake. His movements for the past week were a mystery.

According to press reports at the time, at least one person had heard from him. Starlet, model, singer, and occasional paramour Soraja Vučelić had picked up a call from the hacker just a couple of days before the alarm was raised. In the call, he said he would be going away, possibly to Thailand. In any case, it would allow him to get away, start fresh. What he'd wanted to do when he came to Montenegro, but never got the chance.

Vučelić hesitated. She already had everything she wanted. She was well cared for, well off, and well known. She had legions of admirers and a head for both business and people. She was booked to drive a Lamborghini into a swimming pool for a TV commercial in a couple of months' time. She told him she would be staying put. Čujović asked if she had a friend he might take instead.

Vučelić did have a friend, as it turned out—a Croatian girl she'd bonded with on the reality-show circuit. Barbara Segetin and Vučelić had, said *Celebrity Big Brother* viewers, even started looking alike. Segetin agreed to go with him, and according to Vučelić quotes in the press, the hacker then gave her 15,000 euros, to be split between the two ladies.

And so in the dark days of December, in a car that did not belong to them, Miloš Čujović and his companions, among them an intelligence contact, purred through the early-morning city-center traffic, and headed northwest. Past the old military airbase one last time and out through the Podgorica suburbs. The hacker, the spook, and the starlet crossed Nikola Tesla Street and swept out through the half builds, graffiti, and terra-cotta roofs. Then the city was swallowed by a final darkness as the E80 autoroute took them into the mountains.

The Čakor Pass, where they entered Kosovo that night, is

subject to icy winds that blow cars over the edges and down the mountainsides. The border itself is at 6,066 feet in altitude. The perilous mountain road, closed during the Kosovo war, is tarmacked only on the Montenegrin side of the border. The six-hour drive was painfully slow, but they weren't held up by border checks.

They had hotels booked for them in Lišak, outside Mitrovica, the majority-Serbian main city of Kosovo's Serb enclave, then Gračanica, close to Pristina Airport. They were given plane tickets. Accommodation, arranged by the authorities, was laid on for them by an infamous Serbian paramilitary warlord and self-proclaimed "king of cocaine" known as Joca Amsterdam.

Kosovo was at another of its periodic boiling points. There was a price on the head of a man named Oliver Ivanović.

Tanned and slim in his midsixties, with steely hair and a soft southern Balkan accent, Ivanović was a popular man around Mitrovica. But his constituency had limits. Among the local crime lords and nationalists, he was as popular as a Kosovo Serb politician turned antimafia whistle-blower is ever going to be. The former leader of Kosovo's Serbs, he had become a key partner in negotiations with the United States, NATO, and the EU—a moderate who backed dialogue with the Albanian majority. It was a principled, moderate stand, in a time and place that was baying for extremes. He was no friend of the ultranationalists or Serbian Honour, of Knights Templar International (KTI), or of Russian agitators and their bands of hackers and propagandists. A social media campaign denouncing him as a "traitor" and "quisling" was taken up by radio and TV channels. One popular TV show placed a target on his forehead. A Serbian Radical Party speaker asked when someone would "put a stop to his meddling."

His office had been attacked, burned down, and then his wife's apartment was firebombed. His car had been blown up. He was uninjured, but the security forces had made no secret of the fact that they thought he had it coming.

Quietly, internet traffic built around the so-called clash of cultures in Kosovo. YouTube, Twitter, Facebook, and email accounts inflamed tensions. The flood of engagement converted into a flood of extremists, loaded with a flammable cocktail of guns, drugs, and stoked-up grievance. Soon the towns and villages of northern Kosovo were bursting with would-be defenders of the line, pumped up and looking for trouble. "Kosovo Serbs in North Kosovo are not afraid of Kosovo Albanians," an exasperated Ivanović told reporters. "They're more afraid of other Serbs! The local criminals and thugs who ride in SUVs without license plates." The Serbian Honour group was an ultranationalist right-wing organization allied to the remnants of the Serbian Internet Army, into whose social and political orbit some of the muscle in Čujović's own Serb-Montenegrin government-sponsored gang had begun to drift. There were far-right groups all over the place, turning Kosovo into a factory for fake news and heists. The paramilitaries. The international Christian supremacist agitators. The terrible nexus between organized crime, the government, and the secret police. All funding, sponsoring, and consuming disinformation campaigns, information attacks, and cyber aggression by the gangs of Podgorica and Belgrade.

Through the 2000s, the Belgrade cyber warriors had not gone away; they had risen. Some, like Čujović, became harnessed to the security services; others spanned out into high-tech abroad, from San Francisco to Dubai. But still many more learned how to take their talents and keep hustling. Through the 2000s and 2010s, Serbia, Montenegro, Kosovo, and Macedonia had emerged as the world's leading generators of a phenomenon that would come to be known as fake news—a bigger drag on Western democratic processes than any official policies by Russia and China combined. Like people on borderlands everywhere, like their nonaligned Cold War parents and their *hajduk* and *partizan* grandparents, they knew how to triangulate between the powers on either side. And they had seen in Google's and Facebook's engagement-first business model a chance to get paid twice: once by the enemies of the United States and its Western allies, to hack into the processes and populations that powered democracy using the skills they had perfected under bombardment, and once by the very same American platforms who delivered the viral load.

By 2014, the Balkan disinformation ecosystem looked very much like the schoolkid hacker scene of Belgrade in 1998. Its target was the same network of Western alliances. Its methods were the same, too: the infection of individual timelines, and individual users, with the right viral information, so that large real-world outcomes would be effected.

Small traces drifted into our lives, washed onto the shores of our consciousness. They were the poorly worded "Stories from Around the Web" that the very same legacy media who dismissed the internet, now cash strapped and not too worried about where it got its next cent from, carried beneath their stories as ads. So familiar yet so easily shrugged off. They were there in faked-up, too-good-to-be-true recipes and celebrity reveals. They were part of our online ecosystem, yet even as we clicked them, we never saw them. One neat trick after one neat trick.

And then they erupted, in forms that would not be so shocking to us if only we had been tracing them in the deep, exploding into already tense and polarized spaces like bombs dropped into an elevator shaft. They erupt in the form of QAnon, and COVID-19 disinformation, and 5G. They erupt with stories of crimes supposedly committed by immigrants but "covered up by the MSM," or deepfakes of politicians. They erupt, claiming the EU is about to ban something British, or Turkey is set to join, as they did shortly before the United Kingdom's Brexit referendum, or that the 2020 election was won by Trump. Like Croatian Mind Hackers and the Black Hand itself, they were engaged in nothing less than causing the centrifuges of democracy itself to break down.

By 2014, Belgrade had become the world's production house for far-right and antidemocracy movements wanting to brand themselves as standing up for a racially pure, Christian West. Ubavka Janevska, a senior investigative journalist in Macedonia's internet hub Veles, told the BBC in 2016 that in the city of Skopje alone, she'd identified seven separate "teams" peddling misinformation online, each comprising "hundreds of schoolchildren, working individually," to pump subversive digital signals into America and Western Europe. Data was the new oil, all right, but it was filling digital Molotov cocktails thrown against the machinery of the networked West, as well as powering its high-tech machinery.

In the wake of Ukraine's overthrow of Russia-friendly dictator Viktor Yanukovych, Russia began to pursue a policy of low-cost, high-impact investments in farms along these lines. They industrialized them in media parks in St. Petersburg and Moscow, with names like the Internet Research Agency, and turned once proud brands like RIA-Novosti into twenty-four-hour fake-news operations working in English and targeting the West with sensationalized disinformation. Best of all, through Google ads, the West paid. It was a savage irony that a US online tool part-founded by the NSA would siphon the West's greatest security threat since the Cold War straight into American homes.

In December 2016, after Trump's victory in the US presidential elections in which disinformation pumped into US social media sites like Facebook and YouTube figured prominently, a team of BBC reporters tracked down one of these teenage disinformation teams that had begun working together as factories. Their business model was so elegant that they no longer required a criminal underground or patrons from elsewhere. The teens had worked out that America was, in fact, happy to incentivize them financially to hack its own electoral process. The reporters worked with these attention hackers to nail down their finances. One claimed he "worked on the fakery for only a month and earned about 1,800 euros (£1,500)," reported the BBC. "But his mates, he claims, have been earning thousands of euros a day."

It is impossible to overstate the importance of this financial model—in which the likes of Google and its YouTube platform, Facebook, and others actively rewarding "engagement" through automated advertising become the funding engine of syndicates and governments working to push destabilizing disinformation into Western democracies.

"The economic differential makes it absolutely inevitable," says Eastern Europe disinfo specialist Dr. Jovan Byford. "They simply make money from American consumers by creating inflammatory and misleading content. You no longer need these shadowy backers funding them, like they had in 1999. They don't need patrons— their patrons are the victims of their own disinformation, in America and Western Europe. Americans, Australians, Brits, Germans, click and share, and Google rewards the producer of the disinformation accordingly. It's absolutely baked into the business model of the social internet."

By the 2010 London mayoral election that gave Boris Johnson his first term as mayor, the tactics used by the Far Right British National Party (BNP) embraced the methods of these Balkan viral-content factories. They had begun circulating appeals and canvassing by zipping it in with illegal music shares that their target demographic would be likely to download. Under the tutelage of Čujović's colleagues and compatriots, perhaps even unknown to Cujka himself, the BNP's teams spent the 2000s subverting Napster, LimeWire, and Torrent sites. It was the Serbian method in reverse. Files labeled with popular Brit-pop or American EDM acts would unzip on download to reveal not the movie or album claimed, but selections of viral clips, memes, and propaganda for the Far Right.

Patrolling the lanes of the dark web and illegal download sites from 2008 to 2014, I found files from the BNP masquerading as a new album from Babyshambles, the side project of the Libertines'

Pete Doherty. Unzipping the archive to release what appeared to be 103 megabytes of music, my hard drive was suddenly home to extremist Islamophobic literature, doctored photographs and addresses from the BNP's mayoral candidate for London claiming to reveal murders, and antiwhite hate crimes committed by Muslims in London that had been "covered up by the mainstream media." Zip files purporting to be everything from Eminem's then new album to *Breaking Bad* episodes were in fact videos from Knights Templar International, Atomwaffen, and Britain First, all pushing that same idea—that they were calls to alarm, revealing what the MSM would not report. And time and again, they would find their way into "respectable" news sources. Established news organizations like the *Daily Telegraph* in Britain uncritically laundered these BNP videos—about fictitious stabbings and killings of white British girls by Muslim attackers—onto its own news site. They treated the BNP's "it's not being reported, but it happened" claims as fact either without checking or in full knowledge because the videos provoked the clicks that fed their online business model. Campaigning councillors and politicians acknowledged the need to "crack down" in the wake of these stabbings and to "acknowledge the understandable fears of the public." The fact that not one of the incidents had happened did not prevent them from leading mainstream discourse and steering policy.

The pattern repeated across America, Canada, and Australia, with neo-Nazi, racist, and antidemocratic organizations such as Stormfront, all fed by Russian and Yugoslav terrorist organizations, pushing for a clash of civilizations against Islam. Ironically, by 2014, these methods had been embraced by the Islamic State itself, which realized that claims about violent Muslim hordes were being laundered so uncritically into media and government policy that it could use the same dynamic to cast a shadow far greater than its capacity for action and use the polarization and paranoia it created to recruit and grow from there.

Russia was also on the move. In 2015, a host of extreme right-wing, ultranationalist, and neofascist heirs apparent convened at a new event held in St. Petersburg, Russia. The International Russian Conservative Forum was organized by Russian ultranationalist Yuri Lyubomirsky and attended by many of Europe's leading far-right voices, including Udo Voigt of Germany's far-right National Democratic Party, Roberto Fiore of Italy's Forza Nuova, and Georgios Epitideios of Greece's neo-Nazi Golden Dawn.

The timing was no accident, coming hard on the heels of neighboring Ukraine's Maidan Square protests in favor of joining the EU and the subsequent riots and overthrow of Russia-sponsored dictator Viktor Yanukovych. Russia ran its disinformation and covert invasion of the Crimean peninsula, Vladimir Putin open to funding groups who could muddy the waters around just what the EU meant anyway. It was the perfect counterpoint. The more the EU was portrayed online as homosexualized, weak, permissive, corrupt, and under siege from the very forces of difference and openness it avowed, the better to woo wavering nations such as Ukraine with the prospect of a new Russia-led sphere, one that was virile, tough, disciplined, virtuous, and pure-blooded.

If there is a Ground Zero for the explosion of Russian online disinformation operations on the West, this was it. Organizer Yuri Lyubomirsky confirmed that delegates from the far-right groups concerned were "exclusively" from the European Union. But of course, the West's press were concerned only with what they saw happening in Ukraine. They did not consider for a moment that the conference was more akin to a global sales-training exercise for giving the West its own nervous breakdown. "Even as Moscow denounces anything it views as a manifestation of fascism abroad and prepares to mark the anniversary of the victory over Nazi Germany," reported former US State Department and CIA chief Paul A. Goble of the conference, "the Russian authorities are hosting tomorrow a meeting of Europe's neo-Nazis, extreme nationalists,

and anti-Semites who share one thing in common—their unquali-
fied support for Vladimir Putin." One British nationalist paused on
a photograph of Putin riding a bear, topless. "Obama and America,
they are like females," he said. "They are feminized men. But you
have been blessed by a man who is a man, and we envy that." Jared
Taylor, whose American Renaissance website incites racial conflict
in the United States and whose conferences featuring the Ku Klux
Klan and US neo-Nazi groups, railed that the United States "wor-
shipped diversity" and "is the greatest enemy" of traditional values
anywhere. Discussion groups and workshops ceded into content
captures—speeches were dressed with flags, photographers ready
to generate social assets.

For other delegates at the conference, in Peter the Great's "Window on the West," it was also an arms show for cyber war. The far-
right agitators, anti-Western fringe figures, and rabble-rousers did
not come to Putin's city alone. There also flocked to St. Petersburg
those hopeful for introductions to collected hacker groups, digital
media studios, and cyber warriors from across Europe and the United
States, including figures from the Serbian, Macedonian, Montenegrin, and Russian hacker undergrounds, while their American and
British fringe counterparts linked up online to discuss methods and
technologies. The atmosphere was that of a premission briefing.

The Balkans represented a place pitched between East and West
that came packed with skilled cyber warriors and online disinformation specialists—plus access to every digital platform banned in
Russia itself or flagged as suspicious by Western authorities. Best
of all, it bordered the EU. It was the revolving door for cash and
influence. And with Montenegro about to vote on membership, the
battleground was set. Suddenly, these hacker gangs were rolling in
commissions, as millions of dollars in hard currency washed into
the Balkan groups. The month after the conference in 2014, the
syndicate surrounding Miloš Čujović began an online campaign
of hacking and defacing websites, replacing them with the logos

of white-clad Christian knight crusaders and hacking money from Western governments, businesses, and individuals. The money made its way to reinvestment—growing the networks needed to mount a serious challenge to American and EU political will and social cohesion—and onward to extremist groups to pay for a massive arms buildup on the borders, where Serbian Kosovo met Albanian Kosovo. Čujović's own "handler" for the Zagorje mafia clan and intelligence agencies, the one-eyed, perma-shades-wearing, gold-dripping hacker gang enforcer Vidoje Stanišić, himself began posting material on his Facebook account that echoed the style and sometimes the content of Knights Templar International and Serbian Honour groups. Little that he or anyone who came into contact with these groups posted was ever overt. Memes, T-shirt slogans, visual gags, all were sly winks that would go over the heads of most, but connect with those who knew. They were just covert enough to be attributed to irony, misguided humor, or a love of history. In fact, they had become a sly declaration of war against both the Muslim world and the "soft" democratic governments in the West.

The growth of ultranationalism in the Balkans collided with an enhanced ability to bring it into the world, particularly when combined with wealthy patrons who could mobilize its troops. Russia-funded online operations flocked to the borders from America, Italy, Greece, Poland, Scandinavia, Austria, Britain. Western KTI members promptly began appearing in viral online videos that flooded through Facebook and YouTube, addressing the camera crew from "behind enemy lines" with Christian Serbs in Kosovo, standing in front of heavily armed men in combat fatigues, and soliciting donations for stockpiles of weapons and ammunition for Serbs to fight the Kosovo Albanians. "KTI's jokey memes, nationalist videos and far-right material are shared across 14 Facebook pages, which have earned 2.5 million likes from the social network's users—including three serving British MPs," wrote the

Balkan Investigative Reporting Network's Marija Ristic, after her BIRN/BBC investigation that revealed KTI's giant network of moneymaking social media sites, websites, and viral content hubs "that dwarfs those of mainstream media and political organisations." The investigation finally forced Facebook to remove fourteen different moneymaking presences for the group.

The presences ran the same familiar scam. They would process disinformation into alerts that looked like news or vlog posts. Sometimes a terrible incident would be claimed; furthermore, it had been "covered up by the mainstream media, who you won't see reporting this."

"They run appeals for legal funding, and they sell patriotic memorabilia and tat and things like that," says a Serbian investigator who's followed the group for years but declines to be named out of safety concerns. "You wouldn't know them, a lot of the time, they sell flags and things in online shops, their own e-commerce, even eBay. You could mistake it for the kind of things old people or nationalists like. They are directly funding KTI activities."

In America, insurgent neo-Nazi and pro-Russia groups spread through the same digital ecosystems. The same people that had been employed crowdsourcing and laundering inflammatory and anti-American fake news stories for Russia's Pravda.ru in the 2000s had now moved their presences directly to the United States. Presences like the prolific Atossa were now posting, meming, and amplifying disinformation direct to American social feeds on behalf of Stormfront and other American Nazi groups.

As the 2016 US presidential election approached, for-profit fake-news operations based in the former Yugoslavia became the most shared links on Facebook. In 2018, I asked one of the original Black Hand hackers who'd been busy making viral anti–Hillary Clinton content, setting up disinformation sites, and amplifying through social media what had gotten him involved. "Dollars," he shot back. Two Belgrade media-agency types had come to him for some consultancy initially, as he'd been making it on and off for twenty years since the NATO bombardment and now freelances in media. Besides, he said, for him with the Clintons, it had been personal since they bombed Serbia.

Yet on the Eastern European disinformation networks rolled, picking up funding: from lobbying and nonprofits in Russia itself to right-wing extremist groups and nationalist parliamentary parties across Europe, American conservative and Christian groups, and Western digital platforms that were delighted with the engagement metrics. The more inflammatory, conspiracy centric, and fantastical, the more viral, the more profitable, for everyone. Trump swept to power, while Brexit "knocked Britain to the ground, and it will not get up for a very long time," in the words of Russian ambassador in London Aleksandr Yakovenko. It wasn't until August 2020 that Facebook was finally forced to stop recommending any political groups to its users worldwide when its own internal investigators found that one of its most popular political groups was a disinfo operation in the former Yugoslavia.

And still, the surprises that should have surprised precisely nobody kept pouring in. In the week before the January 6 riots at the US Capitol, an astonishing 87 percent of all news links on "free-speech first" social media platform Parler loved by the American Far Right were from disinformation operations. The conversation was dominated by the single most popular news site referred to on the platform, American Conservatives Today. It was an operation run between Macedonia and Serbia. The borderlands became the global workshop and broadcast HQ for extremist groups targeting the West. Not only that, but it is one who all agree brings hundreds of millions of dollars into these fractious mafia states each year, but which because of its illicit nature shows up on not a single economic report.

When we talk about dark money influencing war and peace in America, this is the darkest of all. It flows like ether, invisible and untrackable, across the lines we draw on maps, through our lives and our timelines, our networks and our servers. It flows from individuals, from governments, from lobby groups and fringe parties, from Alphabet and Meta, from you and from me. It flows from the movement of your pupils and the scroll of your fingertips. The Dark Matter of our lives is created where the Eastern and Western internets come together, the money machine and the mayhem machine, Silicon Valley and subversion.

The internet was supposed to cut out the middlemen. But in the global, public-participation online game of Total War, those who position themselves not on one side or the other but in the middle are the winners, if they can keep their heads.

At 8:17 on the icy morning of January 16, 2018, as he was entering his party's office in North Mitrovica, the Kosovo politician Oliver Ivanović was hit by six bullets fired by the occupants of a passing Opel Astra. He was killed instantly, the bullets ripping through his heart and throat.

The Kosovo media and police reported that the car resembled the one in which Čujović had fled Montenegro to Kosovo. Police briefings immediately seized on the young hacker. The investigation into Ivanović's murder soon turned to his journey from Montenegro, then out of the country. But despite their briefings, and the joint efforts of Serbian and Kosovo-Albanian law enforcement, the murder of Ivanović remains tantalizingly unsolved.

Several reports suggested that Čujović has fled to Thailand. "Montenegro does not have an extradition treaty with Thailand," says reporter Marko Vešović, the investigator who's followed Čujović from the beginning. "That's why people like Čujović go, or are taken there."

Since the Thai military took power in 2008, it has courted Russia and China openly. This has made it harder for the United States to extradite suspects and turned this tropical Las Vegas by the sea into a haven for fugitives wanted on suspicion of international crimes, terrorism, or hostile activity. This in turn has given it a reputation as a global center for cyber mercenaries. It is not an option open to everyone. But for the best, most productive of their battery-farmed cyber mercenaries, intelligence handlers are always willing to go the extra mile. He'd been placed in Pattaya, a vice-riddled seaside resort identified by an American diplomatic cable from 2005 as a magnet for fugitives from international justice who wanted to vanish amid the seedy 24/7 trades in illegal gambling, sex, and narcotics or just to blend in among fugitives and outsiders from all corners of the world.

"Chinese hackers using Pattaya as their base," reported the Thai press in 2019, quoting Thai cops as saying that the phenomenon was growing and their number-one fear was cyberterrorism. Here, hacker conferences are held under palm trees and in hotel bars, not chilly conference centers. They are often attended by US, Chinese, and Russian intelligence working undercover. Russian master hacker Dmitry Ukrainsky lives and runs a yacht-rental business here—or he did, until it was mothballed pending a diplomatic tug-of-war over his extradition to the United States on cybercriminal charges. The Russian government continues to fight for him to be returned to Moscow, comparing him to Viktor "Merchant of Death" Bout, the Russian arms dealer arrested in Bangkok in 2008 and currently serving time in a US jail.

I tried to follow progress for Čujović, even engaging a private detective in Pattaya. But he seemed to flicker on and off like a faulty beacon. Whenever a sighting put him at a particular spot, Thai police would say they had followed the lead and it had been a dud—a standard MO. Thai immigration police commissioner Lieutenant General Wiboon Bangthamai told the *New York Times* back in 2011 that officials at remote border posts were often plagued by sudden and inexplicable computer failures when notable fugitives entered Thailand illegally. "Officers would break the computers and let them in," he sighed. Čujović reportedly had a Thai liaison officer from the security forces.

Many questions remain in Čujović's story. Did he carry out one last favor for Serbia's spooks to earn his permanent exile in the sun of Southeast Asia's Sin City? Or was he deliberately placed close to the scene of the crime, an unwitting patsy, to ensure that he never came home again? For months afterward, reports circulated that his erstwhile handlers had simply needed to make sure he was implicated in a high-profile murder, so that he would never return under his own steam and testify to all the things they had asked him to do. For them, it was insurance. It was, he is believed to have told associates, a witness-protection scheme with a difference. "The hacker was taken out of the state and is no longer available to the judicial authorities, so he can no longer testify about criminal operations," says Vešović. "It is a solution that keeps the wolves full and the sheep in number."

Those who claim to have spoken to Čujović after he vanished say he sounded relieved that the investigation meant he could never return. He'd needed to get away from the police themselves. Perhaps the high-speed internet meant that he could carry out his old work just as well here as anywhere. Perhaps this was a golden opportunity to truly begin again. Start a business. Use his undeniable talents in some other way.

He had a new career in a new town. He could still do what he wanted, but now he could do it without being a celebrity or getting locked up in the hackers' battery farm of ZIKS to pursue government cyber missions in secret. The loose ends back home tied themselves. His ex-wife and mother of his child, Bojana, is now in a steady relationship again. It's with the deputy prime minister and coordinator of the Montenegrin Security Services, a government high-roller called Dritan Abazović—a man plagued by scandals. When the romantic relationship between the former Mrs. Čujović and the head of state security was revealed, Bojana mentioned on her Instagram, "My boyfriend has an encrypted phone so that Cujka doesn't hack him," but opposition figures say it's to cover up Abazović's own shady dealings with the hackers.

Fully plugged into the Western internet, furnished with Microsoft developer centers, and funded by European development cash, the old networks that formed around that room in Belgrade University did not fade away as the war stopped. They simply carried on. They were the hackers, the cyber insurgents, the digital rebels who never stopped. As Mirjana Drakulic had prophesied, they simply found new causes.

Today, Serbia's president, and the architect of its pivot away from the EU and toward Russia and China, is one Aleksandr Vučić. He works closely with Montenegrin security. He defies Western sanctions on Russia in the wake of the Ukraine invasion. He has made Serbia essential, funneling cash from its neighbors in Montenegro and the EU, through to the Kremlin. And he is the strange, flickering connector between events in this story.

Vučić was a journalist before he was a politician, laundering the reputations of Serb paramilitaries in Bosnia in the 1990s. Later, during Kosovo, he served as information minister under Milošević. It was on his watch that the Belgrade University hacking teams were set up and plugged into their global counterparts in China and Russia. On his watch, Colonel Svetozar Radišić's Group 69 within the army was rehabilitated for the duration of the bombardment, as the world's first cyber-disinformation group.

Like Nikola Tesla, the Serbian visionary whose picture hung in the hacking group's room—a secret iconography that cast them in the mold of the lone, misunderstood tech visionary and not Milošević—Vučić and the rest of the cyber group's creators saw a world ruled by the moves of unseen forces in the omnipresent ether of our physical lives. Like Tesla, he harnessed these forces to create something the world had never seen before. And like Tesla, he would see his inventions taken up and turned into money and power beyond imagination by people and countries with more muscle. Only where Tesla in New York found himself courted, copied, and discarded by Edison and America, Vučić found himself courted by Russia and China.

Without the Serbian hackers' viral load and its arrival in our system, the world would be a different place. Without the teen-hacker network, there would perhaps be no Kremlin bot swarms or troll farms in St. Petersburg, no teen hacker camps in Shenzhen. Without his rehabilitation of Group 69, there would be no RT, no QAnon, perhaps no Trump presidency, no Brexit, no Russian invasions of its neighbors. Europe and America would be different places today.

Perhaps it was fitting that in 2022, when the blowback from the Ukraine invasion turned the tables against Russia's weaponization of fake news and the hacker underworld, it would not be the West who would lead or win the fight in cyberspace.

It would be a new, hungrier challenger who would humble the Eastern internet's own behemoths. And they would do so under conditions that mirrored uncannily those in Kosovo twenty-three years earlier.

The mystery of just how the West—the mightiest and most technologically advanced power in the history of the world—has seemed so flat-footed against the subversion of the Eastern internet would be solved by Russia itself. Just not in the way it had planned.

Chapter 21

The End of Everything

History repeats itself not as recitation, but as meme. Its message makes it to us on the voices, currents, and static that crackle through cyberspace, turning and twisting it into nothing but noise. If we're very lucky, we might catch its first signal. We might learn something about that big bang that caused it in the first place.

The West's ascent to cyber hegemony through the 1990s coincided with the end of the Cold War and chaos in the East. Western soft power through the internet was corporate. In 1999, that meant the Pentagon could consider cutting whole countries off from the internet itself. Even today, sanctions against Russia are the result of an ordered and strong corporate world, prepared to work with its government. But in the years since 2014, Russia and China have transformed themselves digitally. They each have their own parallel digital ecosystems to differing degrees, in the Great Firewall and RuNet. By 2019, China was the world's most online country, with almost three times the users of the United States. Russia was sixth, level with Japan. The two countries had brought the Eastern internet from the shadows and put it to work as global muscle. It served their economic, foreign policy, and homeland security goals. Everything from government services to health care and shopping to love delivered to mobile-first populations. Their national neuroses around the digital gap with America was finally vanquished. From security to business, Russia and China were online, and they were back—not just as superpowers, but as cyber powers.

But there the similarities cease. China's rise came on the back of a nationwide economic surge. Its hacker armies, influencers, and rock stars were by and large pleased to work for the national project. But in Russia, things were complicated. The country that had wrestled with its own internet back in the 1980s but could never overcome its leaders' deep suspicion of the very idea that people might share information without going through them had found a way to square the circle.

The USSR's postwar determination to boost electrical living was driven partly by the dream of a cleaner, sleeker future that would rise from the rubble of flattened cities and link the growing Eastern bloc together with Lenin's dream of electrification. One of the most popular Soviet cartoon series, released in 1960 as a "filmstrip"—a kind of magic-lantern slideshow for the home popular in the USSR before video technology—promoted a dream of Soviet-wide Skype- and Zoom-type meetings ("Televideophone") and the Internet of Things. ("Igor carefully switched on the machine and dropped the note into the slot. Invisible beams traced the letters on the note in order to carry out the task; automatic ladles measured out what was needed, and special knives quickly chopped up the vegetables.") Its name was *In the Year 2017*.

What the real-world 2017 brought about in the cyberspace of Russia was so uncannily similar, one wonders if Russia's president, eight years old when schools in St. Petersburg were shown the film, had retained some memory of it. Vladimir Putin tasked his technologists and information ministers with creating the Sovereign RuNet—a Russia-wide version of the internet that could be unplugged from the world wide web in its entirety. By restricting the points at which Russia's version of the internet connected to the global web, this would give the government more control over what Russians could or could not access—effectively turning the Russian web into one gigantic intranet. It was sold as a security measure. This way, Russia would be able to resist Western incursions and diverge from Western internet standards with ease. In 2019, the Kremlin claimed it had successfully tested this Russia-only internet, unplugging the country's internet from the web for a spell, with no negative effects. It would now reign supreme over its own corner of cyberspace. In this, it would be like China, in total control of the minutest information—every search result, every social platform—on its own parallel internet, behind the Great Firewall.

This was important to the Kremlin for some very Soviet reasons indeed. First, the country's scale demanded it economically—this was Lenin's dream of "Soviet power plus the electrification of the entire country." Second, it provided control over what its citizens could see. The Sovereign RuNet would mean that while Russians could of course still receive information from the outside world, that information would arrive through easily monitored choke points, just as when the KGB restricted the number of international telephone lines into the Soviet Union to make them easier to tap. Third, it would make it easier to monitor what Russians did. Putin's drive to turn the country into a vast digital panopticon had already led to aggressive monitoring measures—from the persecution of opposition protesters on Facebook or Russia's clone Vkontakte to the government's planting of SORM, the program whereby all Russian internet service providers are obliged to install equipment that gives the government a surveillance back door on all communications carried. His government and its agencies monitor private exchanges and have introduced draconian laws that see people imprisoned for expressing negative views about anything from the country and its politicians to the Orthodox Church. Most recently, it has been used to prosecute citizens and organizations who use the words "invasion" or "war" to describe Russia's invasion of, or war in, Ukraine.

The sweep was on. What had been a chaotic, semiautonomous scene was being brought to heel. The Man was moving in. The Russian internet was going to get branded and corporatized. All those hackers chafing at American control over the internet were about to be brought under control by the Kremlin anyway.

Yet at the very core of the Eastern internet—what had made it so successful as a disruptor—was its otherness. It was born in resistance, and it grew in subversion. Its model of Total Cyber War had prevailed from the bottom up, not top down. It was tactical, not strategic, opportunistic and entrepreneurial, not command and control. Its tendrils had grown in shade, until they shook giants. The mightier and more structured the Russian state and the internet it made in its own image became, the less they were able to conceive of their model's own disrupters.

Just how complete the change, and how strategically Russian malware developers and hackers were now working with the Kremlin, was illustrated in February 2022 by the massive hack and disruption of satellite communications affecting Ukraine on the eve of Russia's military invasion. The methods had moved from the pings and underworld networks used against Estonia and Georgia. This cyberattack used a powerful, broad-based piece of malware called AcidRain to hit the ground-based modems communicating with communications satellites. The satellites targeted were Viasat—a service used heavily by Ukrainian government-operated communications networks. A US-led investigation showed that the attack carried the fingerprints of Russian overseas intelligence service, the GRU—not least in the root of the code.

This is where the rigidity of Russian planning showed its weakness. As Russian forces poured into Ukraine on February 24, 2022, Russian state media began broadcasting the reports it had prepared in advance, purporting to show the progress its army had made, and its leaders saying, "Mission accomplished," to the cameras. But it wasn't. Instead, Ukrainian hackers and disinformation specialists had already begun to deploy techniques for which Russia really should have been ready.

First, they had been hacking into Russia's command chain using their own manufactured identities. Russian drivers began receiving confusing orders on the pace and destination, as Ukrainians hacked into their communications systems. The Ukrainian government immediately issued orders for Ukrainians to fuck with navigation in any way they could—even putting out guidance for changing signs on highways so that they all read "Go and fuck yourself." As Google suspended its live traffic-mapping service for Ukraine, which had been allowing Russia to keep track of Ukrainian movements, Ukrainian hackers went one better, entering fake locator information across the country's landmarks, businesses, and government buildings online. Photos were switched out on Google. Directions suddenly went awry. Russian units relying on the internet to navigate reported receiving haywire coordinates from websites when they looked at routes. They blundered along roads into traps; they waited in empty fields for fuel as night fell; they idled and froze in mud when they should have been rendezvousing with their comrades elsewhere. How could this happen? they asked. They had been told by their own commanders what to expect, and this was not it. The conscripts found themselves in a strange and unwelcoming Upside Down, where no road led to the place it promised.

Russian intelligence began looking for opportunity online. In late February 2022, Ukrainian authorities raised concerns that Russians were putting intelligence jobs up on San Francisco–based knowledge-crowdsourcing site Premise, looking for users to give them information they might have on strategic locations in Ukraine. Premise's owners denied that any work was being done by individuals who were tied to Russian entities. "Premise tasks were deployed to help our customers in the international humanitarian space understand exactly what was happening on the ground," it said. "These tasks—which asked for Contributors to report on local conditions like road closures, the state of health facilities, and food availability—had been running alongside many other surveys and observational requests for months prior to Russia's invasion."

Ukrainian sources claimed in turn that Ukrainians had been flipping the model across the internet, placing reports and dropping pins everywhere of bridges and craters that were fake, in an attempt to fill Russian scrapers with so much junk data that nothing the Russian forces wanted was reliable. Humans and bots sent fake reports of activity to Russian comms channels, swamping them with bad intel.

The units who weren't being waylaid by bad directions were lighting up the deep web with their own locations. As the Russian columns advanced, Ukrainian women in Kharkiv began seeing likes from Russian soldiers in the area; the likes became a reliable indicator of the direction of travel of those columns. "I actually live in Kyiv but changed my location settings to Kharkiv after a friend told me there were Russian troops all over Tinder," said one Ukrainian user. "I couldn't believe my eyes when they popped up trying to look tough and cool. One muscular guy posed up trying to look sexy in bed posing with his pistol. Another was in full Russian combat gear and others just showed off in tight, stripy vests." All of them offered ID, photos, and a willingness to give away their upcoming plans in the hope of a hookup. Obliging Ukrainian hackers began to scale the operation, running networks of AI-generated bots with fake profiles swarming likes on those soldiers and messages of the "Hey, I'm hot and horny, where are you?" variety, catfishing Russian soldiers into divulging information about their orders and next location. They even deepfaked random faces onto clips of porn stars and camgirls to make them all the more tempting, the employees at a Ukrainian deepfake start-up helping them get started.

Next, the Ukrainian kids began showing up gaps in the official narrative coming from the superpower—turning every citizen into a reporter with a mobile phone and a video camera. Quickly, Russia's attempts to claim success or precision were discredited. Likely Putin apologists were "inoculated" against Russian reports with preemptive shareable assets and memes warning them of the disinfo being used against them.

The Russian internet had grown. The Kremlin had come to rely on it to service and monitor the population. In 2022, it made a temptingly giant-sized target. Ukrainian specialists were all very well, but this called for mass participation.

For anyone who had been watching NATO struggling more than twenty years earlier, it was clear what was coming next. Ukrainian prime minister Mykhailo Fedorov pulled the trigger at 3:38 p.m. local time on February 26. "We are creating an IT army," he tweeted. "We need digital talents. All operational tasks will be given here: t.me/itarmyofukraine. There will be tasks for everyone. We continue to fight on the cyber front. The first task is on the channel for cyber specialists." The link led to a Telegram channel, and the jobs rolled out in real time, by the minute. The Russian state security service and intelligence services went offline, then Russian news agency TASS.

In the twenty-three years since Belgrade, the technology might have changed, but the principles had not. Hacks start and end with humans. Swollen by global diasporas and hacker collectives Anonymous and others, Ukrainian hackers began dismantling the hermetic seals around Russia's sovereign plot of cyberspace. Pointed by Ukraine's leaders, billions of pulses rose, coagulated, and formed ping-of-death attacks, sending every vital public vector of Russian command, control, disinformation, and financing out of action. Who knows what may happen, but as of this writing, the much-anticipated "digital Pearl Harbor" once again was not happening.

In great swaths, Russia's communications, financial, business, and government infrastructures went dark. Russian space and satellite agency Roscosmos went down, cutting links with its databases, then Gazprom's own bank, then the Russian Ministry of Defense itself. The rest followed in quick succession—Russian public-services portal, Moscow State Services, the government of the Russian Federation, the president's office, Russia's own Google clone Yandex. Then the tax office, the entire customs and borders service, Russia's state pension fund. As a coup de grâce, next to vanish was Roskomnadzor—the Russian federal executive agency responsible for monitoring, controlling, and censoring the Russian mass media—and the Russian internet itself. Then the whole edifice of Kremlin financing and oligarchy: Metaloinvest, Lukoil, Magnet, Norilsk Nickel, Surgetneftegas, Tatneft, Evraz, NLMK, Sibur Holing, Severstal, NNC, Russian Copper Company, TMK, Yandex, Polymetal International, Uralkali, Eurosibenergo, OMK, Sberbank, VTB. The Bank of Russia went down after that. The hit list kept rolling on Telegram, targets identified, locked in, then the words "Tango Down" signifying the hack had been successful. Russian hackers, for their part, hacked back. But the effect was muted. It highlighted only what NATO had found out two decades before: that global online opinion is a force multiplier. Ukraine could count on attacks not just from within the country, but from around the world.

"I'm not aware of a government calling for random people to DDoS and hack banks and such before. I think this is a milestone moment," said former senior threat intelligence analyst for Microsoft turned cybersecurity sleuth Kevin Beaumont. "Also, since almost all Western governments are supporting Ukraine, giving weapons and providing cyber assistance, it creates an awkward situation where the West is proxy supporting hacktivist groups. The list of targets has been expanded out to cover some cloud services . . . and Google assets." Companies from Microsoft to Elon Musk's SpaceX got involved too, ensuring that Ukrainian cities stayed connected—and Ukrainian civilians and military alike could keep their online activity at peak levels, even when Russian attacks damaged the country's signals infrastructure.

"We may look back on this as the first Great Information War," wrote political investigative journalist Carole Cadwalladr. "Except we're already eight years in. It began in 2014. The invasion of Ukraine is the latest front. And the idea it doesn't already involve us is a fiction, a lie."

The international cyber volunteer battalions—equivalent to the diaspora spammers of 1999—came native to social media.

One of the oddest and most effective phenomena was the rise of NAFO, or the North Atlantic Fellas Organization. A Twitter-based movement devoted to swamping Russian disinformation on the platform with pro-Ukrainian memes and information drops from accounts with Shiba Inu dog ("the Fella") avatars, NAFO's initial meme was created in May 2022 by Twitter artist @Kama_Kamilia. It quickly became a viral sensation. By calling other Fellas onto a Russian disinformation post, Twitter users could effectively "dog-pile" it, drowning out the initial post with corrections, debunkings, and counterpoints before it gained traction.

Even this global, online, real-time, public participation war had room for specialists. A resurgent Anonymous declared for Ukraine, quickly taking down the Russian streaming equivalents to Netflix, Wink and Ivi and replacing their entertainments with live footage of Russian military destruction and death in Ukraine. It then turned Russian live TV channels Russia 24, Channel One, and Moscow 24 to broadcast on-the-ground footage of the carnage in Ukraine that the Russian government was busy denying. Within hours, they'd hijacked all Russian state TV, turning it into live broadcasts of a war the Russian people were being gaslit into believing did not exist. By early March, Russian battle plans, location information, and leaked data from Russian soldiers' unsecured radio communications were circulating online, having been lifted by Trojans, interceptions, and social engineering and passed to Ukrainian forces. It was a chilling reminder of my NATO leak, and just how vulnerable armed forces on strategic deployment are. Falsified communications transmitted by the Ukrainians' own department of chaos turned Russian soldiers on themselves. On February 26, a Russian Black Sea Fleet

warship began shooting down planes from its own air force, bringing at least one Russian plane down in a bizarre and unforced
"friendly fire" attack. The following day, Russian columns outside
the Ukrainian city of Kharkiv reportedly engaged and destroyed
each other in a fatal shoot-out.

As NATO had two decades before, the Russian authorities
denied they had been hacked at all. Across Vkontakte and Russian forums, TV, and hashtags, it pulled posts, suppressed content,
deprioritized hashtags. Russian influencers spoke out against the
war and then fell silent. Russia has begun to sever its social links.
Content on the invasion is censored inside Russia. Calling it an
invasion carries the prospect of an eight-year prison sentence. It
begins a messaging arms race between Russian authorities with
their internet kill switches and the viral agents who need to get
through. Links spread that allowed cell-phone users outside Russia
to send internet messages as SMS to random Russian phone owners
or put voice calls through to any cell phone inside Russia, so people
anywhere could plead personally and untraceably with whoever
answered.

Russia's assumptions are as full of blind spots as NATO's were
all those years ago. For all its apparent success blanketing the West
in disinformation, it is no less blinkered to the disrupters coming
its way. As traditional media is censored and Twitter, Facebook,
and YouTube at least partially restricted by Russia, something inevitable yet no less unexpected by the Kremlin's strategists happens.
The cyber resistance moves to channels that exist far beyond the
spectrum of government watchfulness. As I write, I am watching
Russian users of illegal download lockers, torrenting sites, special-
interest forums, porn websites, and online games send arms and
ammunition money, downloadable bots that turn your computer
into a vector for DDoS attacks and phishing against targets in
Russia, malware and information on the war, and Russian positions around the world. World of Warcraft, Roblox, and Second

Life—still popular in Russia and Eastern Europe—are awash with anti-Putin posters, pro-Ukraine products, and links to hacker targets to bring down. In Second Life, a Ukrainian armed forces fundraising office has appeared that takes in-game cash in exchange for Ukraine-themed scripts and merchandise. I chat to one avatar there while users of a BDSM disco are plastering it with "Fuck Putin" signs and Ukraine flags. The coder behind the avatar is cruising the game looking for groups, communities, bars, or avatars expressing sympathy with Putin and then hacking their accounts, where real-world information, email addresses, and credit-card info for in-app purchases are stored. He's then diverting payments to the Ukrainian front line. He's not alone. At one bazaar, in-game communities are offering script tools to take down "IRL targets." Another developer in-game is offering bots for Ukraine to deploy on Windows and Linux and "turn your machine into a patriotic bomb." On Pornhub, creators' accounts turn themselves over to messages of support for Ukraine or post morale-boosting videos of themselves having sex while Russia is trying to blow up their neighborhood, while Russian-language preroll ads come pregnant with malware.

File sharers using the Unarchiver application to open their downloads onto their PCs are directed to a payment link to send funds instantly to the Ukrainian army's front line. After just over a week, by March 8, file sharers worldwide had donated more than $350 million (10.6 billion Ukrainian hryvnia) to Ukraine's fighting forces. A Kyiv-based app called Reface that's popular with Russian users uses AI to superimpose users' faces onto celebrities' bodies. Now, it watermarks every image of users' face swaps with the "Stand with Ukraine" slogan and one-click buttons to send funds to the fighters, turns its in-app backgrounds into scenes from the destruction of Kyiv, and pushes notifications about the reality of the war to users' phones. Reface's Ukrainian founder Dima Shvets said that going through leisure channels like this deepfake and games was now "the only way" to reach young Russians.

Ukraine's pirate-hacker economy, nurtured for so long by the Ukrainian intelligence services as well as by the Russians eager to inflict economic drain on the West, is blowing back against Russia.

Two decades have turned Kyiv and Odessa—the birthplace of CarderPlanet and its global network of cash siphons on the West—into thriving Silicon Valley East hubs themselves. And now, like the teenagers of Belgrade groomed and turned into neophyte cyber warriors by the West to which they had so aspired, and by which they had been spurned, the young of Ukraine and its diaspora are turning their networked power on the neighboring superpower who should have seen this coming.

As the screen flickers in the night, these pulses of information are redrawing war for the twenty-first century. This is not in the old, strategic interplay between the forces, diplomacy, and intelligence of states; instead, it is the interplay between strategy and disrupter. The unceasing contest between the execution of commands, on the one hand, and the quantum foam of possibility that stays and subverts them, on the other.

It is not strategy, or weaponry, but the viral spread of antistrategy across the unseen pathways of the world that has changed the way wars are fought. This froth of distributed digital will has turned the binary states of war and peace—of combatant or civilian, of friend or foe—into something far harder to see, let alone fight.

In retrospect, we can see the years between Kosovo and Ukraine were just the grinding of the gears, a period of adjustment. What the internet had done to big media, publishers, record companies, travel agents, TV, it had slowly been telling us it was doing to governments, to war itself. The Kosovo hacks. The cover-up. The Dark Guests. The Russian Business Network. Estonia, Georgia, Crimea, Trump, Brexit, QAnon, Ukraine. It had all been the sound of gears crashing. The space between Kosovo and Kyiv was the long, extended Kodak moment of the old ways of warfare. There was no doubt that traditional, physical military might hold sway on the field, as it had in Kosovo—though that military might prove to be less clear-cut in Ukraine. But what this new form of Total Cyber War did was broaden the context. It made the larger, stronger belligerent hostage to forces that were unpredictable and often mounted in unseen ways, drained resources, sapped morale, diverted attention and force. All the things, in fact, that BadB and the Russian-sponsored networks had spent the 2000s exporting.

When during the shelling of Kyiv in early March 2022 one Ukrainian in-game developer talks to me about "attention hacking" with his code, I can't help thinking of the Croatian Mind Hackers, the Black Hand, and the Department of Chaos, and all that they could have told us sooner, if we'd been willing to listen.

And I see it all laid out, in the blinking grid that crosses the dark expanse between East and West.

Here's Jamie Shea of NATO, floundering and covering up the true origins and collateral damage of wave after wave of cyberattacks in 1999, standing before the herd of nodding legacy media delegates on their graveyard shifts in Brussels, and briefing the existence of imaginary human spies instead of using the encounter to learn and evolve.

There, in their trench coats and brogues are my MI5 men. Leaning across the table at me, frowning as I tell them about Anti-Smyser-1 and trying to steer me away from "all that techie stuff" so they can get to the real threat. Here's General Wesley Clark, whose aircraft stopped one war but bore and dispersed a far stranger one to the four winds, turning tech lobbyist in that oak-paneled room in the sunlit Washington, DC, morning in a bid to stem the uncanny and destabilizing flow of Dark Matter from the United States to the Balkans, Pakistan, Russia, China, the Middle East, pushing Washington and Wall Street to invest in a tech solution to a human problem.

But you can't command Dark Matter to stop flowing on the

global currents of the web. They are the strange quarks, the quantum particles of our big world. We don't see them, only survey what they have wrought. And as for where they'll be next? We can only follow the curve. Watch for where generals and politicians, big tech and big war, the megafauna of our world, still charge and blunder, oblivious to the Empire of the Invisible that surrounds them.

Sometimes, if we're lucky, we catch a glimpse. We see Miloš Čujović, in court or on the yachts with the oligarchs, or limping away down a street in Belgrade like Verbal Kint, clutching a mutilated hand. We see SharpWinner and his band of Peter Pans, posing for tabloids in a rising China, or on the wall of the millions of college kids who study his moves, or Script and BadB at that restaurant in Odessa, raising their toast to draining the West and fucking with American presidents and financial markets. Flyman, in a former ad-agency office in St. Petersburg buying and selling war for cryptocurrency. The Lost Boys, in those high-rises in Belgrade, Kyiv, Skopje, watching the rivers light up orange and red to the sound of alarms and explosions. They flicker, and they are gone. Vanished into islands of asphalt, puffs of smoke, or lines of code. They don't die; they just go dark, until the next time.

Ukraine may hold out against a physically overwhelming force, or it may not; even if it does, the costs have already been catastrophic. Like Serbia, like Russia and China, it may fall in the dimension of the physical and rise in cyberspace. In the quantum world, nothing is binary. War and peace as states may even be obsolete; we are left only with the unceasing, entrepreneurial push for advantage, in a dimension that maps only loosely against anywhere on earth.

All along, ours was a failure not of technology or might, but of imagination.

Western governments, militaries, and intelligence communities, who thought they could solve every problem by speaking to powerful leaders about treaties and strategies. The cybersecurity industry, throwing technological solutions at human riddles. Silicon Valley, forever trapped by its simultaneous claims that it can influence users more by better targeting, and that it is, in the words of Mark Zuckerberg, "a pretty crazy idea" to think it could influence anything like an election.

Even under attack, we are blinded by our own insistence on the advantages we hold—economic and military supremacy, freedom of speech and markets—to things not seen but whose presence weighs on us. We sit at a strange, clouded threshold in our understanding of cyber war. We are Victorian London's cholera doctors. We witness the lethal effects of invisible agents on the population in which we live, but see only vague and deadly miasmas everywhere. They are incomprehensible and toxic simply because we don't yet believe in the reality of their lives, or understand what causes them to erupt into our subterranean networks. In our anxiety, our lack of agency, we see only all-powerful, malign, and invisible forces moving among us. Instead of witchcraft or miasmas, we give them names like China and Russia.

We struggle with the quantum nature of a wholly alien model of cyber war. We fail to realize that like life itself, it has evolved along two parallel but very different lines.

We cling to the old idea that history is made by the big beasts and famous men, because that is what our famous men tell us. Militaries, intelligence services, governments, and corporate actors are easy for us to picture, to photograph shaking hands and testifying and cutting ribbons. They give interviews, make speeches, tell us stories about why the world works the way they say it will.

Yet our world is fundamentally uncanny. Putin says something, and the opposite happens. In the wake of 9/11, the War on Terror was providing a daily example of how a loose, distributed network of code-switching individuals could strike blows in an undefendable way against the West—even as long, drawn-out, generational blowback based on the US response to the Twin Towers attacks. Even in the United States, the phrase was "Forever Wars." People entering the workplace in 2020 had been born to the budgetary, human, and moral drain of costly and bewildering actions in Iraq and Afghanistan. Those actions themselves left vacuums, into which flooded ISIL, warlords of all stripes, and the Taliban. President George W. Bush had declared "Mission Accomplished," and then Americans had lived two decades with the drain of trying to justify that claim. Perhaps the same would await Russia in Ukraine, just as it had in Soviet Afghanistan. The great evolutionary step that the Eastern cyber warriors' methods represented was not simply that cyber war could be carried out as a continuous, unlimited, and entrepreneurial push for advantage in ways that combined sabotage, hacking, information attacks, and denial of service. It was that *these things were autonomous*. They were more effective, more innovative, and more likely to spread carried out by civilians, nonstate actors, overseas communities, or anyone at all than by government or military.

Policy, strategy, these big beasts ride and are tossed with us on a flickering mass of potential actions and potential consequences that we cannot possibly see, or, having seen them, know what they will cause. This is the battle Western intelligence agencies are losing. Just as the US military has been attempting to shoot tornadoes by fighting against the distributed model of cyber conflict with outdated weapons like diplomacy and technology, so our governments have been asleep on the job.

We may not be, ultimately, the masters of our own houses or destinies. There are no binaries, no combatants on the field. No civilians off it. War itself is no longer an act, but a contagion. War itself has gone viral.

Rather than make attacks on enemy capability for which the target—America in this case—could predict and prepare, the very point of Total War was that the attacks were not strategic, and so could not be anticipated. America would defend its military installations and its government networks? Here come attacks on private utilities. Utilities get defended? Private citizens get attacked. On the level of the motivation of the individual, there would be method, but those individual motivations and methods, opportunities spotted, and times chosen would be so varied and widespread that they could not be foreseen effectively. They were, like Twain's worst swordsman in the world, dangerous to the best, because they did not do *the thing they ought to*.

This new form of war was not easily defendable, because it could come in any way, against any vector, at any time. Its commitment to spectacle, to *lulz*—the highest-prestige coin of the internet— meant it was always on a self-perpetuating search for novelty. This was war that jumped and mutated in real time. It fed on its opponents' richness, mass, and complexity. It was war gone *viral*.

It was America's misfortune to be the biggest and mightiest army in the world. After the Cold War, it had basked in its supremacy and taken the opportunity to dismantle much of its standing force of spies trained on Eastern Europe, as well as its signals teams. It was a huge target, and the things that were attacking it were simply too small for it to see.

Now we stand,

> *as on a darkling plain,*
> *Swept with confused alarms of struggle and flight,*
> *Where ignorant armies clash by night.*

No wonder we are anxious. We can walk through our lives, unaware that we are vectors for attack. We may even be the attackers. Our phones, our computers, our social presences are the sleeper agents.

And as I write these last words, watching the roaring destruction play out again, our journey into the age of chaos seems to have come full circle at last. I think about the people on those bridges and the flashing darkness and rocket fire in 1999. The slogan they carried on their placards and shirts was, after all, a prophecy for the new way of war. We understand too late, but finally in the red glare and the din, we know at last what those kids in Belgrade, the flickering, twilit pioneers who unleashed the new age, were trying to tell us. We are all targets.

Acknowledgments

I could not have completed this book without the encouragement, help, input, and inspiration of the following people, all of whom came through in one way or another when it really mattered, somewhere along the way.

Voja Antonić, Branimir Makaneć, Sam Raim, Humfrey Hunter, Lorella Belli, Jonathan Lyon, Rebecca Watson, Fred Francis, Annette Wenda, Niyati Patel, Chris Nolan, Monika Oluwek, Mike Giarratano, Mary Ann Naples, Michelle Aielli, Michael Barrs, Alison Delafave, Mark Galeotti, Janez Škrubej, Milenko Marković, Bojana Robovic, Zoran Rosic, Branko Stamenković, Bosko R, Marko Vesovic, Darko Popović, Slobodan Marković, Andrej Petrovski, Jessikka Aro, Drazen Pantić, Jelena Subotić, Jelena Cosić, Nikola Milosević, Aliide Naylor, Dr Mirjana Drakulic, Ratimir Drakulic, Ashley Kiedrowski, Diana Smite, Adam Lusher, Dr Jessica Barker, Nikola Marković, Bozidar Spasic, Milica Spasic, Ivana Damnjanović, Nigel Tallantire, Zelijko Mirković, Mikko Hypponen, Andrei Soldatov, Milos Vasić, Chris White, Kelly Hignett, Dr Jovan Byford, Victor Petrov, Mary Jo Murphy of *The Washington Post*, Valerie Hopkins, Dejan Mihaijlović, Jože Buh, Milan Kovačević, Dorothy Denning, Dessislava Stoyanova, John Sweeney, Radoslav Leovać, Goran Aleksić, Sean Robbie, Siân Lake, Saska Cvetkovska, Sasa Zivanović, Branko Lestanin, Rowan Manning, Rebekah Billingsley, Damjan and Saša, Jane Mulkerrins, Graham Dobby, Rhys Williams, Paul Clements, Giles Dilnot, Tess Roberts, Paul Martin, Miroljuba Benatova, Vuk Cvijić, Annabel Engels and Ori Ellman, and Jamie Lambert and

Mira Marković (not that one) for help getting me under the skin of 1990s Belgrade and into the offices and operations of Politika. On a personal level, thank you to Ayla Aysel, Galit Haviv-Thomas, and Eddy Temple-Morris for being actual lifesavers without knowing it, likewise Fiona McFall, Al Ahmed, Richard and Marlena Millard, Sami and Sarah Hassan, Lila, and others for their patience; to Graham Sullivan (the British Branimir Makanec, by whom I had the luck to be taught); to teachers Dru Derrick, Laura Cope, Alistair Donaldson, Jacqui Grice, Jeremy Points, Sue Evans/Sue George, Enid Bywater-Lees, Richard Hamilton, and Ron Piper for everything. Thank you also to David, Linda, and Andrea Potter. And all at Dentsu Creative. Thanks too to Vickie Fawcett, Veronique Rhys-Evans, Dan Ambrosio, and Alison Dalafave.

My research assistant on this book was Hanna Andersson, and her hard work, humor, and drive were invaluable.

In addition, my thanks and huge props to the following people for inspiration: Fifi Rong and Milo Lombardi, everyone at the Organized Crime & Corruption Reporting Project (OCCRP.org) and the Balkan Investigative Reporting Network (BIRN.eu.com), Balkan Insight (balkaninsight.com), Bellingcat, the Yugoslavian Wars Archive (yugowarsarchive.org), and Lily Lynch's amazing Balkanist organization; Natalia Antonova (whose resources for open-source intel and geolocation at nataliaantonova.substack.com point to the potential future for citizen involvement). All the NAFO Fellas and Saint Javelin. Likewise all at Bellingcat, and on citizen drone use, Faine Greenwood. Catherine Baker's work on Balkan culture is invaluable, as is Scott J. Henderson's on Chinese hacker culture, Irina Borogan and Andrei Soldatov on Russian security culture. In the research for this book, a point that should be abundantly clear was driven home. Loss of initiative is largely on tech businesses, governments, academia, lawmakers, and militaries not just for thinking too rigidly, but for being blind to their own assumptions. This is undeniably a function of homogeneity. The work of vastly different people like Safiya Umoja Noble, Dr. Emma L. Briant, Asher Wolf, Joan Donovan, Mark Stevenson, Timnit Gebru, Shireen Mitchell, Brooklyne Gipson, Elad Segev, Virginia Eubanks, and organizations such as Blacks In Cybersecurity and Cygenta are not just valuable, but are part of the answer, if tech and governments will only listen.

I owe a further, far broader debt of thanks to friendly faces and voices within technology companies, intelligence workers, and outriders, from Las Vegas to Kyiv, Belgrade to Tel Aviv, Moscow to Milan, and Hong Kong to London; and to the many government and military employees past and present who made time to walk me through points, ideas, and events that first seemed complex, and made them seem very simple.

There are countless more who either wish to remain anonymous here, or in some cases whose real names I never knew. To these mind-hackers everywhere, yes even the ones who spent their time fucking with mine or my phone, who claimed to be different people entirely, thank you for teaching me more than you know.

Matt Potter, January 2023.

Follow me on Twitter: @MattPotter
www.mattpotter.com

This book was powered by:

Goat
Električni Orgazam
The Limiñanas
Disciplina Kičme
Gorky's Zygotic Mynci
King Swamp
Kid Acne
David Bowie
Run The Jewels
Anti-Pop Consortium
Liz Phair
All Them Witches
Flying Lotus
The Anchoress
Valley Of The Sun
Dawn Of The Replicants
King Gizzard & The Lizard Wizard

Selected Bibliography

First and foremost, the body of work by brave and brilliant reporters in Serbian and Montenegrin news organizations such as *Blić, Danas, Kurir, Večernje Novosti, Portal Analitika, Pobjeda, Vijesti, Dan,* Radio Belgrade, and *Monitor* has been invaluable, especially in tracking the stories of the hackers during the bombardment, and Čujović and his generation; and the whistleblowers and cops in the Balkans who undertook personal risk to get the stories, archives, court records, and other material to me. Please join me in supporting their bravery and dedication.

Books

Alberts, Gerard, and Ruth Oldenziel, eds., *Hacking Europe: From Computer Cultures to Demoscenes.* London: Springer, 2014.

Benic, Kristian. *Geeks Behind the Iron Curtain.* Edited by Ana Penovic and Boris Licina. Zagreb: Jasno & Glasno, 2012.

Cassidy, John. *Dot Con: The Greatest Story Ever Sold.* New York: Penguin, 2003.

Clarke, Richard A., and Robert K. Knake. *Cyber War: The Next Threat to National Security and What to Do About It.* New York: HarperCollins, 2010.

Collin, Matthew. *This Is Serbia Calling: Rock'n'Roll Radio and Belgrade's Underground Resistance.* London: Serpent's Tail, 2001.

Earley, Pete. *Comrade J: The Untold Secrets of Russia's Master Spy in America After the End of the Cold War.* New York: Putnam, 2007.

Galeotti, Mark. *The Weaponisation of Everything.* New Haven, CT: Yale University Press, 2022.

———. *We Need to Talk About Putin.* London: Penguin/Ebury, 2019.

Goldman, Marshall. *Oilopoly: Putin, Power and the Rise of the New Russia.* London: One-World, 2010.

Henderson, Scott J. *The Dark Visitor: Inside the World of Chinese Hackers.* N.p., 2007.

Higgs, John. *Stranger than We Can Imagine: Making Sense of the 20th Century.* London: Orion, 2015.

Hu, Tung-hui. *A Prehistory of the Cloud.* Cambridge, MA: MIT Press, 2015.

Judah, Tim. *The Serbs: History, Myth and the Destruction of Yugoslavia.* New Haven, CT: Yale University Press, 2009.

Kaplan, Fred. *Dark Territory: The Secret History of Cyber War.* New York: Simon & Schuster, 2016.

Karatzogianni, Athina. *The Politics of Cyberconflict.* Routledge, 2007.

LeBor, Adam. *Milosevic: A Biography.* London: Bloomsbury, 2003.

Maurer, Tim. *Cyber Mercenaries: The State, Hackers and Power.* Cambridge: Cambridge University Press, 2018.

McCaughey, Martha, and Ayers, Michael D., eds. *Cyberactivism: Online Activism in Theory and Practice.* London: Routledge, 2003.

Merrin, William. *Digital War: A Critical Introduction.* London: Routledge, 2019.

Noble, Safiya Umoja. *Algorithms of Oppression: How Search Engines Reinforce Racism.* New York: New York University Press, 2018.

Perlroth, Nicole. *This Is How They Tell Me the World Ends: The Cyber Weapons Arms Race.* London: Bloomsbury, 2021.

Peters, Benjamin. *How Not to Network a Nation: An Uneasy History of the Soviet Internet.* Cambridge, MA: MIT Press, 2017.

Pomerantsev, Peter. *Nothing Is True and Everything Is Possible.* London: Faber, 2017.

———. *This Is Not Propaganda.* London: Faber, 2019.

Saunders, Robert A. *Ethnopolitics in Cyberspace: The Internet, Minority Nationalism, and the Web of Identity.* Lanham, MD: Lexington Books, 2017.

Segev, Elad. *Google and the Digital Divide: The Bias of Online Knowledge.* Elsevier/Oxford.

Skrubej, Janez. *The Cold War for Information Technology: The Inside Story.* N.p.: Strategic Book, 2013.

Soldatov, Andrei, and Irina Borogan. *The Red Web: The Kremlin's War on the Internet.* New York: PublicAffairs, 2015.

Spasic, Bozodar. *Lasica Koja Govori ("The Weasel Who Talked"): The Spasic Dossier.* Belgrade: Knjiga Komerc, 2000.

Stamenković, Branko. *Cyber War and Cyber Crime: Responding to the Governance Challenges (in partnership with DCAF),* Belgrade Forum, June 2012.

Stewart, Christopher S. *Hunting the Tiger: The Fast Life and Violent Death of the Balkans' Most Dangerous Man.* New York: Thomas Dunne Books, 2008.

Verton, Dan. *The Hacker Diaries: Confessions of Teenage Hackers.* New York: McGraw-Hill/Osborne, 2002.

Papers and articles

"The Science of Making Americans Hurt Their Own Country," Anne Applebaum, *Atlantic,* March 19, 2021.

"Anchoring and Objectifying Neocortical Warfare: Re-presentation of a Biological Metaphor in Serbian Conspiracy Literature," Jovan Byford, The Open University, 2022.

Cosic, Jelena, Ivan Angelovski, Lawrence Marzouk, Maja Zivanovic, and Visar Prebreza. "Serbian Monarchists, British Right-Wingers Plot Kosovo 'Resistance.'" Balkan Insight/BIRN, November 3, 2017.

"A View of Cyberterrorism Five Years Later," by Dorothy Denning, *Readings in Hacking, Counterhacking, and Society* (K. Himma ed.), Jones and Bartlett Publishers, Boston, 2006.

"Balkan Hackers: War in Cyberspace," Dr Mirjana Drakulic, Ratimir Drakulic, 14th BILETA Conference: "Cyberspace 1999: Crime, Criminal Justice and the Internet," College of Ripon & York St. John, York, 1999.

Gault, Matthew. "Ukraine Busts Alleged Russian Bot Farm Using Thousands of SIM Cards." *Vice*, February 9, 2022.

Gerovich, Slava. "Mathematical Machines of the Cold War: Soviet Computing, American Cybernetics and Ideological Disputes in the Early 1950s." *Social Studies of Science* 31, no. 2 (2001): 253–287.

"The Rise of China's Hacking Culture: Defining Chinese Hackers," William Howlett IV, California State University, San Bernardino, June 2016.

"China's Hacker Army," Mara Hvistendahl, *Foreign Policy*, March 2010.

Jones, Ken M. "Cyber War: The Next Frontier for NATO." Calhoun Institutional Archive of the Naval Postgraduate School, 2015. https://citeseerx.ist.psu.edu/viewdoc/download?doi=10.1.1.982.836&rep=rep1&type=pdf.

"Bloggers, Hackers and the King Kong Syndrome," Jeroen de Kloet, University of Amsterdam, January 2009.

Lestanin, Branko, and Professor Zelijko Nikac. "The Fight Against Cyber Crime in Republic of Serbia." Nis, 2017. https://www.academia.edu/42755559/FIGHT_AGAINST_CYBER_CRIME_IN_REPUBLIC_OF_SERBIA.

Lewis, James Andrew. "The Economic Impact of Cybercrime and Cyber Espionage." Center for Strategic and International Studies/McAfee, 2013. https://www.csis.org/analysis/economic-impact-cybercrime-and-cyber-espionage.

"NATO Kosovo plan leaked on net," Adam Lusher and Sean Thomas (pseudonym for Matt Potter): London, *Sunday Telegraph*, 2 April 2000.

"Razvoj Računarkih Mreža U Jugoslaviji I Srbiji 1970–1996 (Computer Networks in Yugoslavia and Serbia, 1970-1996)," PhD Thesis of Dr Slobodan Markovic, Digital Advisor at UN Development Program.

Martin, Diego A., and Jacob N. Shapiro. "Trends in Online Foreign Influence Efforts." Princeton University, 2019. https://www.readkong.com/page/trends-in-online-foreign-influence-efforts-6626592.

Messmer, Ellen. "Kosovo Cyber War Intensifies: Chinese Hackers Targeting US Sites, Government Says." CNN, May 12, 1999.

———. "Serb Supporters Sock It to NATO, US Web Sites." CNN, April 6, 1999.

Office of the Director of National Intelligence. "Foreign Threats to the 2020 US Federal Elections." US National Intelligence Council: Intelligence Community Assessment, declassified March 15, 2021. http://www.dni.gov.

"Annual Address to the Federal Assembly of the Russian Federation," Vladimir Putin, Kremlin.ru, 8/7/2000.

Rossokhovatsky, Diana, and Olga Khvostunova. "Why Russia Needs a Sovereign RuNet." Institute of Modern Russia, 2019. https://imrussia.org/en/analysis/3029-why-russia-needs-a-sovereign-runet.

"Security After 9/11: Strategy Choices & Budget Tradeoffs." Washington, DC: Center for Defense Information, 2003. https://www.files.ethz.ch/isn/28261/security-after-911.pdf.

Shahbaz, Adrian. "Freedom on the Net, 2018: The Rise of Digital Authoritarianism." Freedom House, 2018. http://www.freedomhouse.org.

"Parasecurity and Paratime in Serbia: Neocortical Defence and National Consciousness." Maja Petrović Šteger, *Times of Security*, Routledge, 2013.

Weise, Zia. "Ukraine Blames Russia for Cyberattack Against Government Websites." *Politico*, January 16, 2022.

United Nations Office on Drugs and Crime. "Crime & Its Impact on the Balkans and Affected Countries." March 2008. https://www.unodc.org/documents/data-and-analysis/Balkan_study.pdf.

"Yugoslavia Grows Ripe for Computer Boom," *New Scientist and Science Journal*, 9th September 1971.

For a more exhaustive list of material and links, go to mattpotter.com

Sources

Introduction: Pandora's Box

Machado Pureza, Gabriel. "Dotcom Bubble Meaning." *Wall Street Mojo*. www .wallstreetmojo.com/dotcom-bubble.

"A Brief History of Computer Viruses & What the Future Holds." www.kaspersky .co.uk/resource-center/threats/a-brief-history-of-computer-viruses-and-what-the -future-holds.

"Moral Combat: Nato at War." *Panorama*. BBC, 2000. Archived at: www.yugowarsarchive .org/index.php/moral-combat-nato-at-war.

Lusher, Adam, and Sean Thomas [Matt Potter]. "NATO Kosovo Plan Leaked on Net." *Sunday Telegraph*, April 2, 2000. Unavailable online.

Cromwell, Bob. "History of Cyberwar." https://cromwell-intl.com/cybersecurity /cyberwar/history.html.

"NATO Creates Computer Virus That Reveals Its Secrets." *Times*, June 18, 2000. Unavailable online.

"Help Net Security." Nat-Sec Mini Letter, no. 19 (June 26, 2000). https://packetstorm security.com/files/22221/netsec19.txt.html.

Chapter 1: Rebel Code

"Yugoslavia." https://broadwcast.org/index.php/Yugoslavia.

"The Visit of Apollo 15 Astronauts in Slovenia." https://www.gov.si/en/news/2019 -06-01-the-visit-of-apollo-15-astronauts-in-slovenia/.

"Yugoslavia Grows Ripe for Computer Boom." *New Scientist and Science Journal*, September 9, 1971.

Watson, Paul. "In Death, 'Arkan' Is Still Larger than Life as Media Speculates." *Los Angeles Times*, January 21, 2000. https://www.latimes.com/archives/la-xpm-2000-jan -21-mn-56326-story.html.

Higginbotham, Adam. "Beauty and the Beast." *Guardian*, January 3, 2004. https:// www.theguardian.com/theobserver/2004/jan/04/features.magazine67.

Wood, Paul. "Gangster's Life of Serb Warlord." BBC News, January 15, 2000. http:// news.bbc.co.uk/1/hi/world/europe/605266.stm.

"Arkan, Death of a Warlord: Special Report." BBC News, January 20, 2000. http:// news.bbc.co.uk/1/hi/world/europe/611826.stm.

Stewart, Christopher S. *Hunting the Tiger: The Fast Life and Violent Death of the Balkans' Most Dangerous Man.* New York: Thomas Dunne Books, 2008.

Markovic, Dr. Slobodan. "Razvoj Računarkih Mreža U Jugoslaviji I Srbiji, 1970–1996 [Computer Networks in Yugoslavia and Serbia, 1970-1996]." PhD thesis.

Makanec, Branimir. "My Grandfather Came into the Room, Kissed Me and I Never Saw Him Again. I Don't Even Know Where His Grave Is." November 22, 2020. https://www.vecernji.hr/vijesti/moj-robot-robi-je-68-bio-prava-senzacija-setao-se -zagrebackim-ulicama-i-dobacivao-curama-1447912.

Apollo Guidance Computer: Chandler, David L. "Behind the Scenes of the Apollo Mission at MIT." *MIT News,* July 18, 2019. https://news.mit.edu/2019/behind-scenes -apollo-mission-0718.

Škrubej, Janez. *The Cold War for Information Technology: The Inside Story.* N.p.: SPRA, 2014.

Chapter 2: Enter the Web

Kontrabant: "General Info for: Komtrabant 2 (#ID: 21603)," release date 1984, https:// spectrumcomputing.co.uk/entry/21603/ZX-Spectrum/Kontrabant_2.

ZX Spectrum: http://retrospec.sgn.net/users/tomcat/yu/ZX/TextAdv/Html/Kontrabant .php.

Ventilator 202: https://hyperleap.com/topic/Ventilator_202.

"How People Used to Download Games from the Radio," https://iqfy.com/how-people -used-to-download-games-from-the-radio/.

Hyperinflation: Zeljko Bogetic, Pavle Petrovic, and Zorica Vujosevic, "The Yugoslav Hyperinflation of 1992–1994: Causes, Dynamics, and Money Supply Process," *Journal of Comparative Economics* 27, no. 2 (1999): 335–353, https://www.researchgate .net/publication/4969125_The_Yugoslav_Hyperinflation_of_1992-1994_Causes _Dynamics_and_Money_Supply_Process.

Milica Stojković, "Hyperinflation in Yugoslavia: An Example in Monetary History," *Open Journal for Studies in History* 2, no. 2 (2019): 43–48, https://www.google.com /url?sa=t&rct=j&q=&esrc=s&source=web&cd=&ved=2ahUKEwjSsuzK2qz 4AhUNhFwKHVafAvsQFnoECAsQAw&url=https%3A%2F%2Fcenterprode .com%2Fojsh%2Fojsh0202%2Fcoas.ojsh.0202.03043s.pdf&usg=AOvVaw0kiPiJ -Av8EeJ4lMTstecG.

Paul Toscano, "The Worst Hyperinflation Situations of All Time," CNBC, February 14, 2011, https://www.cnbc.com/2011/02/14/The-Worst-Hyperinflation-Situations-of -All-Time.html.

Gonggrijp and XS4ALL: "Welcome Address by Rop Gonggrijp (Hacker & Activist)," https://conference.hitb.org/hitbsecconf2010ams/index.html%3Fpage_id=838.html.

Drazen Pantic: Interviews recorded by the author.

Zoran Rosic: Series of interviews by the author.

Mirjana & Ratimir Drakulic: Interviews by the author.

Crna Ruka: Julie Moffett, "World: Computer Hacking Becoming a Global Threat," Radio-FreeEurope RadioLiberty, November 9, 1998, https://www.rferl.org/a/1090064 .html.

Laurence Peter, "War of Words on the Internet," BBC News, October 25, 1998, http://news.bbc.co.uk/1/hi/world/monitoring/200708.stm.

Sasa Milosevic, "Serbia: Gaddafi's Cyber Army Oppose Rebels and NATO," Global-Voices, March 30, 2011, https://globalvoices.org/2011/03/30/serbia-gaddafis-cyber-army-oppose-rebels-and-nato/.

Dorothy E. Denning, "A View of Cyberterrorism Five Years Later," Calhoun, 2006, https://www.google.com/url?sa=t&rct=j&q=&esrc=s&source=web&cd=&ved=2ahUKEwikmv_Z4Kz4AhXDilwKHVFCAoEQFnoECCAQAQ&url=https%3A%2F%2Fcore.ac.uk%2Fdownload%2Fpdf%2F36729634.pdf&usg=AOvVaw2XG_x_b-zMk7eOVqcRcCGQ.

Athina Karatzogianni, *The Politics of Cyberconflict* (London: Routledge, 2006).

Martha McCaughey and Michael D. Ayers, eds., *Cyberactivism: Online Activism in Theory and Practice* (New York: Routledge, 2003).

"Serbian Hackers Against NATO," *Novosti*, March 26, 2011, https://www.novosti.rs/vesti/naslovna/aktuelno.69.html:324445-Srpski-hakeri-protiv-NATO.

"Top 15 ExYu Hakerskih Napada," *Internet Dnevnik* (blog), July 31, 2017, https://ircdnevnik.wordpress.com/2017/07/31/%F0%9F%8C%90-web-top-10-exyu-hakerskih-napada/.

Croatian Hacker Army: http://temat.4ever.cc

Goran Katlevic: Mirjana Drakulic and Ratimir Drakulic, "Balkan Hackers War in Cyberspace," paper presented at "Cyberspace 1999: Crime, Criminal Justice and the Internet," York, March 29–30, 1999, https://www.google.com/url?sa=t&rct=j&q=&esrc=s&source=web&cd=&ved=2ahUKEwilsNeG4qz4AhVLiFwKHWRwCxQQFnoECAYQAQ&url=https%3A%2F%2Fwww.bileta.org.uk%2Fwp-content%2Fuploads%2FBalkan-Hackers-War-in-Cyberspace.pdf&usg=AOvVaw3cBrE0ZkXJ7gc8xd8MYg0T.

Jovan Ananiev and Strasko Stojanovski, "Nationalistic Competition over Internet: Legal Regulation and Social Impact," https://www.google.com/url?sa=t&rct=j&q=&esrc=s&source=web&cd=&ved=2ahUKEwilsNeG4qz4AhVLiFwKHWRwCxQQFnoECAUQAQ&url=https%3A%2F%2Feprints.ugd.edu.mk%2F1455%2F1%2FNationalistic%2520strugle%2520over%2520internet%25203.doc&usg=AOvVaw0Gk2kBiWk79LEBv_E0n4zY.

Eligible Receiver: "Lt. Gen. Kenneth A. Minihan, USAF," NSA Historical Figures, https://www.nsa.gov/History/Cryptologic-History/Historical-Figures/Historical-Figures-View/Article/2014245/lt-gen-kenneth-a-minihan-usaf/.

Fred Kaplan, "Inside 'Eligible Receiver': The NSA's Disturbingly Successful Hack of the American Military," March 7, 2016, https://slate.com/technology/2016/03/inside-the-nsas-shockingly-successful-simulated-hack-of-the-u-s-military.html.

Fred Kaplan, *Dark Territory: The Secret History of Cyber War* (New York: Simon and Schuster, 2016).

Moonlight Maze: Will Gragido and John Pirc, "Seven Commonalities of Multivector Threats," *Cybercrime and Espionage*, https://www.sciencedirect.com/topics/computer-science/moonlight-maze.

"Ancient Apt Tools Can Evolve into Current Trends," Kapersky, https://www.kaspersky.com/cyber-attack-moonlight-maze.

Chris Doman, "The First Cyber Espionage Attacks: How Operation Moonlight Maze Made History," *Medium.com* (blog), July 7, 2016, https://medium.com/@chris _doman/the-first-sophistiated-cyber-attacks-how-operation-moonlight-maze -made-history-2adb12cc43f7.

Nikolay Pankov, "Moonlight Maze: Lessons from History," *Kaspersky.com* (blog), April 3, 2017, https://www.kaspersky.com/blog/moonlight-maze-the-lessons/6713/.

Chapter 3: Hacker Nation

Hacks on challenging images of Serbs: Mirjana Drakulic and Ratimir Drakulic, "Balkan Hackers War in Cyberspace," paper presented at "Cyberspace 1999: Crime, Criminal Justice and the Internet," York, March 29–30, 1999, https://www.google .com/url?sa=t&rct=j&q=&esrc=s&source=web&cd=&ved=2ahUKEwjOke-B5a z4AhWSmFwKHS9iDlYQFnoECDAQAQ&url=https%3A%2F%2Fwww.bileta .org.uk%2Fwp-content%2Fuploads%2FBalkan-Hackers-War-in-Cyberspace.pdf &usg=AOvVaw3cBrE0ZkXJ7gc8xd8MYg0T.

Svet Computerra: http://www.zik.com/

http://www.kosova.com/

http://www.vjesnik. com/

Chapter 4: Electronic Child Soldiers

ISPs: "Internet Links to Yugoslavia Under Fire," May 13, 1999, http://www.converge .org.nz/pma/sinte.htm.

Infosky: Interviews with Zoran Rosic, Drazen Pantic, and Slobodan Markovic.

Shut off satellite internet to Yugoslavia: https://www.kosmoplovci.net/hc/digest /articles/may/0028.htm.

The young swarming online in Belgrade: Mirjana Drakulic and Ratimir Drakulic, "Balkan Hackers War in Cyberspace," paper presented at "Cyberspace 1999: Crime, Criminal Justice and the Internet," York, March 29–30, 1999, https://www.google .com/url?sa=t&rct=j&q=&esrc=s&source=web&cd=&ved=2ahUKEwjLobvgg 634AhUNg_0HHXf5D7MQFnoECAkQAQ&url=https%3A%2F%2Fwww.bileta .org.uk%2Fwp-content%2Fuploads%2FBalkan-Hackers-War-in-Cyberspace.pdf &usg=AOvVaw3cBrE0ZkXJ7gc8xd8MYg0T.

White House vanishes: Chris Nuttall, "Kosovo Info Warfare Spreads," BBC News, April 1, 1999, http://news.bbc.co.uk/1/hi/sci/tech/308788.stm.

"White House Computer Network 'Hacked,'" BBC News, October 29, 2014, https:// www.bbc.co.uk/news/technology-29817644.

"Kosovo 1999: Hacking the Military Report," IvyPanda, November 16, 2019, https:// ivypanda.com/essays/kosovo-1999-hacking-the-military/.

Ellen Messmer, "Kosovo Cyber-War Intensifies: Chinese Hackers Targeting U.S. Sites, Government Says," CNN, May 12, 1999, https://www.google.com/url?sa=t&rct =j&q=&esrc=s&source=web&cd=&ved=2ahUKEwiX4e2DhK34AhV5h_0HHV hlBeEQFnoECAYQAQ&url=http%3A%2F%2Fedition.cnn.com%2FTECH%2Fco mputing%2F9905%2F12%2Fcyberwar.idg%2F&usg=AOvVaw1YiHi6CB0vvwBB zysBq6fc.

Myriam Dunn Cavelty, *Cyber-Security and Threat Politics: US Efforts to Secure the Information Age* (New York: Routledge, 2007).

Microwave ovens: Interview with Marko Milosevic; author's own monitoring. **Some additional discussion here:** http://margo.student.utwente.nl/el/microwave /mladen_story.html (site now defunct).

"Old News Item on Iraqi Air Defense; New Questions," http://www.casi.org.uk/discuss /2000/msg00596.html.

Mekon, "Microwave Ovens as Radar Decoys??," August 9, 2001, https://groups.google .com/g/rec.aviation.military/c/L9fqK0190-U.

"TIL That the Yugoslavian Army Used Microwave Ovens to Fool NATO into Dropping Million Dollar Radar Jammers in Empty Fields," Reddit.com, https://www .reddit.com/r/todayilearned/comments/n9484/til_that_the_yugoslavian_army _used_microwave/.

Windows 99: "New!!! Windows 99 and Internet Explore 6: Beta Version, Created by NATO, Tested in Yugoslavia," https://www.mi.sanu.ac.rs/vismath/tart/index .html.

"Postcard Windows 99: NATOsoft Version Yugoslav Anti NATO 1999, Kosovo, Serbia," Rakuten.com, https://fr.shopping.rakuten.com/offer/buy/2837320598/carte -postale-windows-99-natosoft-version-yugoslav-anti-otan-1999-kosovo-serbie .html.

Chapter 5: Black Jet Down

Dario Leone, "An In-Depth Analysis of How the Serbs Were Able to Shoot Down an F-117 Stealth Fighter During Operation Allied Force," Aviation Geek Club, March 26, 2020, https://theaviationgeekclub.com/an-in-depth-analysis-of-how-serbs-were -able-to-shoot-down-an-f-117-stealth-fighter-during-operation-allied-force/.

Trevor Filseth, "The Amazing Story of How a Stealth Fighter Was Shot Down," National Interest, June 14, 2021, https://nationalinterest.org/blog/buzz/amazing -story-how-stealth-fighter-was-shot-down-187658.

Sebastien Roblin, "That's Embarrassing: In 1999, Yugoslavia Shot Down an F-117 Nighthawk," National Interest, August 13, 2020, https://nationalinterest.org/blog/reboot /thats-embarrassing-1999-yugoslavia-shot-down-f-117-nighthawk-166788.

Ivana Nikolic, "Serbia Keeps Downed US Stealth Bomber on Show," Balkan Transitional Justice, March 27, 2015, https://balkaninsight.com/2015/03/27/serbia-keeps -memory-on-fallen-nighthawk/.

Katsuji Nakazawa, "Analysis: Mystery of 1999 US Stealth Jet Shootdown Returns with Twist," Nikkei Asia, June 3, 2021, https://asia.nikkei.com/Editor-s-Picks/China-up -close/Analysis-Mystery-of-1999-US-stealth-jet-shootdown-returns-with-twist.

Dale Zelko: Blake Stilwell, "How an Air Force Pilot Became Friends with the Man Who Shot Down His F-117," Military.com, https://www.military.com/military -life/how-air-force-pilot-became-friends-man-who-shot-down-his-f-117.html.

Hasard Lee, "F-35 Pilot Explains How 1950s Tech Shot Down a 'Stealth Fighter,'" Sandboxx, September 21, 2021, https://www.sandboxx.us/blog/an-f-35-pilots-take -on-the-only-stealth-fighter-lost-in-combat/.

Darrell Whitcomb, "The Night They Saved Vega 31," *Air Force Magazine*, December 1, 2006, https://www.airforcemag.com/article/1206vega/.

Michael B. Prosser, "Memetics: A Growth Industry in US Military Operations" (master's thesis, Marine Corps University, Quantico, School of Advanced Warfighting, 2006), https://apps.dtic.mil/sti/citations/ADA507172.

We are all targets: Michael Dobbs, "Targets Hit Bull's-Eye for Defiant Serbs," *Washington Post*, April 9, 1999, https://www.washingtonpost.com/wp-srv/inatl/longterm/balkans/stories/belgrade040999.htm.

Jamie Shea: John Schwartz, "Yugoslavs Hacking at NATO Computers," *Washington Post*, April 1, 1999, https://www.washingtonpost.com/wp-srv/inatl/daily/april99/hackers040199.htm.

609th Info War squadron: Jason Healey, "Claiming the Lost Cyber Heritage," Air University, June 1, 2017, https://www.airuniversity.af.edu/CyberCollege/Portal/Article/Article/1198929/claiming-the-lost-cyber-heritage/.

Haiti: Yael Yashar, "Information Warfare," International Institute for Counter-Terrorism, February 26, 1997, https://www.ict.org.il/UserFiles/Information%20Warfare.pdf.

Donald Emmett Elam, "Attacking the Infrastructure: Exploring Potential Uses of Offensive Information Warfare" (master's thesis, Naval Postgraduate School, 2006), Calhoun: The NPS Institutional Archive, June 1996, https://www.google.com/url?sa=t&rct=j&q=&esrc=s&source=web&cd=&ved=2ahUKEwjqzPDn8bH4AhXRh1wKHWW1D4kQFnoECA0QAQ&url=https%3A%2F%2Fcore.ac.uk%2Fdownload%2Fpdf%2F36724816.pdf&usg=AOvVaw3ww8BwEX_j-_o1T_cpYBe1.

Chris Scheuerweghs: Dan Verton, "Serbs Launch Cyberattack on NATO," FCW, April 4, 1999, https://fcw.com/1999/04/serbs-launch-cyberattack-on-nato/195288/.

Chapter 6: Chaos Particle

Nikola Markovic: M. Trajanović and M. Stanković, eds., *6th International ICT Conference: Proceedings* (Niš, Serbia: Regional Chamber of Commerce, 2014), https://www.academia.edu/10518758/Proceedings_of_6th_International_ICT_Conference.

Drakulices and the secret room: Interviews with the author.

Bozidar "the Weasel" Spasic: Interviews with the author.

Chapter 7: The Birth of a Global Brand

Captain Dragan: Nidzara Ahmetasevic, "'Captain Dragan', Man of Many Identities," *BalkanInsight*, April 1, 2010, https://balkaninsight.com/2010/04/01/captain-dragan-man-of-many-identities/.

Jenny Awford, "Serbian Commander Known as Captain Dragan Who Lived as a Golf Instructor in Australia Finally Faces War Crimes Trial for Killing and Torturing Civilians," *Daily Mail*, September 20, 2016, https://www.dailymail.co.uk/news/article-3798120/Serbian-commander-Captain-Dragan-finally-faces-war-crimes-trial.html.

Serbian Internet Army: http://members.tripod.com/srbadija1/.

http://come.to/svi

Svetozar Radišić and Neocortical Warfare: Jovan Byford, "Anchoring and Objectifying Neocortical Warfare: Re-presentation of a Biological Metaphor in Serbian Conspiracy

Literature," *Papers on Social Representations* 11 (2002): 3.1–3.14, https://www.research gate.net/publication/42792728_Anchoring_and_objectifying_neocortical_warfare _Re-presentation_of_a_biological_metaphor_in_Serbian_conspiracy_literature.

Maja Petrović-Šteger, "Parasecurity and Paratime in Serbia: Neocortical Defence and National Consciousness," in *Times of Security: Ethnographies of Fear, Protest, and the Future*, ed. Martin Holbraad and Morten Axel Pedersen (New York: Routledge, 2013).

Chapter 8: Horror Show

Bombing of Chinese Embassy: Dario Leone, "The Night USAF B-2A Spirits Bombed Chinese Embassy in Belgrade," Aviation Geek Club, March 26, 2020, https:// theaviationgeekclub.com/the-night-usaf-b-2a-spirits-bombed-chinese-embassy-in -belgrade/.

Steven Perlstein, "Supply Building Was NATO's Real Target," *Washington Post*, May 9, 1999, https://www.washingtonpost.com/wp-srv/inatl/longterm/balkans/stories /kosovo050999.htm.

"Truth Behind America's Raid on Belgrade," *Guardian*, November 27, 1999, https:// www.theguardian.com/theobserver/1999/nov/28/focus.news1.

Kevin Ponniah and Lazara Marinkovic, "The Night the US Bombed a Chinese Embassy," BBC News, May 7, 2019, https://www.bbc.co.uk/news/world-europe-48134881.

"Stop all war. Consintrate [sic] on your problems. Nothing was damaged, but we are not telling how we got in." https://everything2.com/title/The+Hong+Kong +Danger+Duo

Wallace Wang, *Steal This Computer Book 4.0: What They Won't Tell You About the Internet* (San Francisco: self-published, 2006), https://vdoc.pub/documents/steal-this-computer -book-40-what-they-wont-tell-you-about-the-internet-22l65lldgu60.

Rocky the Chinese Hacker: Ellen Messmer, "Kosovo Cyber-war Intensifies: Chinese Hackers Targeting U.S. Sites, Government Says," CNN.com, May 12, 1999, http:// edition.cnn.com/TECH/computing/9905/12/cyberwar.idg/.

Green Army/Whampoa Military Academy: Scott J. Henderson, *The Dark Visitor: Inside the World of Chinese Hackers* (self-published, 2007), https://ebin.pub/the-dark -visitor-inside-the-world-of-chinese-hackers.html.

1999 Cyberattacks Cost US Businesses $266 Million: William Yurcik, David Loomis, and Alexander D. Korzyk Sr., "Predicting Internet Attacks: On Developing and Effective Measurement Methodology," *Proceedings of the 18th Annual International Communications Forecasting Conference* (2006), https://citeseerx.ist.psu.edu/viewdoc /download?doi=10.1.1.60.4112&rep=rep1&type=pdf.

Chinawill and Wan Tao: Michael Yip, "An Investigation into Chinese Cybercrime and the Underground Economy in Comparison with the West" (PhD diss., University of Southampton, 2010), https://www.academia.edu/2728559/An_investigation _into_Chinese_cybercrime_and_the_underground_economy_in_comparison _with_the_West.

Cult of the Dead Cow—Back Orifice: https://www.f-secure.com/v-descs/backori .shtml.

DDoS figures: V. Anil Kumar, "Sophistication in Distributed Denial-of-Service Attacks on the Internet," *Current Science* 87 no. 7 (2004): 885–888, https://www.jstor.org/stable/24109391.

Chapter 9: Alarms in Virginia

Bill Swallow: Dan Verton, *The Hacker Diaries: Confessions of Teenage Hackers* (New York: McGraw-Hill/Osborne, 2002).

Brian Friel, "Interagency Web Site Hacked by War Critics," Government Executive, April 30, 1999, https://www.govexec.com/federal-news/1999/04/interagency-web-site-hacked-by-war-critics/2855/.

Chapter 10: A Clash of Cyber Cultures

Reports that the US planned to shut down the Yugoslav Internet: Gordana Rajkov, Independent Living Institute of Belgrade, "A Personal Letter from Belgrade, Serbia—Written during the current NATO bombings in Yugoslavia," May 13, 1999, https://www.independentliving.org/docs6/rajkov1999.html.

Leander Kahn, *Wired*, May 13, 1999: "US May Pull Belgrade Bandwidth," https://www.wired.com/1999/05/us-may-pull-belgrade-bandwidth/.

James Rubin denies allegations, as internet is helpful to freedom: "Activism, Hacktivism, and Cyberterrorism: The Internet as a Tool for Influencing Foreign Policy," Dorothy E. Denning, Georgetown University, http://oldsite.nautilus.org/archives/info-policy/workshop/papers/denning.html.

An Assessment of International Legal Issues in Information Operations, 1999: https://cyber.harvard.edu/cybersecurity/An_Assessment_of_International_Legal_Issues_in_Information_Operations.

Jakewick plan: Kaplan, Fred. *Dark Territory: The Secret History of Cyber War.* New York: Simon & Schuster, 2016.

Serbian Angels lift MI6 names: Participant interviews with the author.

Clinton approves plan to raid bank accounts of Serbian leadership: *Time*, July 5, 1999, https://apnews.com/article/fcd2581e450c4efb5d41cbebf1b31009.

Borka Vucic: "Milosevic's Banker Emerges from War Fighting for Cash," Robert Block, *Wall Street Journal*, August 9, 1999, https://www.wsj.com/articles/SB934153990401559655.

John Arquilla on financial targets: "Pentagon kept the lid on cyberwar in Kosovo", Julian Borger, *Guardian*, November 9, 1999, https://www.theguardian.com/world/1999/nov/09/balkans.

Martin Libicki, as above: https://www.theguardian.com/world/1999/nov/09/balkans.

Paul Magis on the NATO servers: CNN, and "Crisis in the Balkans—Serbs' Revenge: NATO website zapped," Amy Harmon, *New York Times*, April 1, 1999, https://www.nytimes.com/1999/04/01/world/crisis-in-the-balkans-serbs-revenge-nato-web-site-zapped.html.

DARPA's Chris White: Interview with the author.

Bill Swallow and Jill Knesek: Dan Verton, *The Hacker Diaries: Confessions of Teenage Hackers* (New York: McGraw-Hill/Osborne, 2002).

Team Spl0it: *Attrition*, Friday, June 11, 1999.

Chapter 11: The Big Bang

Clinton on China nailing Jell-O to the wall: Steven Melendez, " 'Nailing Jell-O to the Wall': How China Shut Down the Open Internet," *Fast Company*, March 9, 2015, https://www.fastcompany.com/3057604/nailing-jell-o-to-the-wall-how-china-shut -down-the-open-internet.

***People's Daily* China on internet users numbers being insignificant:** "China Had 8 Million Internet Users at the End of 1999," *People's Daily Online*, n.d., http:// en.people.cn/english/200001/12/print20000112T122.html.

Yahoo! leaker jailed: Julia Pearlman, "Yahoo! Founder Admits It Helped Jail Journalist over Leaked Warning," Campaign Live, September 12, 2005, https://www .campaignlive.co.uk/article/yahoo-founder-admits-helped-jail-journalist-leaked -warning/505593.

Microsoft collaborating with China on censorship: Stephen Brook, "Microsoft Defends Pulling Plug on Chinese Blogger," *Guardian*, January 6, 2006, https://www. theguardian.com/technology/2006/jan/06/newmedia.media.

Milan Kovačević: Sasa Milosevic, "Serbia: Gaddafi's Cyber Army Opposes Rebels and NATO," New Media Rights, March 29, 2011, https://www.newmediarights.org/drm _digital_rights_management/newmediarights.org/about_us/newsletters?page=78.

"Serbian Hackers Against NATO," *Novosti*, March 26, 2011, https://www.novosti.rs/vesti /naslovna/aktuelno.69.html:324445-Srpski-hakeri-protiv-NATO.

Zoran Rosic: Interviews by the author.

https://globalvoices.org/2011/03/30/serbia-gaddafis-cyber-army-oppose-rebels-and-nato/

Chapter 12: The Cyber Mercenaries

Google's origins in NSA/CIA funding of the Massive Digital Data Systems Project: Jeff Nesbit, "Google's True Origin Partly Lies in CIA and NSA Research Grants for Mass Surveillance," *Quartz*, December 8, 2017, https://qz.com/1145669/googles -true-origin-partly-lies-in-cia-and-nsa-research-grants-for-mass-surveillance/.

Cicada 3301: Mihai Andrei, "Cicada 3301: A Puzzle for the Brightest Minds, Posted by an Unknown, Mysterious Organization," *ZME Science*, February 1, 2021, https:// www.zmescience.com/other/feature-post/cicada-3301-puzzle-brightest-minds -posted-unknown-mysterious-organizationt/.

Michael Grothaus, "Meet the Man Who Solved the Mysterious Cicada 3301 Puzzle," *Fast Company*, November 25, 2014, https://www.fastcompany.com/3025785/meet -the-man-who-solved-the-mysterious-cicada-3301-puzzle.

Chapter 13: A Troll Is Born

FBI working together with Russian FSB in Lubyanka: Kim Zetter, "When Russia Helped the US Nab Cybercriminals," *Zero Day* (blog), November 30, 2021, https:// zetter.substack.com/p/when-russia-helped-the-us-nab-cybercriminals.

Lajos F. Szászdi, *Russian Civil-Military Relations and the Origins of the Second Chechen War* (Lanham, MD: University Press of America, 2008), https://www.scribd.com /book/80750121/Russian-Civil-Military-Relations-and-the-Origins-of-the-Second -Chechen-War.

Jerri Williams, "Episode 141: Bill Kinane—FBI in Moscow, First Russian LEGAT," November 8, 2018, in *FBI Retired Case File Review*, podcast, https://jerriwilliams .com/bill-kinane-fbi-in-moscow-first-russian-legat/.

Brad Thor, *State of the Union: A Thriller* (New York: Atria Books, 2004).

Raf Sanchez, "Old Habits Die Hard: The FBI and the Russian Security Services," *Telegraph*, May 1, 2013, https://www.telegraph.co.uk/news/worldnews/northamerica /usa/10029472/Old-habits-die-hard-the-FBI-and-the-Russian-security-services.html.

Putin's recognition of asymmetric war's value: Russian Defense Ministry's Daily "Krasnaya Zvezda," October 9, 1999.

Sakaguchi Yoshaiki and Mayama Katsuhiko, "Significance of the War in Kosovo for China and Russia," *NIDS Security Reports*, no. 3 (March 2002), https://www.google .com/url?sa=t&rct=j&q=&esrc=s&source=web&cd=&ved=2ahUKEwjFkbTz ts34AhWIh1wKHbKtA1MQFnoECAYQAQ&url=http%3A%2F%2Fwww.nids .mod.go.jp%2Fenglish%2Fpublication%2Fkiyo%2Fpdf%2Fbulletin_e2001_1.pdf &usg=AOvVaw3ozCSUgfTjYbZfC2RQBxLs

Russian Security Concept 2000: "2000 Russian National Security Concept," https:// www.bits.de/EURA/natsecconc.pdf.

Celeste A. Wallander, "Russian National Security Policy in 2000," PONARS Policy Memo, January 2000, https://www.ponarseurasia.org/wp-content/uploads/attachments /pm_0102-5.pdf.

"Russia's National Security Concept," *Arms Control Today*, n.d., https://www.armscontrol .org/act/2000-01/features/russias-national-security-concept.

Putin's address to the All-Russia Meeting of Defence Industry Workers, Nizhny Novgorod, April 2000: http://en.kremlin.ru/events/president/transcripts/21265.

Putin's July 2000 Federal Assembly address: http://en.kremlin.ru/events/president /transcripts/21480.

Sergei Tretyakov: Jonathan Steele, "Sergei Tretyakov Obituary," *Guardian*, July 11, 2010, https://www.theguardian.com/world/2010/jul/11/sergei-tretyakov-obituary.

Pete Earley, *Comrade J: The Untold Secrets of Russia's Master Spy in America After the End of the Cold War* (New York: G. P. Putnam's Sons, 2007).

Roman Vega, Carder Planet, and Boafactory.com: Misha Glenny, *DarkMarket: Cyberthieves, Cybercops, and You* (New York: Alfred A. Knopf, 2011).

United States Attorney's Office, Eastern District of New York, "Ukrainian National Who Co-founded Cybercrime Marketplace Sentenced to 18 Years In Prison," December 12, 2013, https://www.justice.gov/usao-edny/pr/ukrainian-national-who -co-founded-cybercrime-marketplace-sentenced-18-years-prison.

M. E. Kabay and Bradley Guinen, "The Russian Cybermafia: Boa Factory & Carder-Planet," *Network World*, March 23, 2011, https://www.networkworld.com/article /2201010/the-russian-cybermafia—boa-factory—carderplanet.html.

BadB: Andrew E. Kramer, "Hacker's Arrest Offers Peek into Crime in Russia," *New York Times*, August 24, 2010, https://www.nytimes.com/2010/08/24/business/global /24cyber.html.

"Alleged Carder 'BadB' Busted in France: Watch His Cartoon," *InfoSec News*, August 12, 2010, https://seclists.org/isn/2010/Aug/37.

BadB promotional cartoon: https://www.youtube.com/watch?v=EtcKavgS_2k.

Script and arrest by US Postal Service work: "Tracking the Russian Scammers," *Wired*, January 31, 2007, https://www.wired.com/2007/01/tracking-the-russian-scammers/.

Andrei Lugovoi, assassin of Aleksandr Litvinenko, promoted to Russian State Duma to avoid prosecution or extradition: Luke Harding, "Russian Honour for Andrei Lugovoi Is Provocation, Litvinineko Inquiry Told," *Guardian*, March 10, 2015, https://www.theguardian.com/world/2015/mar/10/russian-honour-andrei-lugovoi-provocation-litvinineko-inquiry.

"Litvinenko Suspects Andri Lugovoi and Dmitry Kovtun," BBC News, January 21, 2016, https://www.bbc.co.uk/news/uk-35370621.

http://duma.gov.ru/en/duma/persons/99110999/news/

Chapter 14: Life on the Wire

Robert Boback and Tiversa: Raffi Khatchadourian, "A Cybersecurity Firm's Sharp Rise and Stunning Collapse," *New Yorker*, October 28, 2019, https://www.newyorker.com/magazine/2019/11/04/a-cybersecurity-firms-sharp-rise-and-stunning-collapse.

Russian Business Network: M. Edwards, "What Is the Russian Business Network," ITProToday, November 27, 2007, https://www.itprotoday.com/windows-78/what-russian-business-network.

"A Walk on the Dark Side: These Badhats May Have Bought Your Bank Account," *Economist*, August 30, 2007, https://www.economist.com/unknown/2007/08/30/a-walk-on-the-dark-side.

Peter Warren, "Hunt for Russia's Web Criminals," *Guardian*, November 15, 2007, https://www.theguardian.com/technology/2007/nov/15/news.crime.

Kelly Jackson Higgins, "An Inside Look at the Russian Business Network," DarkReading, January 11, 2008, https://www.darkreading.com/risk/an-inside-look-at-the-russian-business-network.

US House of Representatives Special Hearing, "Inadvertent File Sharing on Peer-to-Peer Networks: How It Endangers Citizens and Jeopardizes National Security," transcript, July 29, 2009, https://www.govinfo.gov/content/pkg/CHRG-111hhrg54009/html/CHRG-111hhrg54009.htm.

Chapter 15: The New Russian Way of War

Estonia's cyber development: "E-stonia, the Most Connected Country in the World," https://accessr.eu/en/projets/e-stonia-the-most-connected-country-in-the-world/.

Elizabeth Schulze, "How a Tiny Country Bordering Russia Became One of the Most Tech-Savvy Societies in the World," CNBC, February 8, 2019, https://www.cnbc.com/2019/02/08/how-estonia-became-a-digital-society.html.

"Estonia, the World's First Digital Republic," Killik & Co., n.d., https://www.killik.com/the-edit/estonia-the-worlds-first-digital-republic/.

Cyberwar: Damien McGuinness, "How a Cyber Attack Transformed Estonia," BBC News, April 27, 2017, https://www.bbc.com/news/39655415.

Emily Tamkin, "10 Years After the Landmark Attack on Estonia, Is the World Better Prepared for Cyber Threats?," *Foreign Policy*, April 27, 2017, https://foreignpolicy

.com/2017/04/27/10-years-after-the-landmark-attack-on-estonia-is-the-world-better
-prepared-for-cyber-threats/.

Stephen Herzog, "Revisiting the Estonian Cyber Attacks: Digital Threats and Mul-
tinational Responses," *Journal of Strategic Security* 8, no. 4 (2011): 49–60, https://
www.jstor.org/stable/26463926.

Rain Ottis, "Analysis of the 2007 Cyber Attacks Against Estonia from the Information
Warfare Perspective," https://ccdcoe.org/uploads/2018/10/Ottis2008_AnalysisOf
2007FromTheInformationWarfarePerspective.pdf.

Involvement of Nashi and Konstantin Goloskov: Victor Yasmann, "Russia: Monu-
ment Dispute with Estonia Gets Dirty," RadioFreeEurope RadioLiberty, May 4,
2007, https://www.rferl.org/a/1076297.html.

Gadi Evron, "Authoritatively, Who Was Behind the Estonia Attacks," DarkReading,
March 17, 2009, https://cyber-peace.org/wp-content/uploads/2016/11/Authoritatively
-Who-Was-Behind-The-Estonian-Attacks_.pdf.

Jose Nazario on absence of smoking gun from the Russian government: "Estonian
DDoS: A Final Analysis," May 31, 2007, http://www.h-online.com/security/news
/item/Estonian-DDoS-a-final-analysis-732971.html.

Script: http://fipip.ru/raznoe/pingi.bat

Student in Tallinn Dmitri Galushkevich arrested for Estonia hacks: Jeremy Kirk,
"Student Fined for Attack Against Estonian Web Site," *Computerworld*, January 24,
2008, https://www.computerworld.com/article/2538983/student-fined-for-attack
-against-estonian-web-site.html.

Charles Arthur, "That Cyberwarfare by Russia on Estonia? It Was One Kid...in Estonia," *Guardian,* January 25, 2008, https://www.theguardian.com/technology/blog
/2008/jan/25/thatcyberwarfarebyrussiaon.

Sergei Markov claim: "I Kill Spammers," *Spam* (blog), May 7, 2013, http://itsspammail
.blogspot.com/2013/05/blog-post_1884.html.

Georgia cyberwar: John Markoff, "Before the Gunfire, Cyberattacks," *New York Times*,
August 12, 2008, https://www.nytimes.com/2008/08/13/technology/13cyber
.html.

"Georgia-Russia Conflict (2008)," https://cyberlaw.ccdcoe.org/wiki/Georgia-Russia
conflict(2008).

Donald L. Buresh, "Russian Cyber-attacks on Estonia, Georgia, and Ukraine, Including Tactics, Techniques, Procedures, and Effects," *Journal of Advanced Forensic Sciences* 1, no. 2 (2021): 15–26, https://openaccesspub.org/jafs/article/1686.

Tulip Systems' Tom Burling: Peter Svensson, "Russian Hackers Continue Attacks on
Georgian Sites," *Sydney Morning Herald*, August 13, 2008, https://www.smh.com.au
/technology/russian-hackers-continue-attacks-on-georgian-sites-20080812-3tpo
.html.

"Russian Hackers Hit Georgian Websites," *Irish Examiner*, August 14, 2008, https://
www.irishexaminer.com/world/arid-20069841.html.

"Russian Hackers Attack Georgian Websites," CBS News, August 12, 2008, https://
www.cbsnews.com/news/russian-hackers-attack-georgian-web-sites/.

Chapter 16: Storms and Deserts

US Department of Defense lost data: Mustafa Canbolat and Emrah Sezgin, "Is NATO Ready for a Cyberwar?" (master's thesis, Naval Postgraduate School, 2016), https://core.ac.uk/download/pdf/81223436.pdf.

Alexander Klimburg and Heli Tirmaa-Klaar, "Cybersecurity and Cyberpower: Concepts, Conditions and Capabilities for Cooperation for Action within the EU," April 2011, https://www.europarl.europa.eu/RegData/etudes/STUD/2011/433828/EXPO-SEDE_ET(2011)433828_EN.pdf.

Black Hand in Libya: Sasa Milosevic, "Serbia: Gaddafi's Cyber Army Oppose Rebels and NATO," GlobalVoices, March 30, 2011, https://globalvoices.org/2011/03/30/serbia-gaddafis-cyber-army-oppose-rebels-and-nato/.

Philip J. Cohen, "The Ideology and Historical Continuity of Serbia's Anti-Islamic Policy," *Islamic Studies* 36, nos. 2–3 (1997): 361–382, https://www.jstor.org/stable/23076201.

"Libyan Opposition Accuses '50,000 Serb Hackers,'" b92, March 24, 2011, https://www.b92.net/eng/news/society.php?yyyy=2011&mm=03&dd=24&nav_id=73415.

Iva Martinovic and Charles Rechnagel, "Ultranationalist Serbs Organize Pro-Qaddafi Campaign," RadioFreeEurope RadioLiberty, March 24 2011, https://www.rferl.org/a/serb_ultranationalists_rally_for_qaddafi/2348963.html.

Dejan Vuletić: https://www.researchgate.net/profile/Dejan-Vuletic.

Chapter 17: The Google Archipelago

Milos Čujović biographical details: "Trial and Judgement of Judge Vesna Mostrokol in the Case of Milos Čujović, Natasha Golovic and Nebojsa Boskovic," Podgorica High Court, Montenegro, December 5, 2019.

Miloš Čujović criminal past: https://www.vijesti.me/tag/28488/milos-cujovic.

Interviews with Branko Stamenković, chief prosecutor, cybercrime, Belgrade, and others.

Čujović three fingers cut off: http://mondo.rs/a259466/Info/Drustvo/Mafija-odsekla-prste-hakeru-iz-Beograda.html.

Čujović in Serbia: http://www.dan.co.me/?nivo=3&datum=2015-03-16&rubrika=Hronika&najdatum=2016-01-25&clanak=529891&naslov=Hakeru%20prona%B9li%20mobilni%20u%20%E6eliji.

http://www.dan.co.me/indexprovjera.phtml?nivo=3&datum=2014-06-16&rubrika=Hronika&najdatum=2015-04-14&clanak=486213&naslov=U%20Mandi%E6evoj%20%E6eliji%20prona%F0eni%20telefoni.

2012 trial with the Zagorje criminal gang: https://www.portalanalitika.me/clanak/uhapen-vidoje-stanii.

Golden Goose phenomenon for hackers in Russia: Photon Research Team, "Life in Prison: The Cybercriminal Perspective," *Digital Shadows* (blog), January 27, 2022, https://www.digitalshadows.com/blog-and-research/life-in-prison-the-cybercriminal-perspective/.

Čujović and the Zagorje gang sentenced in Podgorica: http://volimpodgoricu.me/2016/05/18/podgorica-hakeri-osudeni-na-20-godina-zatvora/.

Chapter 18: Dark Guest, Red Guest

China's hacker culture: Mara Hvistendahl, "China's Hacker Army," *Foreign Policy*, March 3, 2010, https://foreignpolicy.com/2010/03/03/chinas-hacker-army/.

Scott J. Henderson, *The Dark Visitor: Inside the World of Chinese Hackers* (self-published, 2007).

Scott Henderson, "Beijing's Rising Hacker Stars...: How Does Mother China React," *IO Sphere* (Fall 2008): 25–30, https://www.google.com/url?sa=t&rct=j&q=&esrc =s&source=web&cd=&ved=2ahUKEwjrwc2U4c34AhW7QEEAHS_iAZsQFno ECB0QAQ&url=https%3A%2F%2Fcommunity.apan.org%2Fcfs-file%2F__key% 2Fdocpreview-s%2F00-00-06-09-67%2F2008_2D00_09_2D00_01-Beijing_2700_s -Rising-Hacker-Stars-_2800_Henderson_2900_.pdf&usg=AOvVaw2TwxDOTW Drwkq7bEOqm5Sk.

Mara Hvistendahl, "Hackers: The China Syndrome," *Popular Science*, April 23, 2009, https://www.popsci.com/scitech/article/2009-04/hackers-china-syndrome/.

David Barboza, "Hacking for Fun and Profit in China's Underworld," *New York Times*, February 1, 2010, https://www.nytimes.com/2010/02/02/business/global /02hacker.html.

State sponsorship of hacking: William Howlett IV, "The Rise of China's Hacking Culture: Defining Chinese Hackers" (master's thesis, California State University, San Bernardino, 2016), https://scholarworks.lib.csusb.edu/etd/383/.

Mitch Edwards, "China's Green Army: Capitalism Defeats China's First Hacking Group," *Medium.com* (blog), March 28, 2018, https://medium.com/@theCTIGuy /chinas-green-army-capitalism-defeats-china-s-first-hacking-group-d4c73631d2ca.

Chinese universities cranking out hackers: Dakota Cary, "China's Next Genera-tion of Hackers Won't Be Criminals. That's a Problem," TechCrunch, November 12, 2021, https://techcrunch.com/2021/11/12/chinas-next-generation-of-hackers -wont-be-criminals-thats-a-problem/?guccounter=1&guce_referrer=aHR0cHM 6Ly93d3cuZ29vZ2xlLmNvbS8&guce_referrer_sig=AQAAAC67HRWg4koLjch Aoj0HvJxhRwb2qSceK54c85yTOJzcmebR89cCFoHPrIxTo5uhcvLKsXOIvU r8yIIejsXhgj-Xx8XlE80eu0mDpiN1YmhsMwkPUZbrKy29zYX—MxbpvTZqRt9 iscMmtx899b34_Sviqs0jjnA7r7wr679okox.

Attacks on Japanese websites: "Chinese Hackers Attack Japanese Websites," *Irish Times*, August 14, 2001, https://www.irishtimes.com/news/chinese-hackers-attack -japanese-websites-1.393185.

Fake Apple store: Melanie Lee, "Fake Apple Store in China Even Fools Staff," Reuters, July 21, 2011, https://www.reuters.com/article/us-china-apple-fake-idUS TRE76K1SU20110721.

Legal battle between Chinese hacker groups: William Howlett IV, "The Rise of Chi-na's Hacking Culture: Defining Chinese Hackers" (master's thesis, California State University, San Bernardino, 2016), https://scholarworks.lib.csusb.edu/etd/383/.

SharpWinner's autobiography: Mara Hvistendahl, "China's 'Pirate' Army," esglobal, March 10, 2010, https://www-esglobal-org.translate.goog/el-ejercito-pirata-de-china /?_x_tr_sl=es&_x_tr_tl=en&_x_tr_hl=en&_x_tr_pto=sc.

Hacking live contest for students at China's Southeastern University: Catalin Cimpanu, "Chinese Universities Connected to Known APTs Are Conducting AI/ML Cybersecurity Research," *Record*, March 11, 2021, https://therecord.media/chinese -universities-connected-to-known-apts-are-conducting-ai-ml-cybersecurity-research/.

Chapter 19: Ignorant Armies

Stuxnet: "An Unprecedented Look at Stuxnet, the World's First Digital Weapon," *Wired*, November 3, 2014, https://www.wired.com/2014/11/countdown-to-zero-day-stuxnet/.

Ron Rosenbaum, "Richard Clarke on Who Was Behind the Stuxnet Attack," *Smithsonian Magazine*, April 2012, https://www.smithsonianmag.com/history/richard -clarke-on-who-was-behind-the-stuxnet-attack-160630516/.

EvilCorp: Joe Tidy, "Evil Corp: 'My Hunt for the World's Most Wanted Hackers,'" BBC News, November 17, 2021, https://www.bbc.co.uk/news/technology-59297187.

Chapter 20: Darkness Visible

Čujović and Soraja Vučelić relationship: http://www.informer.rs/vesti/hronika /47962/ZENA-ROBIJASA-IZ-SPUZA-FINGIRALA-KIDNAPOVANJE-Izmislila -otmicu-da-se-muzu-osveti-za-Soraju.

Fake news: Emma Jane Kirby, "The City Getting Rich from Fake News," BBC News, December 5, 2016, https://www.bbc.co.uk/news/magazine-38168281.

Elise Morton, "Step Inside Macedonia's Fake News Hub, Where Teens Are Making Big Bucks," *Calvert Journal*, December 5, 2016, https://www.calvertjournal.com/articles /show/7302/step-inside-macedonias-fake-news-hub-where-teens-are-making-big -bucks.

Sarah Morrison, "Russian Information Operations" (PhD diss., Swinburn University of Technology, 2021), https://researchbank.swinburne.edu.au/file/2ce9bdba-af2e -4638-9758-1f129a237e79/1/Sarah_Morrison_Thesis.pdf.

Activities in Kosovo and the Balkan borders of Europe: Andrew Learmonth, "Probe Links Britain First Founder Jim Dowson to Anti-Muslim Groups in Balkans," National, May 2, 2018, https://www.thenational.scot/news/16197745.probe-links -britain-first-founder-jim-dowson-anti-muslim-groups-balkans/.

Matthew Collins, "Jim Dowson: The 'Invisible Man' of the Far Right and the Kosovo Connection," Hope Not Hate, May 1, 2018, https://hopenothate.org.uk /2018/05/01/jim-dowson-kosovo-connection/.

András B. Göllner, "Creatures in the Budapest Hills, Part 2," *Hungarian Free Press*, April 30, 2017, https://hungarianfreepress.com/2017/04/30/creatures-in-the-budapest-hills -part-2/.

"Britain First's Founder Jim Dowson Guards Europe's Frontier" (video), n.d., https:// www.dailymail.co.uk/video/news/video-1345767/Britain-founder-Jim-Dowson -guards-Europe-s-Frontier.html.

"BBC and Al Jazeera English Release BIRN-Backed Documentaries," BIRN, May 4, 2018, https://birn.eu.com/news-and-events/bbc-and-al-jazeera-english-release-birn -backed-documentaries/.

"Scottish Far-Right Activist Denies 'Stirring Up Tensions' in Kosovo," *Scotsman*, May 2, 2018, https://www.scotsman.com/news/politics/scottish-far-right-activist-denies -stirring-tensions-kosovo-1429959.

"The Invisible Man of Britain's Far Right—Jim Dowson KTI," YouTube, May 13, 2018, https://www.youtube.com/watch?v=EDe5Pong8eM.

Katharine M. Millar and Julia Costa Lopez, "Conspiratorial Medievalism: History and Hyperagency in the Far-Right Knights Templar Security Imaginary," *Politics* (July 2021), https://journals.sagepub.com/doi/10.1177/02633957211010983.

Alex Hern, "Facebook Bans Far-Right Groups Including BNP, EDL and Britain First," *Guardian*, April 18, 2019, https://www.theguardian.com/technology/2019/apr/18 /facebook-bans-far-right-groups-including-bnp-edl-and-britain-first.

The Far Right and Serbia: Hannah Lucinda Smith and Milivoje Pantovic, "How Europe's Far Right Found Friends in Serbia," *Times*, March 23, 2021, https://www .thetimes.co.uk/article/serbian-president-vucic-regularly-spoke-to-leader-of-violent -far-right-group-mp-claims-r8m35kbnd.

"Documents," BIRN, http://www.birnsource.com/sq/documents?page=25.

Heidi Beirich, "The Transatlantic Connections Between American And Southeastern Europe's White Supremacists," Global Project Against Hate and Extremism, November 12, 2020, https://globalextremism.org/post/balkans/.

Marina Lažetić, "'Migration Crisis' and the Far Right Networks in Europe: A Case Study of Serbia," *Journal of Regional Security* 13, no. 2 (2018): 131–178, https://pdfs .semanticscholar.org/a7bb/d1d932665a731a381f16a3e559844a744588.pdf.

Stefan Lang, "Not unto Us, O Lord, but unto Thy Name Give Glory: The Knights Templar and the KTI," *History's Shadow* (blog), May 10, 2018, https://historysshadow .wordpress.com/tag/jim-dowson/.

The Far Right and Russian connections: Max Seddon, "Racists, Neo-Nazis, Far Right Flock to Russia for Joint Conference," *BuzzFeed*, March 22, 2015, https://www. buzzfeednews.com/article/maxseddon/europes-far-right-comes-to-russia-in-search -of-shared-values.

Matthew Collins, "Home from Russia, with Hate," Hope Not Hate, March 24, 2015, https://hopenothate.org.uk/2015/03/24/home-from-russia-with-hate/.

Neil MacFarquhar, "Right Wing Groups Find a Haven, for a Day, in Russia," March 22, 2015, https://www.nytimes.com/2015/03/23/world/europe/right-wing-groups-find -a-haven-for-a-day-in-russia.html.

Tom Porter, "Kremlin's Links to British Far Right Stretch Back Decades, Experts Warn," *International Business Times*, September 2, 2017, https://www.ibtimes.co.uk/kremlins -links-british-far-right-stretch-back-decade-experts-warn-1605441.

Gabrielle Tetrault-Farber, "Russian, European Far-Right Parties Converge in St. Petersburg," *Moscow Times*, March 22, 2015, https://www.themoscowtimes.com/2015/03/22 /russian-european-far-right-parties-converge-in-st-petersburg-a45010.

Anton Shekhovtsov, "Russian [sic] Building International Alliance of Far-Right Parties and Organizations," Ukraine Solidarity Campaign, April 8, 2022, https://ukrai nesolidaritycampaign.org/2022/04/08/russian-building-international-alliance -of-far-right-parties-and-organizations/.

Milos Čujović flees Kosovo after Ivanovic murder with Barbara Segetin: "The Special Prosecutor's Office of Kosovo Expanded the Investigation into the Murder of Oliver Ivanovic," *Danas*, January 4, 2019, https://www.danas.rs/drustvo/specijalno-tuzilastvo-kosova-prosirilo-istragu-o-ubistvu-olivera-ivanovica/.

"A Preliminary Investigation into the Murder of Oliver Ivanovic Was Not Renewed," *Newsbeezer*, January 4, 2019, https://newsbeezer.com/serbiaeng/a-preliminary-investigation-into-the-murder-of-oliver-ivanovic-was-not-renewed/.

Abazovic and the fake diplomat: "Škrelja: Fake Diplomat and Forger Simijanović as Abazović's Mentor and Advisor in the Betrayal of Civil Montenegro," *Aktuelno*, June 19, 2021, https://www.aktuelno.me/english/skrelja-fake-diplomat-and-forger-simijanovic-as-abazovics-mentor-and-advisor-in-the-betrayal-of-civil-montenegro/.

Abazovic and Čujović's wife: "Scandal That Can Endanger National Security: Abazovic in Relationship with Hacker's Ex-Wife?," *Aktuelno*, June 9, 2016, https://www.aktuelno.me/english/scandal-abazovic-in-relationship-with-hackers-ex-wife/.

Group 69: Martin Holbraad and Morten Axel Pedersen, eds., *Times of Security: Ethnographies of Fear, Protest, and the Future* (New York: Routledge, 2013).

Chapter 21: The End of Everything

Russia's massive cyberattack on Ukraine in February 2022: David E. Sander and Kate Conger, "Russia Was Behind Cyberattack in Run-Up to Ukraine War, Investigation Finds," *New York Times*, May 10, 2022, https://www.nytimes.com/2022/05/10/us/politics/russia-cyberattack-ukraine-war.html.

Russian forces using Premise app to crowdsource info: Byron Tau, "Premise Mobile-Phone App Suspends Ukraine Activities After Accusations Fly," *Wall Street Journal*, February 26, 2022, https://www.wsj.com/livecoverage/russia-ukraine-latest-news-2022-02-26/card/premise-mobile-phone-app-suspends-ukraine-activities-after-accusations-fly-8FDnhZe9raunaIJ4HV66.

"San Francisco–Based Premise App Suspends Activities in Ukraine," NBC Bay Area, February 27, 2022, https://www.nbcbayarea.com/news/local/san-francisco-based-premise-app-suspends-activities-in-ukraine/2823493/.

Louise Matsakis, "California-Based App Premise Battles Accusations of Helping Russian Military," *Yahoo! News*, February 26, 2022, https://news.yahoo.com/california-based-app-premise-battles-023006409.html.

"Is Russia Using Premise Mobile App to Compile Human Intelligence in Ukraine?," *Business Today*, February 27, 2022, https://www.businesstoday.in/latest/world/story/is-russia-using-premise-mobile-app-to-compile-human-intelligence-in-ukraine-324075-2022-02-27.

Tinder as a weapon: Zoe Strimpel, "Inside Ukraine's Tinder War," *UnHerd*, June 3, 2022, https://unherd.com/2022/06/inside-ukraines-tinder-war/.

Severija Bielskyte, "How Tinder Became a Weapon in the Russia-Ukraine War: Swiping in Solidarity," *Huck*, March 21, 2022, https://www.huckmag.com/perspectives/how-tinder-became-a-weapon-in-the-russia-ukraine-war/.

Tim Hanlon, "Russian Soldiers Sending Flirty Tinder Messages to Ukrainian Women 'Ahead of Invasion,'" *Mirror*, February 24, 2022, https://www.mirror.co.uk/news/world-news/russian-soldiers-sending-flirty-tinder-26314943.

Jesse O'Neil, "'Sleeping with the Enemy': Russian Troops Try to Pick Up Ukrainian Women on Tinder," *New York Post*, February 24, 2022, https://nypost.com/2022/02/24/ukrainian-women-say-russian-troops-are-flirting-with-them-on-tinder/.

Sharan Sanil, "From Russia with Love: Ukrainian Women Bombarded with Tinder Likes from Invading Soldiers," Man's World India, n.d., https://www.mansworldindia.com/more/news/ukraine-russia-tinder-soldiers-dating/.

The Ukrainian Twitter Army: "Ukraine Creates 'IT Army'—Says 'Hack These Russian Companies,'" *Stack*, February 26, 2022, https://thestack.technology/ukraine-it-army/.

James Pearson, "Ukraine Launches 'IT Army,' Takes Aim at Russian Cyberspace," Reuters, February 26, 2022, https://www.reuters.com/world/europe/ukraine-launches-it-army-takes-aim-russian-cyberspace-2022-02-26/.

"Meet the IT Army of Ukraine, the Army of Volunteers Working to Hack Russian Sites," *Entrepreneur*, March 15, 2022, https://www.entrepreneur.com/article/422315.

Cat Zakrzewski, "4000 Letters and Four Hours of Sleep: Ukrainian Leader Wages Digital War," *Washington Post*, March 30, 2022, https://www.washingtonpost.com/technology/2022/03/30/mykhailo-fedorov-ukraine-digital-front/.

Kevin Beaumont (GossiTheDog), "'I'll Just DDoS a Russian State Bank List.' Spoiler: here's where your traffic goes and potentially impacts," Twitter, February 26, 2022, 4:33 p.m., https://twitter.com/gossithedog/status/1497686331706720259?lang=en-GB.

Russian warship shoots down its own plane: "Ukrainian Armed Forces: Russian Warship Accidentally Shoots Down Friendly Military Aircraft," *Kyiv Independent*, February 26, 2022, https://kyivindependent.com/uncategorized/ukrainian-armed-forces-russian-warship-accidentally-shoots-down-friendly-military-aircraft.

Reface AI: https://hey.reface.ai/.

About the Author

Matt Potter is an investigative journalist, broadcaster and screen-writer. He contributes regularly to the *Washington Post*, BBC and others. He is the author of *Outlaws Inc: Flying with the World's Most Dangerous Smugglers* and *The Last Goodbye: A History of the World in Resignations*. He lives in London.

www.mattpotter.com
Twitter: @MattPotter